Governments and Professional Education

SRHE and Open University Press Imprint
General Editor: Heather Eggins

Current titles include:

Governments and Professional Education

Edited by Tony Becher

Society for Research into Higher Education
& Open University Press

Published by SRHE and
Open University Press
Celtic Court
22 Ballmoor
Buckingham
MK18 1XW

and
1900 Frost Road, Suite 101
Bristol, PA 19007, USA

First Published 1994

Copyright © The Editor and Contributors 1994

All rights reserved. Except for the quotation of short passages for the purposes
of criticism and review, no part of this publication may be reproduced, stored in
a retrieval system, or transmitted, in any form or by any means, electronic,
mechanical, photocopying, recording or otherwise, without the prior written
permission of the publisher or a licence from the Copyright Licensing Agency
Limited. Details of such licences (for reprographic reproduction) may be
obtained from the Copyright Licensing Agency Ltd of 90 Tottenham Court
Road, London, W1P 9HE.

A catalogue record of this book is available from the British Library

ISBN 0 335 19135 5 (hb)

Library of Congress Cataloging-in-Publication Data

Governments and professional education / edited by Tony Becher.
    p.   cm.
  Includes bibliographical references and index.
  ISBN 0–335–19135–5
  1. Professional education—Cross-cultural studies.   2. Education
and state—Cross-cultural studies.   I. Becher, Tony.
  LC1059.G68   1993
  378'.013—dc20   93–1136
                                                          CIP

Typeset by Graphicraft Typesetters Ltd., Hong Kong
Printed in Great Britain by St Edmundsbury Press Limited
Bury St Edmunds, Suffolk

Contents

Conclusion

Contributors

Tony Becher is a Professor of Education at the University of Sussex. He has researched widely on qualitative aspects of higher education, and has a current interest in professional training. His books include *British Higher Education* (1987), *Academic Tribes and Territories* (1989) and *Process and Structure in Higher Education* (with Maurice Kogan, 2nd edition 1992).

Michael Burrage was recently a Research Associate of the Center for the Study of Higher Education at the University of California, Berkeley. His work on the professions in the United States, France and Russia has appeared in a number of American and European journals and two volumes edited with Rolf Torstendahl for the Swedish Collegium for the Advanced Study of the Social Sciences at Uppsala. He is a lecturer at the London School of Economics.

Elaine El-Khawas is Vice President for Policy Analysis and Research at the American Council on Education, a non-governmental organization representing higher education in the United States. A sociologist, she has published many studies interpreting recent trends and issues facing academe, most notably in an annual report titled *Campus Trends*. Her current interests focus on academic staffing issues.

Mary Henkel is Senior Lecturer in Government at Brunel University. Her main areas of research have been in evaluation studies and the impacts of higher education and research policies. Her books include *Government and Research* (with Maurice Kogan, 1983) and *Government, Evaluation and Change* (1991). She has taught on three different social work courses.

Julian Lonbay is Senior Lecturer in Law and Director of the Institute of European Law at the University of Birmingham. He is active in a number of national and international bodies, and has undertaken research for the Law Societies of the British Isles on the mutual recognition of professional qualifications in Europe as well as an enquiry for the Law Society of England and Wales and the Department of Employment on the training needs of solicitors in an international context. His recent publications include *Training Lawyers in the European Community* (1990) and *International Professional Practice* (1992, with L. Spedding).

Hannes Siegrist is Associate Professor in the History Department and Co-Director of the Center for Comparative Social History at the Free University of Berlin. He has published on business history and on the history of white collar employees and professions (lawyers, engineers) in the nineteenth and twentieth centuries. His recent articles and books deal with the comparative history of lawyers and the bourgeois middle classes in Europe.

Lennart G. Svensson is Associate Professor of Sociology at the University of Gothenburg. His main research has been devoted to the Swedish university system and he has published three volumes in Swedish on this theme as well as *Higher Education and the State in Swedish History* (1987). His present research relates to professional practice in different occupational groups: professional work and bureaucracy in the process of decentralization; ethics and rhetorics in the discourse of professionals in meetings; and education and social work.

Sir William Taylor is a Visiting Professor in the University of Oxford and Honorary Visiting Fellow of Green College, Oxford. He was formerly Vice Chancellor of the University of Hull, and from 1984 to 1993 Chair of the Council for the Accreditation of Teacher Education. His books include *Society and the Education of Teachers* (1969), *Research and Reform in Teacher Education* (1978), *Metaphors of Education* (ed.) (1984) and *Universities under Scrutiny* (1987).

Rolf Torstendahl is Professor of History at the University of Uppsala. He has written books on the career patterns of Swedish engineers and the origins of the training of engineers in Sweden and is working on a comparative study of the professional careers of engineers. Among his recent books are *The Formation of Professions* and *Professions in Theory and History* (both edited together with Michael Burrage in 1990), *Bureaucratisation in Northwestern Europe, 1880–1985: Domination and Governance* (1991) and *State Theory and State History* (1992).

Johannes Vang has held senior academic appointments in surgery in the Universities of Lund and Kuwait, and is currently Professor of Technology Assessment at the University of Linköping. He was for seven years medical director of the hospitals in a region of Sweden. More recently he has been a staff member at the WHO Regional Office for Europe in Copenhagen and a consultant to its Department of Health Services. He has taught and published in a variety of fields, including surgery, metabolism, health care administration and health policy.

Preface and Acknowledgements

As a number of contributors to this volume imply, the professions are facing a difficult period, and one in which governmental intervention seems in a number of countries to have become more active than at any other time in their long existence. That intervention has commonly taken the form of exercising a direct control over the process or the outcomes of initial training. An examination of the relationships between the state and professional education therefore seemed a timely theme for the *Precedings* of the 1993 Annual Conference of the Society for Research into Higher Education.

It will be clear from the most cursory glance that the contents are not based on a uniform editorial requirement. The authors were given a free hand within the overall specification implied by the title of the book, rather than being enjoined to write to a detailed presentational formula. This strategy has the limitation of allowing for a wide variety of approaches, with the attendant absence of direct comparability between one contribution and another. The compensating advantage is that it gives rise to a series of explorations on the theme of governments and the professions which are abundant in their range of perspectives and exemplifications. In an attempt to capitalize on this richness, the final chapter is designed to draw together the main strands of the argument.

There is a clear emphasis throughout the text on the international aspects of professionality and professional education. This emerges in most of the discussions of particular professions in Part 1, and is underlined in the different country-based contributions in Part 2. Unfortunately, the latter is not as extensive as had been intended. Two contributions, though negotiated and agreed well over a year before the editorial deadline, failed to materialize in an appropriate form. By the time it had become clear that they would not be forthcoming, it was already too late to commission alternative authors. Accordingly, one Western and one Central European component are missing from the pattern of the volume as originally planned. It is to be hoped that the existing contributions will nevertheless provide a

varied and thought-provoking account of the issues of professional education and of the diverse relationships it enjoys with the state, at a time during
which – as has already been remarked – established arrangements are being
held in question in almost every country.

Interestingly, the changes are not always in the same direction: centralized systems appear to be decentralizing at the very same time that decentralized systems seem to be embracing a greater measure of centralization.
But it can nevertheless be contended that the underlying political pressures
are in many countries shifting from the control of curricular content and
process towards a more detailed concern with educational outcomes. One
might mark the change in general terms as from regulation to accountability.

This and other salient issues are explored in the chapters which follow:
it must be for the reader to make up his or her mind which are of the most
significance. There is certainly no shortage of choice on offer.

Acknowledgements

I would like to express my gratitude to Hugh Glanville, Heather Nicholas
and Penny Searls for their help in preparing the material in this volume for
publication.

Tony Becher

Introduction

1

The Professions, State and Government in Theory and History

Hannes Siegrist

Introduction

The professions are regarded as pillars of modern society, reflecting its rationality and division of labour. In their practice they are concerned with core values and scarce resources, and apply rational knowledge efficiently and 'regardless of person'. That is at any rate what is expected of the doctor treating a patient or of the engineer or industrialist managing costly or scarce resources. Barristers and solicitors dealing with conflicts about property and honour, law and order are regarded as representatives of modern civil society and the constitutional state. Teachers of all levels, who command cultural knowledge and transmit social and cognitive competences, are considered to be among the elite of modern secularized culture. The spectrum of functions carried out by these professions ranges from routine operations, which can also be carried out by non-experts, through the application of abstract knowledge to concrete situations, to scientific innovation and the creation of new meanings. The history of the professions goes hand in hand with the social processes of modernization and rationalization: with professionalization and bureaucratization, with the development of 'school cultures' and the meritocratic system, and with juridification, medicalization and technical and economic progress.

The activities of the professions affect public interest and common welfare in many ways. For this reason even states, governments and legislature always take an interest in the organization, deployment and control of the professions. This was already the case before the modern era, but it remained so in modern times, even when many professions and activities were deregulated as a result of the introduction of freedom of trade. In the nineteenth and twentieth centuries, however, public interest in the professions did not manifest itself everywhere or in uniform fashion. It took various forms, depending on the type of knowledge and the profession in question. It also depended on the type of state and political culture, as well as on the ideologies, the concepts of order and the needs of the professions and their clients. Traditions, mentalities and fashions lend a particular colouring to each set of conditions. The relationship between the professions, the state and the public is thus shaped by a particular historicity. No single theory of the professions would be adequate to comprehend this, nor is there just one path to professionalization.

In this chapter, I will present some reflections and generalizations concerning the relationship between state and government on the one hand, and the professions on the other. I will begin by asking whether, why and how this relationship has been dealt with in the literature. Then I will present three historical-sociological basic models of professions and professionalization, which may be clearly distinguished from one another by virtue of the degree of state intervention and the kind of political control they have been subject to. The chapter will conclude with a look at the long-term development of professional organizations and the relationship between state and professions.

The state, government and professions in the literature

There is frequent mention in the literature of the ideal profession, abstracted from all local and historical singularities. This ideal concept may be described as follows. A profession is a particular sort of full-time occupation, the practice of which presupposes a specialized (and possibly scientific) educational background. Specialized education allows the professional to secure practical and theoretical expertise relevant to his or her field as well as to acquire general knowledge and a sense of ethical values. Knowledge that is utilized 'selflessly' for the common welfare regardless of person is guaranteed through examination and licence. Therefore only experts are, properly speaking, in the position of fulfilling certain functions and providing particular services. The professions demand, therefore, exclusive control over certain areas of operation and service as well as freedom from external supervision. Organized professional groups possess autonomous control over admissions and licensing policies. With reference to competence, ethical standards and the importance of efficiency for society and the common good, professions lay claim to special rewards and a higher social and economic status. 'Professionalization' thus means the process that transforms an activity or function into a profession. Many authors concern themselves with the whole complex. Others focus more on the transformation of knowledge, education and examination. A third group concentrates on the way the market is structured and protected. A fourth group is concerned with analysing the organization and status of the professions.

This concept of the ideal profession does not fully tackle the question of state and political intervention in the process of professionalization. Indeed, the subject of state and government has long been more or less neglected in research on the professions (overviews of the considerable literature have been provided by Dingwall and Lewis 1983; Siegrist 1988b; Burrage 1990; Jarausch 1990b). The structural-functional approach has placed the relationship between expert and client in the foreground. This gives the impression that the superiority of the expert over the client, and the high status of the professional in society, rest exclusively on expert knowledge, which is indispensable for the functioning and general progress of modern society. The highly qualified professional is concerned, unselfishly, with non-personal standards, universal scientific values and an ethic of service (the classic exponent of this view is Parsons 1963). Thus there must not and should not be any interference from state or layman in professional questions. This view was contested by the conflict sociologists of the 1970s, who accused the professions of using the power their superior knowledge gave them over the client in order to enhance their position in the market and in society. According to these sociologists, the strong professional associations, which were established in the age of organized interests to fight for autonomy in all professional questions, exploited their collective power in the market place and prestige in the eye of the public for selfish professional goals. The tenets of expert knowledge, selflessness and concern for common welfare thus became an ideology which legitimated material and social rewards (Johnson 1972; Sarfatti Larson 1977; Collins 1979, 1990).

These critics of the professions are, however, blinkered by the belief that the professions enjoy relatively unrestricted freedom of action to carry out the strategies and 'professional projects' they choose. Their case rests on research which has focused primarily on the aims, programmes and strategies of the organized professions. As a result of this limited perspective they have only an unclear perception of the dynamic relationship between the professions and their environment, and only rarely have they given it close attention. All in all it is evident that a research perspective which is mainly concerned with the superiority of knowledge, market advantage and autonomy of the professional can approach the great problem of heteronomy (subjection to outside control) only through particular problems; for instance, through the problem which preoccupies organization sociologists – the dilemma of the role of the professional in a bureaucracy or in the management of private enterprise (see Kornhauser 1962).

While sociology after 1945 based itself on 'Western' shared values and a universal trend towards modernization, the characteristics of the professions in the individual states and nations seemed less important. Some writers even went as far as to dismiss instances of state intervention, political influence, institutional tradition and national culture as irrational or dysfunctional. So it is not surprising that the question of the relationship of state, government and professions was not in the foreground of sociological research into the professions. Outside the sociological community, on the other hand, there was lively political debate in every country about the role and position of the professions in a liberal, democratic and welfare society. This debate was constantly recharged by new themes, ranging from issues of basic political order to the politics of education, law, health, insurance and technology. The protracted discussions conducted by some parts of the professions in the decades after the Second World War about how government and health service bureaucracies, motivated by welfare state ideals, interfered in the concerns of the self-governing professions are at bottom discussions about the relationship between state and professions. They are of interest as discussions about how the professional idea is conceived and realized in isolation from the state and the market, but they were really part of the great ideological argument about 'freedom versus totalitarianism'. They have little to say about the *actual* relationship between state, government and professions.

Were these discussions, by sociologists on the one hand, and by politicians and professionals on the other, conducted in isolation from each other? It seems to me that the structuralist-functionalist direction taken by American sociology, which prevailed until well into the 1960s and left its mark on all scientific investigation of the professions undertaken in the West, did share common ground with many of the professions' ideas insofar as it marginalized the state and stylized the autonomy of those professions which were regarded as knowing what was best for the common welfare.

It is true that the few studies of the role of the intellectual and the professions in fascism and in the socialist states focused more on the state. But they were often based on the axiom that professions and intellectual occupations could only develop in a 'liberal system', where the state did not intervene. Many apologists for the professions regarded the system that allowed the most autonomy to the professions as the most liberal. In many studies, investigation of the role of the 'state' is just schematic and ideological.

On the European continent, where large sections of the professions discredited themselves and betrayed their professional and humanistic ideals by becoming functionaries and elites of Nazi and fascist systems, ahistorical concepts of professionalization, which ignored the way the professions had allied themselves to the point of total self-surrender with the totalitarian state, were particularly welcome after 1945. Such concepts drew a veil over the past and at the same time presented a programme for the future regulation of the professions which would not be subject to too much state intervention. For many, state intervention meant welfare state programmes threatening their freedom of action and competition from newly rising elites, which were branded as commercial 'seducers' and 'irresponsible' elites of a bureaucratic or socialist 'mass society' (Siegrist 1993).

It was not until the 1960s that political science research into politics, policy-making and neo-corporatism, as well as policy research, paid more attention to the role of professional associations in the system of political power and influence (e.g. Heidenheimer 1980; Torstendahl and Burrage 1990). At the same time educationists, sociologists and historians also began to study the problem of the relationship between the professions and the state in the context of the politics and sociology of education. They called for a reorientation of educational policy and more state intervention. This was not without consequences for the professions.

Gradually even modern social historians turned their attention to the professions, invading a field in which there had hitherto only been hagiographic accounts written by doctors, jurists, teachers and engineers to justify the history of professional associations and occupations. Since then a few historians and sociologists with a historical bent have paraphrased the available histories, self-presentations and programmes of the professional associations, using the concepts and models of the sociology of the professions. They used a trait list to measure the degree to which an occupation or occupational group was qualified to be classed as a profession. Many did not progress beyond the level of theoretical deductions or superficial taxonomies, because they neither considered nor understood the wider network of interrelationships which characterized the history of professionalization on the European continent. They failed to take account either of the particular role of the state and the state system of higher education and qualifications, or of how closely interwoven the history of the professions was with the history of the middle and upper middle classes, and the crisis-prone development of a capitalist and civil society.

In the meantime an interdisciplinary 'professional community' of historians, social scientists and political scientists gradually came into being, which criticized this short-sighted view. The theories and models of the sociologists of the professions might have a heuristic value, but should not become a Procrustean bed. The time perspective should be extended and more attention given to international comparison. Research should focus not only on the professions' self-understanding and aims, but also on the actual developments in the education, work, markets and careers of the members of the professions. In particular the role of states and governments and the importance of legislation and politics should be given closer attention (see Geison 1984; Conze and Kocka (eds) 1985; Siegrist 1985, 1988a, b, 1991; Rüschemeyer 1986; Karpik 1988; Lundgreen 1988; Heidenheimer 1989; Burrage and Torstendahl 1990; Jarausch 1990a, b).

Historians were usually interested in the role of state, government and politics as a matter of course; certainly this interest was not a new discovery for them, as it was for most sociologists, who were only just beginning to bring the problem of the state back as a fit subject for sociological research (Rüschemeyer 1986; Tousijn 1987; Burrage 1989). *Bringing the State Back In* was the emblematic title of a reader by Evans *et al.* (1985). Historians and sociologists were now involved in the same problem: the quest for theoretical understanding of the role of the state in professionalization, and for a concept of the state which took account of this role. On the one hand this involved examining how the concepts of state, government and the legislative process, which were developed in historical and political research, related to the professional model. On the other hand it involved investigating the importance of politics and policies for the various professions.

One result of these investigations is the recognition that 'knowledge' and 'market' are sometimes less significant as factors in the development and attitude of the professions than 'state' and 'politics'. For a time this was regarded as something peculiar to continental Europe, but it is increasingly recognized as true of the UK and the USA (Freidson 1986; Burrage 1989; Göbel 1990). A few authors call, as a matter of principle, for *all* significant actors who have influenced the formation and practice of the professions to be examined within the context of an actor-centred framework (Burrage *et al.* 1990). Only through placing greater emphasis on the actors would it be possible to break free from the formal models of the sociology of the professions. The significant actors, whose importance varies according to time and place, are: the educational institutions and the 'system of knowledge'; state/government and the legislature; the members of the professions and their organizations; the clients and client organizations; the media and public opinion. Further significant influences are the collective memory of the occupational group and institutional traditions, which are able to transcend breaks in the system, whether as conscious inheritance or as unreflecting mentality. The contributions to the present volume demonstrate the richness of this vein.

Professional models and professionalization in historical context

For the most part, the older theories about professions and models of professionalization fail to deal adequately with the role of the state, government and legislation, and they fail in particular to consider the differences between states and nations. In this section, three basic models of professionalization will be described, which differ from one another by virtue of the role and significance of state, government and legislation: the first is the harmonious and gradual transformation of the old corporative professions in England; the second is the liberal professionalization achieved by the occupational groups in the USA; and the third is the professionalization from above, by the state, which was experienced by many professions in many countries on the European continent. This debate goes back far into the nineteenth century, to the time when many of the basic professional models and their associated institutions, practices and concepts came into being. These basic models, though much modified and added to over time, still have an influence today, which is only gradually diminishing.

The traditional corporative professions and the 'weak' state: the special case of England

The development of the English professions in the transition from the dawn of the modern age to the nineteenth and twentieth centuries is characterized by a strong sense of continuity and a gradual transformation of the old corporate model into the modern profession. England is an example of a society which, without a strong bureaucratic central state, but governed by a parliament drawn from social elites, was very careful in the way it treated the professions. The English model – of a professional corporation legitimized in early modern times by a royal charter (a guild or college) and solely responsible for the education and entry into the profession of its members, which was not swept away by a revolution – became something of an exception in the history of professionalization. The right to grant licences remained until well into the nineteenth century, and in some cases until the twentieth century, in the hands of particular regional corporations, professional associations, colleges and universities, and the process of standardization was patchy and slow. This is evident in the cases of both doctors and barristers. When the Medical Act of 1858 created the General Council of Medical Education, its members were drawn from the former corporations, with some government representatives. It put an end to the regional control of licensing and created a general examination in 1884 (Ramsey 1984: 232, 245–9). The traditional way to become a barrister was through co-option by one of the four Inns of Court in London. Candidates for co-option had to have completed five years' practical work in a barrister's chambers and eaten a specified number of dinners in one of the Inns of Court. Masters of Arts or Bachelors of Law of Oxford or Cambridge only had to complete three years of practical work. The first move towards coordinating the education system was made by the General Council for Legal Education, which was set up in 1852 and provided courses for law students. In 1872 an examination was introduced as a formal qualification for entry, but in practice legal education placed more emphasis on practical experience, and entry was still through co-option by a particular Inn (Duman 1983: 21–34, 79–89).

The pattern of barristers and doctors provided the basic model for many other professions, from solicitors and engineers to accountants. They constituted themselves into an 'institution' or association, defined the qualifications for entry into their profession, and supervised the ethical standards and conduct of their members. Many strove for a royal charter to sanction their status and rights (Burrage 1988: 55; Perkin 1989; Torstendahl in this volume). Regulation of the professions was achieved through the agreement of the interested institutions and professions; it was an arrangement among elites. Parliament and the government were often involved in the process, bringing pressure to bear and taking part in the negotiations. In these interventions, the various claims of the rest of society on the professions were given a voice. The actual drafting of laws usually respected the wishes of the professional group, which thereby gained a more rational legitimation for its practices. With regard to the functional areas, which were of more direct concern to the social elites, state and government showed notable restraint and diplomacy – even at times that were in other respects strongly interventionist. The process of professionalization in Britain in the nineteenth and twentieth centuries was characterized by an attitude of cooperation and consensus on the part of the professions, decentralized elites, and a weak state. The old professions accepted a small degree of modernization, but did not have to fear any serious threats to their autonomy. The government showed a similar degree of restraint towards the teaching profession, which for the most part remained under the control of traditional and local institutions and authorities.

The English professional model just described possesses many features of the abstract ideal model described above. It does admittedly fail formally with regard to scientific higher education. But in so far as there was already a considerable increase in the actual proportion of university graduates in the nineteenth century, the English model approaches the ideal model and that of the continental professions (Duman 1983: 24).

Professionalization in the post-revolutionary liberal-democratic societies

The English path to the modern professions differs considerably from the step-by-step process of professionalization that Wilensky – writing against the background of modern American developments – put forward as a generally applicable model. 'Professionalization', according to Wilenksy, begins when (a) a function or part of a profession becomes a full-time occupation. At this point, (b) the occupational group lays claim to certain functions and areas of the profession. In the next phase, (c) the education process becomes more precisely regulated, if possible by means of an academic curriculum at the university. Then, (d) professors and leading professionals establish a professional association, which expands quickly, and (e) ensures that only those who pass the appropriate examination are allowed to practise the profession, which gives them monopoly rights over the profession and all its services. Finally, (f) regulations concerning the conduct and ethical standards of the profession receive more precise formulation, and their observance is supervised by the governing body or council of the professional association (Wilensky 1972).

In contrast to the older English professions, this development starts from a *tabula rasa* or from the point at which trades and professions were open to all. This was the situation after the institutions that had been imported from England were swept away by the liberal, egalitarian and democratic movement of the 1830s (Burrage 1989). (In the twentieth century, new professions like psychologists, social workers, computer experts, etc. found themselves in a similar situation at the outset.) Liberal market principles are given freer rein. The professions must first of all be allowed to develop and take shape. The state, or the legislature, only comes into the process at stage (e), according to Wilensky. The 'state' accords the profession and the rights of the professional group the sanction of legislation only when the profession has reached the stage of enjoying the general acceptance and trust of the public, won entirely by its own efforts.

Many writers consider this pattern to be the American way of professionalization. American sociologists abstracted their model of professionalization from it, relegating state and legislature to secondary roles. Yet, closer scrutiny reveals that the model is of more general and universal applicability: it is relatively typical of post-revolutionary liberal-democratic societies, which keep close watch on their experts' observance of informal social and economic controls, but are reluctant to give the formal endorsement of laws and policies to the position of privilege enjoyed by the expert over his or her client or consumer. This is evident in the example of Switzerland, which as an early liberal and democratic society with a weak bureaucracy and few government institutions, but with its decentralized elites strongly represented in parliament and government, is comparable with the United States (Siegrist 1985). Elements of the model may also be found in certain French professions of the nineteenth century, though in competition with elements of a 'professionalization from above' (Ramsey 1984; Burrage 1988). Many professions in liberal-democratic societies have been developing in a similar direction since the liberalization of the late nineteenth century, but in the large states of continental Europe this trend is impeded by the traditions and pressures of an earlier or revived 'professionalization from above'.

Professionalization from above in a bureaucratic authoritarian state in the nineteenth century

Up to the end of the eighteenth century conditions in large parts of the European continent were similar to those in England. Professional corporations, universities, church, kings and aristocratic and patrician elites determined which members of a society characterized by division of labour could practise a 'professional' function, which competences it required and what status it enjoyed (Siegrist 1988b: 20–2). When the large and medium-sized states on the European continent established a rational and unified state apparatus of rule, government, law and culture in the late eighteenth and early nineteenth centuries, they transformed the professions, functions, education structures, examinations and qualifications of the inherited system in a truly revolutionary fashion, in order to use them for their own purposes. Professional occupations which were concerned with core values and resources, and which were regarded by the state as indispensable for its aims, were refashioned.

Prussia, the Bourbon Kingdom of Sicily, the Hapsburg Kingdom in central Europe and Napoleonic France, and in their train a large number of the countless small and medium-sized states, introduced a programme of educational reform, changing basic education and the systems of qualification, redefining the learned, educated or scientific professions and reorientating the 'professional sector' towards the goal of common welfare prescribed by the state. The aim was to create an elite – in terms of both function and values – of experts who were not only competent and efficient but also loyal and morally unimpeachable, to occupy the high-status positions of civil servants, officials and professionals in private practice. To carry out this aim a unified, national system of qualifications and examinations, regulated in both content and form, was introduced; practice of a profession was restricted to holders of a statutory licence or certificate of authorization; ethical rules were prescribed for the guidance and supervision of methods of practice; and the status, the relationship to the client, the salary scales and fees were all regulated. The former professional corporations were held in contempt as 'intermediary powers'. The members of the professions were left isolated, without an organization and hence without any influence on these developments.

The transformation of the professions often followed in the wake of reform of the civil service. When states increased their control over universities or even established state-wide examinations to take the place of university degrees, their primary aim was to produce efficient and loyal servants (including officers) of the state. This was – to cite only a few examples – the motive behind the establishment of the French engineering schools and medical faculties and the reform of the law and political economy faculties in the German states and the Habsburg empire (Lundgreen 1988; Heidenheimer 1989; Siegrist 1990b). The curricula and examinations were also compulsory for those who did not intend to enter the civil service, but aspired to gain the licence or authorization to practise privately as a lawyer, doctor or engineer. The state determined the structure of the market and through its policies it ensured that, in certain cases, only the certification of warranted professionals was recognized.

Professionals in private practice were only able to exert an influence on the socialization of the next generation and on the examinations insofar as they were permitted to work as professors and masters. In southern and western Europe, and generally in liberal countries, it was more common for professionals who were not civil servants to be involved in the education and examination of the coming generation than was the case in the bigger German bureaucratic-authoritarian states.

At first the states conducted a policy of school cultures. Later many demanded that the university course should be followed by a period of practical experience, to be spent in a junior position (*Referendariat*) in a working environment. The length of this practical term was constantly extended, owing more to questions of the job market and status than to educational considerations. The first to do this were lawyers who wished to enter the civil service, the next were solicitors, then doctors and finally teachers in higher education (Huerkamp 1985; Siegrist 1990a; Titze 1991). The technical professions were influenced by this example, and it was practised in an informal way by engineers employed in private industry.

Another feature of professionalization from above was state control of entry to and practice of the profession. The state intervened in the matter of income, through its salary scale for state-employed professionals and regulated fee structure for privately practising professionals, according the professions tutelage with one hand and privilege with the other.

After the state had disbanded the old professional corporations, in many places it was forbidden for professions to set up their own organizations. Under Napoleon, regional professional associations with compulsory membership were set up in many parts of Europe, particularly for the legal profession, which were closely supervised and had no real autonomy. The councils of these associations, whose members were appointed by the state from among the most senior members of the profession, acted as mediators between state and profession; they were responsible for ensuring that the informal code of professional and ethical standards was observed, and on occasion they articulated the views of the profession. After 1815 many states disbanded these compulsory associations (*ordres* in French, *Kammern* in German). The organizational model survived in only a few areas of southern and western Europe, but was later reinstituted.

All in all the professions which underwent this process of professionalization from above displayed many of the traits of the ideal professional model, from theoretically based knowledge and examinations right through to monopoly of functions and market and high status. But this pattern of development is quite different from English and American professionalization because its impetus did not come from a functional or occupational group striving for autonomy, but from the state, which exercised an extreme form of heteronomy in which other social actors played no role. Despite superficial similarities with the Anglo-Saxon professions this was a fundamentally different model of professionalization, and its individual elements were given a quite different meaning by virtue of their position in this specific constellation. In effect, the model of professionalization from above and its consequences, a phenomenon mostly encountered on the European continent, differs in principle from the English and American model.

As a result of the general liberalization of the market in the late nineteenth century this model of professionalization from above was modified to the extent that the market for services was less closely controlled, and the profession was given somewhat more autonomy, particularly in the sphere of ethical standards. Education and examinations, however, remained in the hands of the state. And a protectionist mentality lingered in many parts of the professions. Every time there was a crisis in the market for services there was a call for state intervention.

A comparative view of professions and professionalization

The models of professionalization presented above are mostly drawn from the history of the older professions, such as lawyers, doctors and engineers. They have been used as models for the newer professions, and it is still possible to generalize from them to a certain degree – even in the case of the teaching profession, particularly university teaching, which oscillated between the model of the subject-specialist public servant and the ethic- and science-based model of the established liberal professions, depending on the country and professional tradition prevailing there.

The three basic models characterized above are derived from generalizations of developments in (a) England, (b) the United States of America and (c) the larger countries of continental Europe. Of course, elements of these historical-generic models can be found in other regions, but in weaker form and with different significance. What has been presented here as a single model or constellation of factors will in practice appear as mixtures of models. This was already the case in France and in many Italian states in the early nineteenth century, because the bureaucratic central state was not strong enough and thus had to take account of the wishes of the elites and professions. Since the liberalization of the authoritarian states in the late nineteenth century, elements of the liberal model of professionalization have become mixed with elements of the model of professionalization from above. In the United States of America and England, on the other hand, elements of the formalization and institutionalization of the 'continental' model have appeared since the late nineteenth century, evoking much discussion.

Conclusion: organizations and tendencies towards convergence

Compulsory 'associations' and voluntary professional 'organizations'

From the mid-nineteenth century the compulsory professional associations (*ordres, Kammern*) – an organizational principle introduced by Napoleon to large areas of Europe originally in order to control headstrong professions – were developed into organs of self-government and won support everywhere. The government regarded them as a useful instrument of indirect control, while the professions regarded them as a means of safeguarding their autonomy. Since the end of the nineteenth century they were used as a model by American attorneys and doctors.

In the course of the nineteenth and twentieth centuries many states – often at the behest of the professions, who had in the meantime organized themselves into voluntary professional organizations – introduced compulsory associations with an elected council. Some became organs of self-government, and the state delegated to them powers of jurisdiction in matters of professional ethics, supervision of tariffs, etc. In contrast with the English professions and institutions, most professional associations had little or no influence in the sphere of education, examinations and admission to the professions. Despite this, the model of the compulsory association, which had originally been most common in the legal profession, was adopted by doctors in the late nineteenth century and then by many other occupational groups, which sooner or later received state recognition (Bieback 1973; Tousijn 1987).

Professions with a compulsory association and self-government received a boost to their status comparable to that given by the granting of a royal charter in England, as it gave them the public legitimation of an institution. In my opinion it is only to this aspect that Rüschemeyer's (1986) concept of 'state-sponsored professionalization' – a euphemism for the professionalization from above of the early nineteenth century – is applicable.

In the corporate systems of fascism and Nazism the principle of the compulsory association was ostensibly extended to further occupations, which were seemingly given more formal power, but in reality the power was undermined since state influence and arbitrary interventions increased and autonomy was reduced. Under the changed conditions of the period after the Second World War the principle of compulsory associations was revived in many areas on the grounds that self-government was regarded as the best bastion of freedom. Only the American occupying authorities tried to get rid of the compulsory associations in Germany, because they were in contradiction of the concept of liberal legal and market structures. The English and French, on the other hand, tolerated the *Kammern* and other compulsorily imposed organizations, even going so far as to strengthen them by giving the organizations of the general practitioners' panel (*Kassenärztliche Vereinigung*) and the solicitors' councils (*Rechtsanwaltskammern*) greater powers than ever, for instance with regard to admission to the professions. Sooner or later the Constitutional Court of the Federal Republic described these powers as 'illiberal'. Since they were incompatible with the Basic Law, they were abolished (Ostler 1971: part V; Lega 1974, for Italy).

Since the nineteenth and early twentieth centuries there have been some professions in most countries which had – and still have – voluntary organizations alongside the compulsory associations. The voluntary organizations developed from old boy clubs, continuing education institutions and fraternities into pressure groups that often had something of the trade union about them. This dualism of compulsory association and voluntary professional organization, sometimes complementing each other, sometimes in conflict, is still characteristic of countries like Germany and Italy.

The voluntary professional organizations established in the course of the nineteenth and twentieth centuries were all in one way or another striving for higher position and status, and for representation of their interests. Their concern was first to fight against outside control on the part of the state and against certain aspects of professionalization from above, then against market pressures, and finally against the organized pressure groups of clients and employers. Some professions set up voluntary professional organizations for all their members regardless of whether they were employers, private practitioners, employees or civil servants. In many places those working in private practice were the first in their group to set up a separate organization. The teachers and state-employed professions, which stood in a particular relationship of loyalty to the state, were slower to set up organizations. The leading privately practising professionals, such as engineers, lawyers and economists, were also late in setting up special employee associations and organizations for different status groups, even though they had already established subject associations.

Political changes and the process of convergence

In the long term, a degree of convergence between professions and between countries was perceptible – a trend that had various causes. Since the parliamentary-democratic state and government model, mixed with federal state and bureaucratic elements, became a general pattern, the professions have a similar political environment all over Europe. The professions everywhere have a greater say in negotiations and decisions about questions concerning their profession, though they have to accept a considerable degree of compromise with the state, with its monopoly over the qualifications system, and also with client and employer organizations. With the spread of the modern welfare state after the Second World War, there has been an increasing similarity in the policies that significantly affect the various professions: social security, education, health, and approaches to legal, economic, technical and industrial issues.

Where differences have remained, they have been due to the presence of political majorities, to the internal structure and power relations of the professions, and to traditions and mentalities. In countries where state control was strong in the nineteenth century, a defensive and protectionist mentality survived the process of liberalization, which not only conducted a rhetorical battle against state influence, but at bottom also rejected the market and any form of negotiation with clients, and demanded government and legal sanctioning of their privileges and monopolies. These concepts of professional autonomy were too strong to be overcome by those minority groups within the professions who were in favour of opening up, and actively creating, new fields of activity and sources of income. In the interwar period there was a revival of fears concerning the market. The Nazi and fascist regimes either closed or restricted entry to the professions in order to strengthen their hold on the functional elites. At the same time they intervened strongly in all relevant issues. The defensive attitude and the strategy of closing entry to the professions remained dominant in many countries until some way into the 1960s. It was relaxed in times when growing markets brought improved opportunities, and in some cases was abolished by high court verdicts, on the grounds that the elements of a traditional defensive policy of closure contravened the constitution. Since the 1980s, because of real or imagined crises of over-recruitment, the professions have repeatedly put pressure on the state to bring in further closures; these were in some cases rescinded by the highest courts, even where they had been introduced by the government or administration. This shows that the state is no longer a unity, as was the authoritarian state of the nineteenth century, but a network of complementary institutions, some of which are in competition with one another (Strath and Torstendahl 1992).

In countries with a longer and stronger liberal tradition, the professions were in general much more innovative and active in creating new markets for their services. Even here there were increasing demands for legal sanctioning of professional claims and for a closed market. These demands were only met if the professionals were able to win more general legitimation through negotiation with other interest groups. In some of these countries the professionals were even inclined to become civil servants, which they considered preferable to the life of a small businessman; this was, for instance, the case for Swedish doctors. West German doctors, in contrast, clung to the ideal of a settled private practice, an ideal enjoyed by little more than half of the medical profession, though it was they who dominated the professional associations (Heidenheimer 1980). The consequences of this professional policy can be seen at the moment in the transformation of the system of medical care in the former GDR.

All in all, in the decades after the Second World War a qualitatively new balance of forces was achieved between state and government, professions and client organizations. In the Western countries, this balance rested on the fundamental conviction, held by the majority of interested parties, that the inordinately strong, one-sided and uncontrollable state intervention suffered by the countries of the socialist bloc was not desirable. As a result of developments in the European Community, changes are taking place in the relationship between state, national government and nationally regulated and organized professions. On the one hand liberalization is opening up new markets for the holders of diplomas, and some professions are already in the process of changing. On the other hand the transnational and trans-government bureaucracy of the European Community, and the lobbies circling round it, are generating new issues and new forces, which present countries and professions with unfamiliar challenges. It is this that makes a political study of the history and sociology of the professions of today so interesting.

References

Bieback, K.J. (1976) *Die Öffentliche Körperschaft. Ihre Entstehung, die Entwicklung ihres Begriffs und die Lehre vom Staate und den Innerstaatlichen Verbänden in der Epoche des Konstitutionalismus in Deutschland.* Berlin, Duncker und Humblot.

Burrage, M. (1988) 'Unternehmer, Beamte und freie Berufe. Schlüsselgruppen der bürgerlichen Mittelschichten in England, Frankreich und den Vereinigten Staaten', in H. Siegrist (ed.) *Bürgerliche Berufe im Internationalen Vergleich.* Göttingen, Vandenhoeck und Ruprecht.

Burrage, M. (1989) 'Revolution as a starting point for the comparative analysis of the French, American and English legal professions', in R.L. Abel and P. Lewis (eds) *Lawyers in Society*, Vol. 3. Berkeley, University of California Press.

Burrage, M. (1990) 'Introduction. The professions in sociology and history', in M. Burrage and R. Torstendahl (eds) *Professions in Theory and History: Rethinking the Study of the Professions.* London, Sage.

Burrage, M., Jarausch, K.H. and Siegrist, H. (1990) 'An actor-based framework for the study of the professions', in M. Burrage and R. Torstendahl (eds) *Professions in Theory and History. Rethinking the Study of the Professions.* London, Sage.

Burrage, M. and Torstendahl, R. (eds) (1990) *Professions in Theory and History: Rethinking the Study of the Professions.* London, Sage.

Collins, R. (1979) *The Credential Society.* New York, Academic Press.

Collins, R. (1990) 'Market closure and the conflict theory of the professions', in M. Burrage and R. Torstendahl (eds) *Professions in Theory and History: Rethinking the Study of the Professions.* London, Sage.

Conze, W. and Kocka, J. (eds) (1985) *Bildungsbürgertum im 19. Jahrhundert. Teil I: Bildungssystem und Professionalisierung in Internationalen Vergleichen.* Stuttgart, Klett-Cotta.

Dingwall, R. and Lewis, P. (1983) 'Introduction', in R. Dingwall and P. Lewis (eds) *The Sociology of the Professions. Lawyers, Doctors and Others.* London, Macmillan.

Duman, D. (1983) *The English and Colonial Bars in the Nineteenth Century.* London, Croom Helm.

Evans, P., Rüschemeyer, D. and Skocpol, T. (eds) (1985) *Bringing the State Back In.* Cambridge, Cambridge University Press.

Freidson, E. (1986) *Professional Powers. A Study of the Institutionalization of Formal Knowledge.* Chicago, University of Chicago Press.

Geison, G.L. (ed.) (1984) *Professions and the French State 1700–1900.* Philadelphia, University of Pennsylvania Press.

Göbel, T. (1990) 'Ärzte und Rechtsanwälte in den USA 1800–1930', *Geschichte und Gesellschaft* **16**, 318–42.

Heidenheimer, A.J. (1980) 'Organized medicine and physician specialization in Scandinavia and West Germany', in A.J. Heidenheimer (ed.) *Public Political Comparisons: Scandinavia.* London, Frank Cass.

Heidenheimer, A.J. (1989) 'Professional knowledge and state policy in comparative historical perspective: law and medicine in Britain, Germany and the United States', *International Social Science Journal* **122**, 529–53.

Huerkamp, C. (1985) *Der Aufstieg der Ärzte im 19. Jahrhundert. Vom Gelehrten Stand zum Professionellen Experten.* Göttingen, Vandenhoeck und Ruprecht.

Jarausch, K.H. (1990a) *The Unfree Professions. German Lawyers, Teachers and Engineers 1900–1950.* Oxford and New York, Oxford University Press.

Jarausch, K.H. (1990b) 'The German professions in history and theory', in G. Cocks and K.H. Jarausch (eds) *German Professions 1800–1950.* Oxford and New York, Oxford University Press.

Johnson, T. (1972) *Professions and Power.* London, Macmillan.

Karpik, L. (1988) 'Lawyers and politics in France 1814–1950: the state, the market and the public', *Law and Social Inquiry* **13**, 707–36.

Karpik, L. (1990) 'Technical and political knowledge: the relationship of lawyers and other legal professions to the market and the state', in R. Torstendahl and M. Burrage (eds) *The Formation of the Professions: Knowledge, State and Strategy.* London, Sage.

Kornhauser, W. (1962) *Scientists in Industry: Conflict and Accommodation.* Berkeley, University of California Press.

Lega, C. (1974) *Le Libere Professioni Intellettuali nelle Leggi e nella Giurisprudenza.* Milan, Giuffre.

Lundgreen, P. (1988) 'Wissen und Bürgertum. Skizze eines historischen Vergleichs zwischen Preussen/Deutschland, Frankreich und den USA, 18–20 Jahrhundert', in H. Siegrist (ed.) *Bürgerliche Berufe.* Göttingen, Vandenhoeck und Ruprecht.

McClelland, C.E. (1991) *The German Experience of Professionalisation. Modern Learned Professions and their Organisations from the Early Nineteenth Century to the Hitler Era.* Cambridge, Cambridge University Press.

Ostler, F. (1971) *Die Deutschen Rechtsanwälte 1871–1971.* Essen, Ellinghaus.

Parsons, T. (1963) 'The professions and social structure', in *Essays in Sociological Theory.* Glencoe, IL, Free Press.

Perkin, H. (1989) *The Rise of Professional Society.* London, Routledge.

Ramsey, M. (1984) 'The politics of professional monopoly in nineteenth century medicine: the French model and its rivals', in G. Geison (ed.) *Professions and the French State 1700–1900.* Philadelphia, University of Pennsylvania Press.

Rüschemeyer, D. (1986) 'Comparing legal professions cross-nationally: from a professions-centered to a state-centered approach', *American Bar Foundation Research Journal* 1986, 415–46.

Sarfatti Larson, M. (1977) *The Rise of Professionalism. A Sociological Analysis.* Berkeley, University of California Press.

Siegrist, H. (1985) 'Gebremste Professionalisierung – das Beispiel der Schweizer Rechtsanwaltschaft im Vergleich zu Frankreich und Deutschland im 19. und frühen 20. Jahrhundert', in W. Conze and J. Kocka (eds) *Bildungsbürgertum im 19. Jahrhundert. Teil I: Bildungsystem und Professionalisierung in Internationalen Vergleichen.* Stuttgart, Klett-Cotta.

Siegrist, H. (ed) (1988a) *Bürgerliche Berufe. Zur Sozialgeschichte der Freien und Akademischen Berufe im Internationalen Vergleich.* Göttingen, Vandenhoeck und Ruprecht.

Siegrist, H. (1988b) 'Bürgerliche Berufe. Die Professionen und das Bürgertum', in H. Siegrist (ed.) *Bürgerliche Berufe.* Göttingen, Vandenhoeck und Ruprecht.

Siegrist, H. (1990a) 'Professionalisation as a process: patterns, progression and discontinuity', in M. Burrage and R. Torstendahl (eds) *Professions in Theory and History. Rethinking the Study of the Professions.* London, Sage.

Siegrist, H. (1990b) 'Public office or free profession? German attorneys in the nineteenth and early twentieth centuries', in G. Cocks and K.H. Jarausch (eds) *German Professions, 1800–1950.* New York and Oxford, Oxford University Press.

Siegrist, H. (1991) 'States and legal professions. France, Germany, Italy and Switzerland, 18th to early 20th centuries', in A. Febbrajo (ed.) *Storia del Diritto e Teoria Politica.* Milan.

Siegrist, H. (1993) 'Die gebildeten Mittelklassen in Westdeutschland 1945–1965', in W. Fischer-Rosenthal, P. Alheit and E.M. Hoerning (eds) *Biographien in Deutschland.* Opladen, Westdeutscher Verlag.

Strath, B. and Torstendahl, R. (1992) 'State theory and state development: states as network structures in change in modern European history', in R. Torstendahl (ed.) *State Theory and State History.* London, Sage.

Titze, H. (1991) 'Lehrerbildung und Professionalisierung', in *Handbuch der Deutschen Bildungsgeschichte*, Vol. 4. Munich, C.H. Beck.

Torstendahl, R. (ed.) (1992) *State Theory and State History.* London, Sage.

Torstendahl, R. and Burrage, M. (eds) (1990) *The Formation of the Professions. Knowledge, State and Strategy.* London, Sage.

Tousijn, W. (1987) 'Tra stato e mercato: le libere professioni in Italia in una perspettiva storico-evolutiva', in W. Tousijn (ed.) *Le Libere Professioni in Italia.* Bologna, Mulino.

Wilensky, H. (1972) 'Jeder Beruf eine Profession', in T. Luckmann and W. Sprondel (eds) *Berufssoziologie.* Cologne, Kiepenheuer.

Part 1

Professional Perspectives

2

Engineers and Governments in a Comparative Perspective

Rolf Torstendahl

Introduction: engineers, professionalism and state policy

Engineers in the present-day societies of Western Europe are so often related to industry that they are commonly regarded as being, by nature, industry's servants – although in the past the relationship was not always so close. The other side of the intimate relationship is, however, that industry has become dependent on its engineers. They are the pillar on which industry leans and the workforce on whose loyalty industry depends. Again, this has not always been the case, and there is thus good reason to consider historical evidence when we are trying to locate engineers in their social setting.

A historical perspective on engineers and on all groups which aspire to a professional standing is rewarding, since professionalism, whatever we mean by this sociological concept (to be explored further below), has not had a constant meaning for any occupational group down the centuries. One of the reasons for change and, in other cases, for relative stability is the policy of the state. For our purposes, the state might be better specified as the government in this case, since we shall not look into the possible influences of different state administrations and departments, even though these have been important in some cases. What will be treated here from a historical perspective is rather a system that manifests a loose relationship between engineers as an occupational group, its professionalism and the governmental policy adopted in relation to that group and its professionalism.

Before we consider engineers as a group, some words on professionalism are required, for this concept is widely used but equally often understood in different ways. This task is addressed in the next section. Then a section is devoted to the different types of professional policies toward engineers pursued by the states in Western Europe, the only part of the world taken into account here, the perspective being mainly limited to Britain, France,

Germany and Sweden. This section deals with state involvement in the British way of establishing the engineering professions, the Continental way of establishing a technological education sponsored by the state and, third, state activities in the protection of titles of engineers. Finally there is an analysis of state-related activities by professional associations based on educational criteria in France, Germany and Sweden, and a brief conclusion.

Professionalism

For those to whom English is a native language the use of the term 'professional' is part of everyday life. This does not mean that English-speaking people have a very clear definition of professionalism, but they have no difficulty in understanding the meaning of expressions like 'doctors and other professional groups' or 'A's ambition was to become a professional and thus he tried to get into the Inns of Court.' Even terms like professionalism and professionalization may be perceived as parts of a familiar vocabulary. (I consciously ignore the fact that 'professional' is ambiguous in English. Another meaning of 'professional' is 'doing something for one's living', as in the expression 'A is a professional golfer' or, for short, 'A is a professional' when the context is clear.)

The term professional, as used in sociological theory, was borrowed from everyday English usage. Of course, the term had to be clarified, defined and made orderly to be used in social science. This was no easy task, and the differences between interpreters were enormous. Theoretical aims steered their efforts in quite different directions. In broad terms we can discern a development from the effort to find a valid taxonomy of occupations to the ambition to find driving forces behind the collective behaviour of groups in the labour market (Saks 1983; Collins 1990). We will confine our perspective here to the latter aspect of professionalism.

Knowledge-based groups

There is no doubting a direct relationship between professional groups and particular bodies of knowledge. This relation is so close, and the knowledge associated with groups so clearly established and rigid, that some authors have wanted to identify the capabilities of professional groups with academic knowledge. They also want to say that professionals are university-educated people or people with education from equivalent institutes (Conze and Kocka, 1985; cf. Burrage *et al.* 1990). This seems to be an exaggeration of the role of formal education in the light of both history and different national practices. For example, the English tradition here has been far less academic than the continental.

The emphasis on formal education has been made for a purpose. A standpoint is taken, or at least indicated, in two major fields of discussion:

the question of the relation between knowledge and skill and the question of how professions relate to guilds. A link between the two is not difficult to find. If guilds are seen as organizations based primarily on skill, then professions become the only means of organizing knowledge-based groups.

There are good reasons to maintain a view of professions as knowledge-based groups. But at the same time it is important to emphasize the impossibility of making a clear distinction between knowledge and skill. The line is blurred, so that some of the teachings within universities extend well into what might be termed skills rather than 'theoretical knowledge', whatever that might be. And if we consider the institutions training lawyers, or surgical and other medical training, or the teaching at the institutes of technology, it is quite clear that 'skill' (taken as the ability to do certain things acquired through imitation of masters of the trade rather than through intellectual understanding) is fundamental for many professionals, if not all (this relation is more fully explored in Torstendahl 1990).

Accordingly, when we see professionals as knowledge-based groups it is important to stress that knowledge is taken to mean not only theoretical knowledge but a mixture of theoretical knowledge and skill. It may even be impossible to distinguish between the two, for example in the history of technology, where the systematization of procedures was from the outset seen by many to be at the core of the field. Therefore, the term 'knowledge-based groups' is used here to refer to knowledge as a broad category, including skill (for further discussion, see Torstendahl 1990).

Obviously, then, we have a difficulty in establishing a distinction between professions and guilds. Even the historical difference is unclear. It is true that many professions arose, or developed an organized form, in a period when guilds were vanishing, but this has to do with how different occupational groups related to power in state and society rather than with definitional criteria. It is also important that some professions have a long history, notably lawyers (sometimes in different professions) and doctors (excluding the surgeons, who rose in esteem rather late) (Sarfatti Larson 1977; Collins 1979, 1981). The emphasis may be said to be more on theory in professions than in guilds, but how much more is impossible to state in absolute terms.

Strategic action

Knowledge-based groups may be interesting for different reasons. One of these is the problem of how they acquire their knowledge; another is what ties them together as a group; a third is how they act as a collectivity. We will touch upon all these aspects in this chapter. First, let us give some consideration to the question of collective action among professionals.

Collective action does not presuppose organization, but it is certainly true that organization is a significant help in defining goals and selecting means in collective action. Professional groups have been early and quick to organize, and professional organization has become a term in sociology. Professional organizations are obviously not voluntary associations of the most general sort – for the benefit of mankind – like temperance associations or working groups for environmental protection. Nor are they exactly like trade unions, which are often taken as examples of the most extreme kind of organized interest, for mostly they are not intended to act through bargaining with employers on salaries for their group members. However, during the past few decades we have seen professional organizations take up such bargaining themselves or move into close cooperation with a true white collar union. For example, the most prestigious professional organization of engineers in Sweden has been absorbed into the trade union of first class engineers, though nominally it preserves a formal separate existence.

Thus organization in itself is only a means, not an end, and does not lead towards any specific end. Consequently, organizations may adopt different strategies to realize the goals which are considered vital to their members. Frank Parkin, in his influential book *Marxism and Class Theory* (1979), differentiates between two types of closure strategies. Exclusionary closure is the form typical of professional organizations, whereas usurpation – i.e. the effort to gain certain economic and other conditions defined by comparison with other groups – is typical of trade unions. Parkin also recognizes a strategy consisting of both elements, which he calls dual closure (Parkin 1979).

The strategies of knowledge-based groups are directed towards the labour market and the closure strategy strives for the exclusion of those who have not acquired the knowledge in question from the practice of the occupation. This may seem to be a clear principle, but confronted with labour market realities it is not very clear in actuality and, particularly, it is difficult in many cases to decide if someone has or has not acquired the proper knowledge. All professional groups therefore rely on approximations of different kinds – some on membership of an organization, some on examinations by the professional body, some on degrees from special educational institutions. This is obviously a field where outside influence can play a role, and where state policy has often concentrated.

State professional policies towards engineers

The interest of states in professions has a long and varied history. States have been interested in using professionals as their servants for specific tasks. It has also been a concern of the state to try to influence both the availability of practitioners of these occupations and their standing in society, relating both to their forms of organization and to their social rewards, including material benefits as well as status (a very informative account of the relations of states to engineers in a long historical perspective is given in Burrage 1992). We will confine the perspective here mainly to the nineteenth and early twentieth centuries. This means that we must leave out the possibility of analysing several interesting early varieties of state interference with the professions; but, on the other hand, engineers were rare before 1800, and the term then mainly referred to a limited number of people in the field of construction. The builders of fortresses and roads for military purposes became organized in 'engineering' corps and, to some extent, architects and master-builders of churches and palaces were also known as engineers, but the usage of the term became established only from around 1800.

The institutions of engineers in Britain

With regard to the mobilization of engineers in professional interest organizations there are noticeable differences between countries in Western Europe. British engineers were beginning to recognize mutual concerns from the late eighteenth century and formed different organizations in order to promote their interests. German engineers got their powerful *Verein Deutscher Ingenieure* (VDI) in the middle of the nineteenth century. French engineers created a general organization that was comparatively weak in 1848, but on the other hand the *anciens élèves* of different schools formed reliable networks. Sweden also developed an association for the promotion of the interests of engineers in the late part of the century. Its mobilization of engineers focused on the best educated, and its influence on the state was limited. Associating for professional interests was thus general but different in aims and in its success in achieving them.

British engineers had been given responsibilities for managing complicated road- and bridge-building enterprises and very advanced canal constructions from the period before the railway era. There were thus some competent people to assemble for the dinners of the Society of Civil Engineers in England, already founded in 1771 with John Smeaton as one of the leaders. Thomas Telford, the renowned canal and bridge builder, indirectly played a great role in the beginnings of the Institution of Civil Engineers, founded in 1818 by Telford's assistants, with an ambitious programme of lectures and discussions (Rolt 1958: 189–92; Prandy 1965: 63–70; Watson 1988: 4–17). From the very beginning the Institution was a voluntary association of select people who were renowned for their accomplishments in civil engineering, and Telford was soon asked to become its president. The institution had an ambition to cover the whole field of engineering and, though encouraging societies for specific technical sub-fields, actively opposed any efforts from such societies to get state recognition of the same kind as the Institution had through its royal charter of 1828 (Watson 1988: 31ff., 52ff.).

The model used by civil engineers was applied by the mechanical engineers in their Institution for Mechanical Engineers from 1847, which from the point of view of the civil engineers was merely a society (Parsons 1947: 15).

Through its charter the Institution of Civil Engineers had managed to gain a specially recognized position in society. The Institution of Mechanical Engineers also claimed recognition and soon became important, not least because of its restricted membership, but was awarded its royal charter only in 1930. Mechanical engineers, as the institution defined them, were 'managing heads of establishments in which engines or machines are made' or establishments where such engines or machines were used. Other mechanical engineers might be admitted to membership if they qualified as 'eminent' (Parsons 1947: 15–16, 88–9). It should be noted that these rules gave owners of workshops a decisive position, and also served to distinguish 'engineering' workshops from manufactures based on handicraft. A mechanical engineer had to have a responsibility for linking power sources to machinery.

The Institution of Electrical Engineers was a later creation, founded by naval officers in 1871 as a society of telegraph engineers, but developed and incorporated in 1888 as an institution of its own through active participation by several members of the Institution of Civil Engineers. It got a royal charter in 1921 (Watson 1988: 53). Still later, in 1922, the Institution of Chemical Engineers was founded; and, last of the great institutions, the Institution of Metallurgists in 1945 (Prandy 1965: 63–105). Thus each of the main specialities of engineering had acquired its own institution. These institutions were an interesting combination of clubs for social intercourse between members, debating societies and organs for the authorization of engineers. Parsons notes that at a quite early stage the letters MIME (later MIMechE) were used to signify that a person was a member of the Institute of Mechanical Engineers, and members were later officially authorized to use this distinguishing mark, still valid more than a hundred years later (Parsons 1947: 30ff.; Prandy 1965: 69). It was quickly exploited as a means of competition. From the very beginning it was an asset to be a member. The dividing line – the 'closure' of the theory of professionalization – lay in the conditions for membership.

The royal charters given to some of the institutions of engineers were a public acknowledgement that the state recognized them and their members. We will come back to the question of 'chartered engineers' but here it will suffice to say that the function of the institutions was clearly regarded as important and in the interests of the state. Authorization was needed. Dabblers could not be allowed to compete on an equal footing with the knowledgeable.

In view of such opinions, or insights into the conditions of the market economy, the institutions gradually introduced a new and more important form of authorization. From the beginning only those who had already become socially independent as managers of industry were admitted, and for them the professional strategy was clearly a market control strategy. To be a member was marketable and non-members were at a disadvantage in the market (Reader 1966: 164ff.; Behringer 1981: 74–81). However, restricted membership excluded most of the competent practitioners in dependent positions. Social criteria proved too narrow to accommodate many of the well-regarded professionals. A new demarcation line had to be set. Formally this redrawing of the boundaries allowed, in all the well-established institutions, a new kind of membership, albeit of a second class.

The demand for widening the membership of the British institutions of engineers gained political support. The Institution of Mechanical Engineers was reluctant, however, to make membership easily available for the broad layers of mechanical engineers. The subordinate forms of membership, graduate and associate, had been in existence for a long time and were complemented with 'associate members' in 1892. (The subtle distinction between 'associates' and 'associate members' was used also by the Institution of Electrical Engineers.) However, all these groups had to be nominated and the honour was rather rare. The Institution of Mechanical Engineers was the last of the major engineering institutions in Britain to accept an entrance examination for associate members of the institution, which was first offered in 1912, in fact a year earlier than the Institution of Electrical Engineers, who had delayed implementing a decision from 1908 (Appleyard 1939: 235–7). Such an examination had been proposed in a Parliamentary Bill in 1888, but had been vigorously resisted by the mechanical engineers. Even in 1912 they seem not to have been enthusiastic about it, though it was accepted. However, this examination did not apply to a full member, who was expected to hold 'a position sufficiently important for his technical qualification to be taken for granted' (Parsons 1947: 47). The model was the Institution of Civil Engineers, where associate members had been introduced in 1878 and where regular examinations of the candidates for this grade of membership were held for the first time in 1897 (Watson 1988: 49–51, 123–6). With the introduction of the examinations for associate membership in the engineering institutions, the conditions for professional recognition changed in Britain. Although formal changes resulted from the introduction of examinations, it was still in the hands of these institutions to decide the conditions. However, the road was opened for national certificates and 'diploma hunting' after the First World War (Cotgrove 1958: 154–66) – not through the activities of the Institutions, but by leaving them in a position to supervise the whole process.

From the beginning of the 1920s the institutions supervised schools which claimed that they taught engineering to their pupils. The Institution of Electrical Engineers in 1922 reported that the entrance of schools into the system of control from the Institution was completely voluntary, but no school was accepted without a scrupulous examination by the Institution, and approval was liable to be revoked by the Institution whenever it was deemed necessary. Examination of the pupils of these schools had to be controlled by inspectors from the Institution (Marsh 1986: 248). Marsh, who has emphasized this aspect of British professionalism among engineers, underlines the fact that the control was never complete, and was always moderated through the influence of the Ministry of Education.

One further step was taken in 1924 when the institutions of engineers became the sponsors of the new general council of the engineering profession

(Marsh 1986: 248). This was important as another mark of the decisive influence of the professional organizations on the profession of engineer in Britain. The influence of the state continued to be secondary, though not totally absent. It consistently but cautiously supported the institutions, for example by the award of Royal Charters to the institutions of mechanical and electrical engineers in the inter-war years. But the recognition was a distinction that reinforced the exclusiveness of the profession and implied no ministerial control of the professional organizations. Nor was there any interference in the extent of their control of engineering education before the Second World War. In 1962, however, the earlier council for cooperation between the institutions of engineers was reconstituted as an Engineering Institutions' Joint Council, replaced in 1983 by a Council of Engineers. The role of the latter body was intended to be more far-reaching: indeed, the initiator of reform, the Finniston Report, argued for a state authority to take over the accreditation of engineers (Marsh 1986: 251–3).

The engineering institutions of Britain have had a special and interesting relation with the state. They had the implicit – or even at times the explicit – blessing of the state from the very beginning, and they gradually got involved in state professional policy. For a very long time, however, they were the main actors in the professionalization process, while the state kept in the background. Recognition and control were left in the hands of the organizations. Recognition of engineers meant 'exclusionary closure' (in Parkin's terminology) and, at the same time, control of personal competence. The basic instrument for such control was examination of knowledge and skill, but this was originally a side entrance, while the main entrance was reserved for property owners of the trade. In Britain there were, thus, some means for the state to influence the professionalization of engineers. Without a doubt these were important. In other countries, however, policy measures had interfered far more in the profession of engineering over a much longer period.

Establishing state schools

There are two roots of technical education that came to be important.in most European countries in the nineteenth century. One of them was the demand from the state, as the incarnation and support of the legal system, for a labour force for specific needs, especially in communications (roads, bridges) but also in mining (with origins in the legal conceptions of a royal prerogative with regard to the use of the entrails of the earth) and construction in general. The other root lay in the developing economy within industry (in a broad sense) and in capitalist agriculture.

Of these two roots the second one became dominant, but most of the schools and institutes that arose from this demand were eager to gain some profit from the prestige of the paradigm for the former, the *Ecole polytechnique*. Therefore historical accounts tend to emphasize the connection with this tradition and to pass over what could not be made to fit into it. The main distinction has been blurred by this process. Only a few schools were formed explicitly to meet the needs of both the state and the private economy for technical expertise. However, many of them developed gradually into this hybrid form. Even the *Ecole polytechnique* went through the same process of attrition, though in the face of a constant deprecation of the *pantouflage*, that is the refusal to finish studies by entering the feeder schools for the civil service, and instead switching into private business (Shinn 1980: 93–7, 167–9). The Royal Institute of Technology in Stockholm changed in the other direction. From the beginning, it had no future civil servants among its students but became, during the last decades of the nineteenth century and the beginning of the twentieth, an important gateway to civil service positions for more than 10 per cent of its graduates, even if they often started in private sector businesses (Torstendahl 1975a: 95). Both these schools were state schools, supported by the state and provided with curricula and tasks by the state, but their purposes were originally totally different.

State policy in engineering has often led to the establishment of state schools and, later, to complete state school systems, that is schools at different but related levels, for disseminating technical knowledge. The fundamental belief has been that technology may be learnt through reading and listening in class and need not be learnt through imitation of how things are done, i.e. that it requires not only know-how but also, or rather, know-what. This presumption has never remained undisputed in the history of technological learning, and through the nineteenth and twentieth centuries there has been a strong undercurrent of scepticism about the 'theoretical learning' of technology, which has affected many political debates and administrative arrangements, even in countries where the tradition of technological schooling has been strong (Torstendahl 1975b: 27–130, examines the debate about 'theory and practice' in technological schooling in Sweden during the period 1810–70).

Technological schools set up by the state gave an education that gradually made it natural for them to give their graduates the status and the title of engineers. As 'engineer' was not an exclusive title at the beginning of the nineteenth century, especially in England, this title only gradually became an asset on the labour market, being used on the continent to signal certain labour relations. The more attractive it became, the more it was open to disputes about its legitimate use. We will come back to state policy regarding the title of engineer, but in order to understand state school policy it is important to emphasize that the main state schools became a key means of acquiring this attractive title. In many cases specialized titles were created to pursue a greater exclusivity (the 'closure' became tighter), but even to become an 'engineer' in general was regarded in France, Germany and Sweden (and certainly many other countries on the continent) as a mark of considerable status, partly in contrast with its more limited social value in Britain. (The low esteem of engineers in Britain was especially complained about in the 1960s and early 1970s: see e.g. Platt 1973; Roberts 1973; Towler

1973.) Thus, state school policy stands at the centre of a fundamental difference between engineers as professionals in European countries.

State educational policy in technology had different forms. The French form was based on specific schools and institutes. The *Ecole polytechnique* (EP), dating from the Revolution (it was opened in 1794), was the first and most prestigious but not the only one. The *Ecole centrale des arts et manufactures* was a private school when it started in 1828, but was taken over by the state in 1851. The local *écoles des arts et métiers* only gradually grew in importance and status, and adult education at the *Conservatoire nationale des arts et manufactures*, though it was organized by the state from its very beginning in the 1820s and had a good reputation abroad, was long regarded as of only secondary importance. There were also state regional schools (for a general overview of the technical schools in France, see Artz 1966). Thus France, even before the middle of the nineteenth century, had a number of specific institutes and types of schools that were only loosely related to each other. In each case it was the school as such that imprinted its status on the student. Behind them stood the state, giving its support for the grading of the technological institutes.

Germany was not unified at the beginning of the nineteenth century and there was consequently no possibility of establishing one state policy. However, in some of the different states (Prussia, Baden and Bayern in the first instances) a similar pattern developed. The state was active from the 1820s in establishing a policy for schooling in technology. The first institutes were in some cases more schools for vocational training than anything else (the *Gewerbeinstitut* in Berlin and the *höhere Gewerbeschulen* had vocational training inherent in their names though they became important technological institutes later). What were known as polytechnical schools were established in, for instance, Karlsruhe and Munich. The states took good care of their schools and improved them, and the consequence was their promotion in the 1860s and 1870s to the rank of *Technische Hochschulen*. Their establishment at this level meant that a differentiated tertiary education in technology was established for a distinguished category of first class engineers. Other schools had to be established to provide technical education at a secondary level. (A general overview of the German technical schools and their development is given in *Das akademische Deutschland*, Vol. 1. Many later specialized investigations are available, none of them going into the variety of schools in the same degree of detail.)

In Sweden a Technological Institute was established by the state in Stockholm in 1827. A parallel institute on a private basis came into being in Gothenburg in 1830, but quite soon this school became totally dependent on the state for its means of survival. The Gothenburg school was quite successful compared with its favoured Stockholm counterpart, but when the latter was reorganized in 1847–50 it was given – by the state – a slightly higher position than the former. This was possible because Sweden had introduced a systematic approach to technical education during this period. When four state schools of a lower level were established, the initiative came from the parliament, with the head of the Technological Institute as the author of the detailed plan. The two levels of state schools were then complemented by a third level of local and municipal schools, mainly for vocational training and of different quality. None of them had a recognized standing comparable with that of the secondary state-school level. A system of technological schooling was thus established and even if there were later adjustments of the relations within this system, its main character as a system was never questioned (Torstendahl 1975b).

Continental state policy on technological schooling in the nineteenth century was important, in that its conscious purpose was to define high quality education and, consequently, generate highly qualified graduates. These engineers – as they gradually came to be called – were thus certified by the state as being first-rate practitioners. In some cases, as very early in Sweden, the state even made an effort to distinguish different levels of graduates, even if those at the lower levels were not officially – and rarely in practice – called engineers until a later period.

The school policy was important in its different forms. It made training at certain educational institutions the instrument for establishing the closure required for the professionalization of engineers. In its continental variety this closure resulted from a technological school system and from the different levels recognized by the state. In the French form the emphasis lay on the individual school and its specific character. Even if forms varied, the state gave the impetus and upheld the system that was the basis for the professionalism of engineers in Continental countries.

Protection of groups and titles

'Engineer' was for a long period not a protected title in any country in northwestern Europe. This is obvious from the history of engineers. At the end of the eighteenth century two categories used the title: those who had relevant positions in state military and civil administrations connected with the title, and those practitioners who had privately decided to adopt its use (John Smeaton is a good example). Of course they had all been trained, but schools for the purpose (excepting the *Ecole des ponts et chaussées*) hardly existed. The title was in the hands of those who used it.

The title 'engineer' is differently related to other titles and to diplomas. There have been two different, but sometimes related, uses of the term. On the one hand it has been used for persons with a certain occupational standing, that is as a designation of their work. In this connection the question of where such persons acquired the appropriate knowledge was of secondary importance. In fact, the employer had the right to decide whether a person was competent or not. On the other hand, the title was used for people who had a training, diploma or charter to define them as engineers. These people would continue to be engineers regardless of how they earned their living. They were defined not through employment but through institutional arrangements sanctioned by the state.

Thus the use of the title 'engineer' was for a long time undefined and ambiguous. Many engineers wanted to change this situation. They used different strategies to achieve their goal. With the rise of institutions in Britain and schools and technological institutes in other countries, the situation changed. The groups formed through this process claimed that the title was more or less in their gift. As the self-taught practitioners did not disappear abruptly, specific combinations with the title of engineer were used. There was no point in introducing such a combination if no possibility was allowed of restricting its use. For that purpose the power of the state was needed.

When engineers began to enter industry as salaried employees in Europe and the United States in the late nineteenth century, they began to be regarded as engineers rather than as managers, foremen, mechanics or holders of any specific position or occupation. This was a general phenomenon in the countries under consideration. Technical experts had been employed in their capacity as experts before, but only occasionally and in small numbers. Some had received an education at one or other of the available technical schools: in Germany at the polytechnic schools which became in the 1860–70s *technische Hochschulen*; in France and Sweden at the schools for higher technical education (though sometimes lower technical education would still allow acceptance as an engineer); and in Britain at one of the few specialized technical schools. However, it is important to note that even after 1880 many of those holding technical positions in industry on the continent had not been educated as engineers in schools but had received a practical training (Boltanski 1985). It is not quite certain that such people, without a technical schooling but employed in technical occupations in industry, were really regarded as 'engineers'. Some of them – it seems from the USA – 'usurped' the title of 'mechanical engineer' or something of the kind. Many were thought of by others and by themselves as belonging to one or other of the technical specialties (Calvert 1967: 14ff.). This was natural, since before 1850 'engineer' by itself was hardly regarded as a title. It had to be qualified with other forms, for instance by 'civil' or 'mechanical' in the English-speaking countries and in Sweden, and by 'civil' (in another sense of the word) in France (Armytage 1965: 99ff.; Calvert 1967: 13–27; Runeby 1976: 3–4; Shinn 1978: 40–7).

In several countries – for instance in Germany – a difference is made between a *Diplomingenieur* and just an engineer, and the specialized title was from its introduction in 1899 a protected title. Thus an important and tricky relation between occupation and title has developed as regards engineers. The establishment of the *Diplomingenieure* as a separate category in part gave the desired effect, but 'engineer' did not become the specific title of the secondary rank.

The British engineering institutions adopted a solution which was in principle very like that of the *Diplomingenieur*. When the Privy Council decided, in 1924, to give the members of the Institution of Electrical Engineers the exclusive title of 'Chartered Electrical Engineer' (Appleyard 1939:

245–6; Watson 1988: 53 – the Civil Engineers had the same arrangement, but from Watson's book it is unclear from what date), the state had involved itself in the protection of a certain title. As with the German title, the state had in effect committed itself to maintaining the exclusivity (i.e. the closure) of a specific professional group. It turned out, however, that engineers in Britain were by no means content with the degree of protection given through the 'chartered engineer' title. After the Second World War the various organizations representing British engineers began to call for the kind of protection given in some other countries to the title of engineer (Platt 1973: 16–17). (Platt's survey of countries covers the USA and Canada plus eight European countries, where he found protection either of the general title or of a qualified variety such as *Diplomingenieur.*)

Elsewhere, the general title of engineer became a matter of dispute in the inter-war period. In France this dispute became acute in the 1920s. At that time *ingénieur* was not only a designation for a type of occupation, and a title for graduates of certain schools, but also a well-established title in public administration, specifically the administration of roads and bridges. When the use of the title was extended, in the 1920s, to an administrative category that had not previously carried it, the trade unions working among engineers became active. This was one of the initial events that ultimately led to the law of 1934 on the title of engineer. Although it began as an affair concerning public sector employees, the outcome was a law concerning who might call himself or herself an engineer. The approved schools, which had the right to confer the title of engineer on their diplomates, were to be continuously reviewed by a *Commission des Titres d'Ingénieurs*, which was set up as a result of the law and which became a permanent institution (Part 2 of Grelon 1986 deals with this question: see especially the contributions of Goutmann, Ribeill – two contributions – and Guillerme). The state became substantially engaged, and the commission that was born became an instrument of state power and policy in professionalization.

Legislation on the permitted use of the title of engineer was also introduced in Spain in 1933. There the law specified, in a quite explicit form, that the state had to confer the title of engineer, or to permit holders of foreign titles the right to use them if they had their education at schools regarded as being of similar standing as the Spanish (Riera i Tuèbols 1986: 332ff.). Further decrees of 1934 and 1935, one of them repeating the entire procedure, show how the question of limiting the use of such a general title as that of engineer is far from a simple matter for a state, especially a state on the verge of civil war (Riera i Tuèbols 1988: 55).

After the Second World War an interest in the limitation of the legal right to use the title of engineer was pursued by the German association, the VDI. Its argument was that the title must be protected in order to give all persons with a technical education career chances that accorded with their competence. The association had a first success with its claims when, in 1965, the parliament of the Federal Republic passed a general and federal law to this effect. This law was subsequently declared null and void by the constitutional court in Karlsruhe in 1969. However, while ruling that it should not be a federal task to make such laws, the decision of the court referred eventual legislation to the *Länder*, where similar laws might be carried through. Consequently, the VDI rapidly sought support in the *Länder* for its policy, and after its acceptance by Nordrhein-Westfalen in 1970 all of them followed suit within a year. What was described as a 'gap in the lawgiving' by the VDI was accordingly bridged (see '*Vorwort*' in VDI 1971, and the relevant parts of the laws reprinted in that volume).

What this section has tried to show (through examples that cannot give a total picture of all the related matters) is the ongoing and gradually growing dependence of the professionalization of engineers on the state, a dependence which has increased in both scope and intensity. The process has not been the same in all countries but, somewhat contrary to expectation, strong associations with a base among engineers employed in private sector industry have been eager to secure the protection of the state for their members and the interests of the profession. The strategy appears to have been similar throughout Western Europe, though the means employed have varied considerably.

Professional policies of associations based on alumni or graduation

French school-based professionalism

The French general association of engineers, the *Société des ingénieurs civils de France*, was founded in 1848, and its specific objective was to make industrial careers attractive and popular among engineers. Its philosophical basis was found in a tradition of Comtism and Saint-Simonianism, and it was similar to the VDI in its cultural aims and collective level of activity (Shinn 1978: 57–8). However, it seems never to have acted in a political setting in the same way as the German VDI (see below), and its ambitions for status were directed not towards the state and the education of engineers but rather against the industrial capitalists and managers of industrial enterprises. It was successful in attracting members in the 1890s and the 1900s, its membership steadily shifting from graduates of the *Ecole centrale* to those of the new engineering schools (Shinn 1978: 66ff.). This is not to say that its influence grew in French society in a related way. There are no obvious traces of such influence. (The only author who has really treated the influence of the engineering organizations in France is Shinn. Several others have dealt with science and engineering education but always with a concentration on the *grandes écoles* and the universities rather than on professional organizations: see Day 1980; Paul 1980; Paul and Shinn 1981/2; Weisz 1983. This emphasis is certainly in itself a sign that educational institution meant more than professional organization, but the influence of the latter could be analysed in more detail.)

In spite of the weak character of the organization of engineers in general,

French engineers stood strong. They may have been better equipped socially than in most comparable countries. Instead of cultivating a professional organization of a general kind, French engineers relied heavily on their alumni organizations, the *associations des anciens élèves* of the specific schools. The *grandes écoles* even had specific names for their students: the *polytechniciens* or the *X*; the *centraliens* from the two most renowned schools; and the *gadzarts* from the *écoles des arts et métiers*. In the French case the names signified real coherence. This was made evident in many ways. When bureaucratic organizations looked for personnel, the *polytechnicien* would be helpful to his younger colleague from the EP, and this internal loyalty tended to exclude others or make things more difficult for them, while the road was smoothed for the people of their own kind. It is important to note that this mutual support system was not limited to the EP, and that the *centraliens* and the *gadzarts* fostered the same type of closed-group attitudes. (The literature touching on the close relations among the *polytechniciens* is vast. See, for instance, Crozier 1963; Boltanski 1982; several of the contributions in Thépot 1985: 109–228. On the *centraliens*, see Lévy-Leboyer 1974; Weiss 1982; Ribeill 1985: 111–26. On *gadzarts*, see Day 1980; Darrigo and Serre 1985.)

Professionalism thus took a special turn in France. Exclusion was a strong element and its main form was the promotion of schoolmates, for professionalization was based not on general educational criteria or diplomas but on allegiance to school ideals. These schools were state initiatives or became part of a state school network. Thus, indirectly, the state was a guarantor of this school-based professionalism.

German organization plus education

The important *Verein Deutscher Ingenieure*, which came into existence in 1856 with earlier students of the Berlin *Gewerbeakademie* as driving forces, had other aims and methods. Its ambition was to obtain a *geistig* – or spiritual – recognition of technology as such in society, as a sphere of life in its own right, standing between science and art. Industry was its medium and the VDI was therefore also interested in industry and of interest to it. Its subsequent policy kept close to its initial ambitions. It became a pressure group for propaganda in the first instance and was involved in few activities aimed at promoting the individual interests of its members. It was rather an organization for the promotion of collective concerns (Manegold 1970: 59–61, 1981; Lundgreen 1981; Scholl, 1981).

The VDI had two main forms of activity that are of interest to us here. One was to publish books and pamphlets for use by engineers. In the inter-war period the series of publications reached sizeable proportions, and the VDI publishing house was recognized and used by official authorities such as the Deutsches Museum in Munich. The other activity was political and consisted of bringing VDI interests to the attention of the cultural ministries of the Kaiserreich and, later, of the Weimar Republic, the Third Reich and the Federal Republic. Its policy interests were essentially concerned with the education of engineers. First, the VDI made its views known on the desirability of reforming the polytechnic schools into *technische Hochschulen*, and it also gained the ear of the administration (Manegold 1970: 61–75, 1981: 143–59). Later, it was concerned with the right of the *technische Hochschulen* to confer doctorates on the students who qualified for the degree. After a long struggle the VDI won its case but the universities managed to equip the rose with a thorn. The degree *Doktor-Ingenieur* was supplied with a hyphen, and not latinized as traditional degrees were when the right was bestowed by the Kaiser first on the Berlin *Technische Hochschule* in 1899 and later in the same year on the rest of the *technische Hochschulen* (Manegold 1970: 282–305; Rürup 1979: 19; König 1981).

The successful and influential organization VDI was thus never itself concerned with implementing educational policies. It established no institutes or educational examinations. It worked indirectly through the state in its educational policy and then only for the collective status of engineers.

Swedish professional organizations among engineers took similar forms to those in Germany. A kind of professional organization was founded in Sweden in 1865 with the Society of Engineers in Stockholm, but a consistent policy could only be formed and carried through from the 1880s, when a competing organization, the Swedish Society of Technologists, took the lead. This association never expanded its membership far beyond engineers graduated from the Institute of Technology, now Royal. Its approach was very much in the same vein as that of the VDI, but it was far less successful in influencing educational and other policies (Runeby 1976: 88–100).

In Sweden, as in Germany and France, the education of engineers was planned by the state and mainly carried out in state schools. In Sweden and Germany education could provide a basis for a career in public service as well as in industry, while in France careers were more strongly determined by school of graduation, though in the twentieth century the migration from the public sphere to the private and in the reverse direction became commonplace and served to integrate the elites of the two sectors (Kaelble 1991: 188ff.). The clear similarities between the Swedish and German situations did not guarantee the effectiveness of the same professional association policy to equal degrees in the two countries. In Britain, with no state control over the education of engineers, the professional associations had to arrange the examination of the quality of engineers, which made them different from their counterparts in the other countries considered here.

Conclusion: the role of governmental policy for professional engineers

The simple relational system of the occupational group, its professionalism and the state or governmental policy, outlined in the introduction to this chapter, has in fact become rather complicated in the period since the early nineteenth century. The institutional forms of the relationships chosen by both state and engineers have been so different and have changed in character so many times that the immediate impression may be more chaotic than is justified.

The states in Western Europe have chosen different means to influence the engineering profession. In the main, the state has not enforced policies contrary to the explicit opinion of the professionals, but it has all the same been active to quite different degrees. The interference of the state was fundamental for the engineering profession on the continent. The initiative came from the governments and the state was the guarantor of the competence of the profession through its maintenance of engineering schools.

This is the main difference between the British and the continental pattern. It must be noted, however, that this is complemented by many similarities. After the creation of schools the state has mainly acted only at the request of engineers, or a selection of them, in relation to their interests. Both the German and the British professional organizations have used their influence in obtaining state backing for their policies. The German organization was for a long period more successful than the British in this respect, but in both countries the organizations concerned worked with the same strategy in mind and using mainly the same means. The strategy was to obtain professional closure, and the exclusion was made more and more rigorous. The means were to influence the state both in the protection of the title and in educational matters – giving the British institutions a right to supervise and making the state set certain levels in Germany.

French and Swedish organizations were not strong enough to influence politics in the same way as their German counterparts, or even to formulate a consistent policy in the same way as the British. However, the state had its own interest in the maintenance of the profession and, during the nineteenth century, the result was similar. In the inter-war years, when French trade unions reacted against certain steps taken by the state administration, the boundary between trade unionism and professionalism seems to have been eroded. The solution was, however, highly traditional from a professional point of view, making the professional closure still stricter. The protection of the title won through this struggle became a central objective for professional policy during the inter-war years and thereafter. Only in a country like Sweden, dominated during this period by social democratic ideology, was this type of state interference not on the agenda.

Professional policies tend to be elitist inside an occupation. The professionals have to refuse recognition to some people through their policy of closure, as otherwise it can have no purpose. It has been possible for strong organizations to mobilize the state for their elitist interests to a large extent, though not to the extent they wanted in Britain in the 1960s and 1970s. States and governments have, however, been less inclined to act on their own initiative after the establishment of continental schools and institutes in the nineteenth century, either in promoting or in counteracting the prevailing professionalism of engineers.

References

Appleyard, R. (1939) *The History of the Institution of Electrical Engineers, 1871–1931.* London, The Institution of Electrical Engineers.

Armytage, W.H.G. (1965) *The Rise of the Technocrats. A Social History.* London, Routledge and Kegan Paul.

Artz, F.B. (1966) *The Development of Technical Education in France, 1500–1850.* Cleveland, Society for the History of Technology.

Behringer, P. (1981) 'Ingenieure und Techniker. Technische Angestellte in Grossbritannien im späten 19. und frühen 20. Jahrhundert', in J. Kocka (ed.) *Angestellte im Europäischen Vergleich.* Göttingen, Vandenhoeck und Ruprecht.

Boltanski, L. (1982) *Les cadres. La formation d'un groupe social.* Paris, Minuit.

Boltanski, L. (1985) 'Cadres et ingénieurs autodidactes', in A. Thépot (ed.) *L'Ingénieur dans la société française.* Paris, Ed. Ouvrières.

Burrage, M. (1992) 'States as users of knowledge: a comparison of lawyers and engineers in France and Britain', in R. Torstendahl (ed.) *State Theory and State History.* London, Sage.

Burrage, M., Jarausch, K.H. and Siegrist, H. (1990) 'An actor-based framework for the study of the professions', in M. Burrage and R. Torstendahl (eds) *Professions in Theory and History. Rethinking the Study of the Professions.* London, Sage.

Calvert, M. (1967) *The Mechanical Engineer in America, 1830–1910. Professional Cultures in Conflict.* Baltimore, Johns Hopkins Press.

Collins, R. (1979) *The Credential Society. A Historical Sociology of Education and Stratification.* New York, Academic Press.

Collins, R. (1981) *Sociology since Mid-century. Essays in Theory Cumulation.* New York, Academic Press.

Collins, R. (1990) 'Changing conceptions in the sociology of the professions', in R. Torstendahl and M. Burrage (eds) *The Formation of Professions. Knowledge, State and Strategy.* London: Sage.

Conze, W. and Kocka, J. (1985) 'Einleitung', in W. Conze and J. Kocka (eds) *Bildungsbürgertum im 19. Jahrhundert,* Vol. 1. Stuttgart, Klett-Cotta.

Cotgrove, S.F. (1958) *Technical Education and Social Change.* London, Allen & Unwin.

Crozier, M. (1963) *Le phénomène bureaucratique.* Paris, Seuil.

Darrigo, R. and Serre, P. (1985) '"Gadz'Arts" et société', in A. Thépot (ed.) *L'Ingénieur dans la société française.* Paris, Éd. Ouvrières.

Day, C.R. (1980) 'Education for the industrial world: technical and modern instruction in France under the Third Republic, 1870–1914', in R. Fox and G. Weisz (eds) *The Organisation of Science and Technology in France, 1808–1914.* Cambridge, Cambridge University Press.

Goutmann, P. (1986) 'La genèse parlementaire de la loi sur le titre d'ingénieur', in A. Grelon (ed.) *Les ingénieurs de la crise. Titre et profession entre les deux guerres.* Paris, Éditions EHESS.

Guillerme, A. (1986) 'La loi du 10 juillet 1934 et les ingénieurs des Travaux Publics', in A. Grelon (ed.) *Les ingénieurs de la crise. Titre et profession entre les deux guerres.* Paris, Éditions EHESS.

Kaelble, H. (1991) *Nachbarn am Rhein. Entfremdung und Annäherung der französischen und deutschen Gesellschaft seit 1880.* Munich, Beck.

König, W. (1981) 'Die Ingenieure und der VDI als Grossverein in der wilhelminischen Gesellschaft 1900 bis 1918', in *Technik, Ingenieure und Gesellschaft. Geschichte des Vereins Deutscher Ingenieure 1856–1981*. Düsseldorf, VDI-Verlag.

Lévy-Leboyer, M. (1974) 'Le patronat français, a-t-il été Malthusien?', *Le mouvement social*, 88, 3–49.

Lundgreen, P. (1981) 'Die Vertretung technischer Expertise "im Interesse der gesamten Industrie Deutschlands" durch den VDI 1856 bis 1890', in *Technik, Ingenieure und Gesellschaft. Geschichte des Vereins Deutscher Ingenieure 1856–1981*. Düsseldorf, VDI-Verlag.

Manegold, K.-H. (1970) *Universität, Technische Hochschule und Industrie. Ein Beitrag zur Emanzipation der Technik im 19. Jahrhundert*. Berlin, Duncker und Humblot.

Manegold, K.-H. (1981) 'Der VDI in der Phase der Hochindustrialisierung 1880–1900', in *Technik, Ingenieure und Gesellschaft. Geschichte des Vereins Deutscher Ingenieure 1856–1981*. Düsseldorf, VDI-Verlag.

Marsh, J. (1986) 'Du cercle privé à l'antichambre de l'Université: les associations d'ingénieurs et l'image de marque des ingénieurs britanniques du XVIIIe siècle à nos jours', in A. Grelon (ed.) *Les ingénieurs de la crise. Titre et profession entre les deux guerres*. Paris, Ecole des hautes études en sciences sociales.

Parkin, F. (1979) *Marxism and Class Theory: a Bourgeois Critique*. London, Tavistock.

Parsons, R.H. (1947) *A History of the Institution of Mechanical Engineers, 1847–1947*. London: The Institution of Mechanical Engineers.

Paul, H.W. (1980) 'Apollo courts the Vulcans: the applied science institutes in nineteenth-century French science faculties', in R. Fox and G. Weisz (eds) *The Organization of Science and Technology in France, 1808–1914*. Cambridge, Cambridge University Press.

Paul, H.W. and Shinn, T. (1981/2) 'The structure and state of science in France', *Contemporary French Civilization*, 6, 154–93.

Platt, K.H. (1973) 'The professions in our national life', in E. G. Semler (ed.) *The Engineer and Society*. London, The Institution of Mechanical Engineers.

Prandy, K. (1965) *Professional Employees. A Study of Scientists and Engineers*. London, Faber and Faber.

Reader, W.J. (1966) *Professional Men. The Rise of the Professional Classes in Nineteenth-century England*. London, Weidenfeld and Nicolson.

Ribeill, G. (1985) 'Profils des ingénieurs civils au XIXe siècle: le cas des Centreaux', in A. Thépot (ed.) *L'Ingénieur dans la société française*. Paris, Éd. Ouvrières.

Ribeill, G. (1986a) 'Des ingénieurs civils en quête d'un titre: le cas de l'Ecole des Ponts et Chaussées (1851–1934)', in A. Grelon (ed.) *Les ingénieurs de la crise. Titre et profession entre les deux guerres*. Paris, Éditions EHESS.

Ribeill, G. (1986b) 'Une institution quinquagénaire: la Commission des Titres d'Ingénieurs. Évolutions et permanences', in A. Grelon (ed.) *Les ingénieurs de la crise. Titre et profession entre les deux guerres*. Paris, Éditions EHESS.

Riera i Tuèbols, S. (1986) 'L'évolution de la profession d'ingénieur en Espagne', in A. Grelon (ed.) *Les ingénieurs de la crise. Titre et profession entre les deux guerres*. Paris, Éditions EHESS.

Riera i Tuèbols, S. (1988) *L'Associació i el Collegi d'Enginyers Industrials de Catalunya, de la Dictatura a la Democràcia (1950–1987)*, Vol. 1. Barcelona, Ed. Magrana.

Roberts, F.B. (1973) 'Our public image', in E.G. Semler (ed.) *The Engineer and Society*. London, The Institution of Mechanical Engineers.

Rolt, L.T.C. (1958) *Thomas Telford*. London, Longmans.

Runeby, N. (1976) *Teknikerna, vetenskapen och kulturen. Ingenjörsundervisning och ingenjörsorganisationer i 1870–talets Sverige*. Uppsala: Studia historica Upsaliensia.

Rürup, R. (1979) 'Die Technische Universität Berlin 1879–1979: Grundzüge und Probleme ihrer Geschichte', in R. Rürup (ed.) *Wissenschaft und Gesellschaft. Beiträge zur Geschichte der Technischen Universität Berlin 1879–1979.* Berlin, Springer.

Saks, M. (1983) 'Removing the blinkers? A critique of recent contributions to the sociology of professions', *Sociological Review*, 1983, 1–21.

Sarfatti Larson, M. (1977) *The Rise of Professionalism. A Sociological Analysis.* Berkeley, University of California Press.

Scholl, L.U. (1981) 'Der Ingenieur in Ausbildung, Beruf und Gesellschaft 1856 bis 1881', in *Technik, Ingenieure und Gesellschaft. Geschichte des Vereins Deutscher Ingenieure 1856–1981.* Düsseldorf, VDI-Verlag.

Shinn, T. (1978) 'Des Corps de l'Etat au secteur industriel: genèse de la profession de l'ingénieur, 1950–1920', *Revue française de sociologie*, 19, 39–71.

Shinn, T. (1980) *Savoir scientifique et pouvoir social. L'Ecole polytechnique 1794–1914.* Paris, Presses de la Fond. nat. des sc. pol.

Thépot, A. (ed.) (1985) *L'Ingénieur dans la société française.* Paris, Ed. Ouvrières.

Torstendahl, R. (1975a) *Dispersion of Engineers in a Transitional Society. Swedish Techncians 1860–1940.* Uppsala: Studia historica Upsaliensia.

Torstendahl, R. (1975b) *Teknologins nytta. Motiveringar för det svenska tekniska utbildningsväsendet, 1810–1870.* Uppsala: Studia historica Upsaliensia.

Torstendahl, R. (1990) 'Essential properties, strategic aims and temporal development. Three approaches to theories of professionalism', in M. Burrage and R. Torstendahl (eds) *Professions in Theory and History. Rethinking the Study of the Professions.* London, Sage.

Towler, F.H. (1973) 'The status of the professional engineer', in E.G. Semler (ed.) *The Engineer and Society.* London, The Institution of Mechanical Engineers.

VDI (1971) *Die neuen Ingenieurgesetze der Länder der BRD.* Düsseldorf, VDI-Verlag.

Watson, G. (1988) *The Civils. The Story of the Institution of Civil Engineers.* London, Thomas Telford.

Weiss, J.H. (1982) *The Making of Technological Man. The Social Origins of French Technological Education.* Cambridge, MA, MIT Press.

Weisz, G. (1983) *The Emergence of Modern Universities in France, 1963–1914.* Princeton, NJ, Princeton University Press.

3

Teacher Education: Backstage to Centre Stage

Sir William Taylor

Teaching as a profession

Is teaching a profession? A great deal of time and ink and energy has over the years been devoted to that question. Despite all that has been written about professions in general, no single agreed definition offers a point of reference. Contemporary academic approaches to professionalism tend to be eclectic. This mirrors everyday usage, which extends the term to groups of employees that lack many of the attributes functionally associated with professional status. So whether teaching qualifies depends on what criteria for professionalism one adopts.

In a succinct statement, Easthope *et al.* (1990) identify four major theoretical positions on the issue of professionalism. A *functionalist* view picks out those traits that distinguish professionals from members of other occupational groups, such as an ethic of client service, control over credentialled training, specialized knowledge and autonomy of practice. A *symbolic-interactionist* perspective turns on public acceptance of claims to status and autonomy. A *neo-Weberian* analysis focuses on the extent to which the members of a profession exercise control over workplace or client group. And *Marxists* concentrate on how professionals serve the purposes of capitalist economies and reinforce capitalist values.

A broad-brush overview of the characteristics of teaching would note: the large number of teachers in comparison with some other occupations that claim professional status; the generally modest level of teachers' rewards; changes in their status that have taken place as a consequence of democratization and the dethronement of once secure academic canons; the continued importance of the ethic of service to student, family and society; the large proportion of women at some levels; comparisons between countries in the extent to which teacher unions and associations play a part in the determination and implementation of educational policy, including policy on rewards and conditions of service; the significant involvement of the state in controlling entry to training, credentials and subsequent employment;

and the new demands that the expansion in the scale and economic importance of education have generated for teacher performance and learning
outcomes.

Such an overview would also have to recognize the differences in status,
reward and power that exist *within* teaching, differences principally determined by the two criteria of student age and academic level. Thus nursery
school and infant teachers generally enjoy lower status and rewards than
those who work in academic secondary schools. Those who lecture to university undergraduates in high-ranking subjects such as medicine or physics
have higher status than those who teach non-vocational adult classes.

Characteristics and criteria

If there is no agreement in the literature about the 'pure' form that would
mark a profession off from other occupational groups, many authors accept
that several dimensions are involved. It is the overall profile of an occupation in accordance with these dimensions that determines whether or not
it is sensible to speak of it as a profession. For example, Turner and Hodge
(1970: 26) speak of four areas of concern:

> (1) the degree of substantive theory and technique in the practising
> of professional or semi-professional activities; (2) the degree of mono-
> poly over claimed professional or semi-professional activities; (3) the
> degree of external recognition of a profession or semi-profession; and
> (4) the degree of organization of a profession or semi-profession.

On the basis of a survey of definitions over the half-century between
Flexner's analysis (1915) and that of Goode (1969), Leggatt (1970: 156)
identifies the most frequently mentioned characteristics as being:

(a) Practice is founded upon a base of theoretical, esoteric knowledge
(b) The acquisition of knowledge requires a long period of education
    and socialization
(c) Practitioners are motivated by an ideal of altruistic service rather
    than the pursuit of material and economic gain
(d) Careful control is exercised over recruitment, training, certifica-
    tion and standards of practice
(e) The colleague group is well organized and has disciplinary
    powers to enforce a code of ethical practice.

In a recent essay, Downie (1990) has also emphasized the fluidity of the
concept of profession, and suggests that the idea of a definition as a fixed
set of necessary and sufficient conditions should be dropped in favour of
overlapping sets of characteristics or 'family resemblances'. Not all these

will be represented to the same extent in all the occupations that can be identified as professional.

Downie identifies five characteristics of a profession: its knowledge base; the provision of a service within a relationship of beneficence and integrity and a set of legal and ethical rights and duties underwritten by a professional institution; a critical function ('the duty to speak out with authority on matters of social justice and social utility'); independence, which is not inconsistent with employee status or state funding; preparation that constitutes an education rather than 'mere training' (i.e. that nurtures a wide cognitive perspective and requires a commitment to the continued development of knowledge and skills within a framework of values).

These characteristics, Downie argues, make a profession *legitimate*. The fact of wide public and political involvement in policy on the structure and content of schooling and the current encouragement of consumerist and market relations in education need not preclude such legitimacy in the case of teaching. But Downie's conclusion is cautious:

> These dangers do exist and are a threat to teaching considered as a profession; but one can only hope that they will not destroy the professions entirely because, as patients, clients, students or pupils, we remain vulnerable and must continue to trust in the knowledge, beneficence and integrity, independence and broad education of the professions. The profession of teaching must be open to general social changes but must maintain a professional integrity through these changes. Despite low morale among teachers at the moment the profession still possesses legitimacy in the eyes of the public.
>
> (Downie 1990: 159)

The reference here to consumerism and market relations is important. The application to teachers of 'classical' definitions of professionalism and claims to status based upon them needs reconsideration in terms of two contrasting political and social movements. One is the advocacy of greater parental choice and the importation of market disciplines into the provision of educational services. The other is the wish to demystify professional power in the interests of greater democratic participation in schooling and a more equal society.

In the interests of tidiness it would be easy to label these two movements as coming from the right and left of the political spectrum respectively. But this would be too facile. There is a populist element in many radical right policies which seeks to empower lay and local influence just as much as the most participatory socialist doctrines – this similarity is sometimes concealed by the contrasting rhetorics of parental and family choice on the one side and of community on the other. Neither movement has much time for what in England is labelled as 'the education establishment', taken to include the organized bodies of educators, with their claims to professional recognition.

Consumers and community

A key document in the recent discussion of professionalism in teaching is Walter Metzger's 'The spectre of professionism' (1987). Metzger argues that, although it was once a term of approbation and respect, 'profession' has lost much of its moral content.

> For historians of recent America, the idea that professionals are effective change-artists and that the changes they foster are for the worse has been given so many diverse applications that it has come to serve almost as an explanatory master-key.
>
> (Metzger 1987: 13)

Metzger identifies attacks on professionalism coming from both left and right, from counter-cultural and neo-Marxist writers as much as from new right economists: 'the anti-professional hosts owed their success to the conflation of left and right [rather than] gaining strength from their ideological purity' (Metzger 1980: 17).

In countries with right-wing majorities in government, the thrust of recent educational reform has been towards making schooling more relevant to the needs of a successful market economy, controlling the demands of education on the public purse, improving the efficiency and effectiveness of teaching and satisfying public and political demand for tangible educational outcomes such as objectively assessed credentials, higher standards of reading and arithmetical competence and socially responsible behaviour.

The means employed to these ends have included: the specification of national objectives (such as President Bush's 1990 statement of what American schools should have achieved by the year 2000); a stress on competition at both individual and institutional levels, the former to encourage high achievement, enterprise and entrepreneurship, the latter to improve efficiency and effectiveness and to provide value for money; standardization of curriculum and modes of assessment and the encouragement of audiovisual and computer-assisted modes of instruction; diminishing the influence of educational bureaucracies and creating two-tier, centre/institution patterns of administration and accountability; and enhancing student and family choice of school by open enrolment and the advocacy of educational vouchers.

The objectives of the left focus on: the improvement of the common school; greater equality of outcome; the provision of a high quality education that can form the basis of effective preparation for a variety of occupations, rather than job-specific training; raising the status and rewards of teachers; enhancing the life chances of minorities and challenging both direct and indirect manifestations of sexism and racism; and returning to local communities some of the power and influence over educational policy and decision-making that they are seen to have lost as a result of centralization.

At a practical level, the means to be employed to these ends are less radical than those espoused by the right. Neighbourhood and non-selective comprehensive schools are already in place. If parents could be assured that they can all offer quality educational experiences and outcomes for their children the pressures for greater 'choice' and the demand for schooling outside the state system would diminish. Where national curricula and assessment exist, social democratic parties do not propose their abolition. Few plan to make state education compulsory. In most countries, the principal providers of private schooling are the churches. In the early 1980s, for example, 70 per cent of private school students in the USA attended Catholic schools, and 22.2 per cent went to Lutheran, Jewish and Evangelical schools (Fowler 1991). Rather similar patterns apply elsewhere, such as in Australia. Even in England, where state and private school attendance are related to a greater extent to income, the Labour Party does not now propose the closing down of the independent fee-paying schools. Teachers' unions tend to be more influential when governments have left-wing majorities, but this does not mean that they always get their own way, as the record of past decades in France and England testifies.

Theorists of the left see a role for teachers that goes beyond the efficient 'delivery' (a term that has been subjected to a good deal of criticism from this quarter) of the curriculum, and that incorporates activity as a 'public intellectual'.

> We believe that teachers need to view themselves as public intellectuals who combine conception and implementation, thinking and practice, with a political project grounded in the struggle for a culture of liberation and justice.
>
> (Aronowitz and Giroux 1991: 109)

The importance of the teacher as an agent of progressive social and political change is emphasized in this literature. A 'radical professionalism' is proposed,

> which means that teachers relate to the communities they serve and recognise students' differential positioning and relations to knowledge. The notion of an apolitical or moral education free of politics is rejected. A radical professionalism undermines the construction of immutable expert knowledge and opens up a debate over the nature and purpose of education which facilitates the development of 'really useful knowledge'. In such a dialogue education becomes a centre of debate and democratic participation and so contributes towards the development of an active citizenship.
>
> (Avis 1991: 278–9)

Professionalization, advocated by some as a means to raise the standing and morale of teachers, is seen as a subsidiary project:

> What is needed for the sort of fundamental improvement in schools that some advocates of professionalization have in mind is a much larger reassessment of our educational priorities as a society and a much broader and more ambitious process of social and political

change. For such a change to occur, we believe, teachers must more closely link their interests with other groups who seek progressive educational reform. This means that teachers will need to participate in political activities around extraeducational as well as educational issues, especially at the local level, and involve groups who are currently disenfranchised in the public debate about educational reform. The aspiration to professionalism further widens the gap that teachers see between themselves and these groups at the very time when greater cooperation and mutual understanding are needed.

(Burbules and Densmore 1991a: 60;
for a contrary view see Sykes 1991)

The last point above finds an echo among those who argue that teachers are not in any case in a position to identify themselves or to be identified with the elite 'expert professions' but should instead be located among a distinctive group of 'craft professions' (Pratte and Rury 1991). On this view, good teaching depends less on the kind of esoteric knowledge normally identified with professional expertise and more on what Donald Schon (1983) identifies as knowledge-in-action. It is this kind of knowledge that is demonstrated by what Schon called the reflective practitioner, a key concept in today's teacher education literature.

Governments and teacher education

Government involvement in teacher education is a subset of its broader responsibilities for the provision and efficiency of schools. In most countries such involvement dates from acceptance of those responsibilities. In England and Wales, the first grant for the training of teachers was made in 1834, soon after money had been made available for the building of public elementary schools. Proposals for the setting up of a state normal school for training teachers collapsed in the face of religious objections. However, grants were made to the colleges established by churches and voluntary bodies. The Elementary Education Act of 1870 did not change this position. It did, however, increase the need for teachers. Over the next ten years the numbers in training tripled.

Responsibility for ensuring that appropriately qualified adults are available in every classroom has sustained a more direct involvement in the education and training of teachers by government – central, state and local – than in education and training for other occupations. In most countries teacher training is now carried out by institutions that are part of a higher education system that enjoys a measure of independence from central or local control. However, governments continue to intervene in teacher education through the funding of students and of institutions, and by controlling the qualifications that teachers must possess in order to be employed in state schools.

While the main focus of such intervention has been to ensure an adequate supply of teachers, the structure and content of courses has also been prescribed in some systems, especially those with state examinations. Elsewhere, the curriculum of teacher preparation has been for the training institutions to determine, although there is an increasing tendency for certificating and employing authorities – as in many parts of the United States – to impose additional examination requirements of their own. In recent years demographic profiles and economic conditions in many developed countries have reduced the importance of teacher supply as a policy priority. In some places – Germany and parts of Australia, for example – there is now a significant excess of supply over demand. Government attention tends now to be focused as much on quality as on quantity.

The reasons for this are not far to seek. Education is in demand: from students and parents for purposes of personal development and the enhancement of life chances; from employers requiring skilled and biddable workers and specialists; from governments wanting to enhance competitive advantage, economic performance and a stable polity. Spending on education in all its forms now accounts for a sizeable proportion of all public expenditure. And educational discontents readily translate into votes.

Practitioners of, for example, engineering, law, medicine, pharmacy and psychology generally exercise greater control through their professional organizations over the accreditation of courses of training and of entry to practice than do teachers. States do not generally recognize the authority of teachers' organizations to control entry to service in state schools, or delegate their own powers in this respect to such bodies. Where independent bodies exist their formal powers are generally advisory (as in the case of the Scottish General Teaching Council). The recommendations of such bodies may be almost always accepted, just as the teaching qualifications awarded by universities are officially recognized, but powers of approval and recognition remain in the hands of the state.

This formal position must be qualified both in space and in time. The actual influence of teachers and their organizations varies not only from one country to another but also within countries as the political climate changes and the fortunes of the right and the left wax and wane.

Gaziel and Tuab (1992: 78) illustrate this point with regard to France:

> in the 1960s, initiatives for educational reform came from government alone, whereas during the 1970s, the teachers' unions were consulted in development of government proposals for reform, but their suggestions were not adopted. In the 1980s, two important changes occurred: teachers' unions were consulted and negotiated with, and their views were accepted by the French government and included as part of the reform proposals.

The distinctions between consultation and negotiation in this passage would have resonances for teachers' union leaders elsewhere. In England and Wales, for example, the teachers' associations were among the bodies consulted by the Government prior to the changes introduced into secondary teacher education in 1992. Insofar as they contributed to the view that the proposal to base four-fifths of the training programme in schools was un-realistic and to the subsequent modification of this proportion to two-thirds, their advice can be said to have been heeded. But this advice was provided by means of a written response to a written request. Whatever the outcome, this is very different from being regularly called in by ministers for face-to-face consultations, both formal and informal – the famous 'beer and sand-wiches at Number 10' – which were seen as a regular feature of relations between government and the unions in the 1960s and 1970s.

Politics and policies

In most countries, national authorities still control significant aspects of teacher education, training and certification (registration). The story of official involvement in teacher education in England and Wales since the seminal McNair Report of 1944 has been written about elsewhere (e.g. Taylor 1969, 1978, 1982, 1984, 1989, 1990; Dent 1977; Perry 1989; Aldrich 1990), and will not be summarized here. The American literature on this theme is extensive. And as a consequence of the development of closer European links, there are now a number of accessible sources of informa-tion on developments in other countries (e.g. Bone and McCall 1990; and the *Journal of the Association for Teacher Education in Europe*).

In many systems, following a trend that began in the United States, the education of all kinds of teachers is now fully integrated into university level studies. This is the case, for example, in Canada, England and Wales and Australia, and the creation of IUFMs (*instituts universitaires de formation des maîtres*) has brought primary training into closer relation to the universities in France. There are also a small number of systems, such as those of Scotland and New Zealand, where both secondary and primary training have until very recently been the responsibility of specialist, non-university institutions, but the restructuring of higher education is now leading to the closer integration of such work with the universities.

Political dissatisfaction with the performance of teachers and of schools in the United Kingdom surfaced in the mid-1970s and has been a signifi-cant feature of public policy up to and including the present day. Govern-ments have intervened to introduce the disciplines of the market place into education, to reduce the power of local authorities, to make schools more directly accountable to parents, to replace long-standing arrangements for school inspection with an audit model that enhances lay influence, to put in place a national curriculum and detailed schemes of assessment and to prepare universal evaluation and appraisal for teachers.

Teacher education began to feature on this agenda in the early 1980s. Responsibility for recommending students for the award of qualified teacher status had rested with the university-based institutes of education ('area training organizations', ATOs) until the mid-1970s, when teacher education was integrated into the overall provision of higher education in universities and polytechnics. The disappearance of the ATOs left a gap in arrangements for making recommendations on the approval of courses to the Secretary of State. For nearly a decade the gap was plugged by a variety of temporary and generally unsatisfactory schemes, in which the part played by schools and by teachers remained formal rather than real. The recommendation process remained effectively in the hands of the university schools and departments of education and the Council for National Academic Awards (which accredited the degrees of the polytechnics and those of the higher education colleges that were not still associated with universities).

Perceived weaknesses in the competencies of newly qualified teachers, documented by Her Majesty's Inspectors; anxieties about standards in the schools; and doubts about the quality of courses of training, especially in respect of the depth of subject studies, the recency and relevance of the school experience of some staff, and the balance of institution-based as compared with school-based work, all came together with the need to devise better machinery to advise on the approval of courses to persuade the Government to establish in 1984 the Council for the Accreditation of Teacher Education (CATE).

In common with other bodies of this kind established at this time and since, all the members were appointed directly by the Secretary of State. The day of large representative bodies with memberships drawn from the educational associations and trade unions was clearly over. Instead, informal consultations took place to achieve a balance between the various interests involved.

The first five years of CATE's work have been documented in detail by Gordon McIntyre (1991). During that period the focus of political and administrative attention was less on teacher education and more on the school. The National Curriculum Council and School Examination and Assessment Council were established and the National Curriculum and system of national assessment put in place. All this had implications for the content of courses, reflected in the revised criteria for the approval of courses of initial training promulgated in 1989. CATE's remit was widened to permit a stronger policy contribution.

Towards the end of the 1980s, attacks on the institutions of teacher education increased both in number and in scope (O'Hear 1988; Hillgate Group 1989; O'Keefe 1990), culminating in Lawlor's (1990) proposal that teacher education institutions be closed. The Government's 1991 initiative to make teacher education much more school based is often attributed directly to these attacks, and to the influence of political advisers and 'right-wing think tanks' on ministerial policy. This is, however, too simple a reading. Other factors were also at work.

First in order of importance, there was a need to ensure that students had adequate time in which to benefit from the developing experience of teachers who had direct responsibility for implementing the National Curriculum and applying schemes of assessment.

A second factor was that the whole field of education and training was paying much more attention to the systematic description and assessment of the competencies that a person should be able to demonstrate at the end of a course and at different stages of a career, rather than to formal prerequisites and credentials.

Third, well-regarded school-based training courses were already operating, notably in Oxford, where the local authority had provided a generous grant to the University Department of Education for this purpose. And, 'in the other place', the Professor of Education and some of his colleagues in the University of Cambridge were advocates of not just school-based but school-led training, in which training schools would be designated and given the money that had hitherto been paid by the Higher Education Funding Councils to universities to support initial training (Beardon *et al.* 1992).

Fourth, another type of school-based training had already been introduced in the form of an articled teacher scheme, leading to the award of a postgraduate teaching qualification after two years of largely school-based work. An increasing number of articles and books were appearing about the training and deployment of mentor teachers in schools, who would be key players in the development of school-based training (for references see Wilkin 1992). Some local authorities were also implementing the provisions of the licensed teacher scheme, which permitted mature candidates to teach at the same time as they followed a part-time course of training that could lead to recognition as a qualified teacher.

A fifth factor was the ability to pray-in-aid international precedents. A move towards giving the school a more important role in training was not limited to this country. There was much discussion in the United States about alternative routes into teaching. Officials and HMI had already studied and reported upon the New Jersey scheme. There was interest in the long-standing German system of placing students almost wholly in schools for the second part of their training.

Finally, at a time when layers of educational management between the centre and the operational units were in the process of being simplified or removed, there was anxiety on the part of institutions, administrators and Ministers that the accreditation process had become excessively bureaucratic, and relied too much on written statements.

In his speech at the North of England Education Conference in January 1992 the Secretary of State for Education announced the Government's intention to make training more school-based. He drew explicit comparisons with the training of other professionals:

> Lawyers and doctors have always spent a key part of their training in supervised pupillage working alongside and under the guidance of the best experienced members of their profession. Theory can be no substitute for this practical training in professions that give person to person services. Student teachers need more time in classrooms guided by serving teachers and less time in the teacher training colleges.

A consultative document was issued shortly afterwards, setting out the Government's proposals. The range of response was wide. Some teachers' organizations welcomed the idea of school-based training, subject to the necessary resources being available. In contrast, an article by the Deputy Editor of the *Journal of Education for Teaching*, entitled 'The political rape of teacher education' (Gilroy 1992), was followed in the subsequent number by an editorial headed 'Mindless imperatives and the moral profession' (JET 1992). There was general agreement, however, that the proportion of school-based work proposed – four-fifths of the one-year PGCE – was too great, and this was modified to two-thirds in the Circular (9/92, Welsh Office Circular 35/92) setting out the Government's decisions that was published in June of 1992.

In this political climate, what are the prospects for greater professional self-government for teachers?

The case for a GTC for England and Wales

Proposals for the self-government of the teaching profession in England and Wales go back at least 130 years. The Medical Registration Act dates from 1858. Within two years it was being suggested that a Scholastic Registration Act was needed. Between 1879 and 1896 there were three attempts to legislate, all of which failed. Following the Education Act of 1899 a Teachers Registration Council was set up, but it did not secure sufficient support among teachers and went out of existence in 1906. A fresh effort was made six years later. By the early 1920s a large proportion of teachers were on the new Register, which automatically qualified them for membership of a Royal Society of Teachers. But membership was voluntary, and the RST did not occupy the high ground of teacher training and supply. The Register was finally abolished by an Order in Council in 1949 (Department of Education and Science 1970).

During the 1950s meetings between teachers' organizations took place with the intention of setting up a General Teaching Council (GTC) with three principal functions:

1 To achieve control over entry into teaching, including control of standards.
2 To exercise the sole right of recognition of a qualified teacher.
3 To control professional discipline.

It was another ten years before the Department of Education and Science was persuaded to establish a working party to 'formulate proposals for the establishment and operation of a Teaching Council; and for national arrangements for advice to the Secretary of State on the training and supply of teachers' (DES 1970: 3).

In the meantime, in the wake of a dispute in Scotland about what teachers saw as a dilution of entry requirements, an official committee on which a majority of the members were serving teachers recommended that there 'should be established a General Teaching Council for Scotland broadly similar in scope, powers and functions to the Councils in other professions' (quoted in Ross 1990; see also Ross 1991). The Teaching Council (Scotland) Act was enacted in 1965. In addition to maintaining a register of teachers qualified to teach in local authority and grant-aided schools, and having the power to remove teachers from this register, the Council reviews courses and makes recommendations on training, and also advises on 'matters (other than remuneration and conditions of service) relating to the supply of teachers'. It is funded by an annual registration fee paid by every teacher in Scotland.

Ross (1990: 127) comments that:

> The powers granted to the General Teaching Council for Scotland are not unduly great but, in contrast with the situation in England and Wales they do, whilst recognizing the ultimate authority of the Secretary of State for Scotland, give the teaching profession a recognized place in the organization and management of the profession. Instead of being left to provide observations on policy initiatives emanating from government, the Scottish teachers are able through the Council to initiate policy discussions.

In recommending the establishment of a Teaching Council for England and Wales, the Weaver Report of 1970 (named after the Chairman of the DES Working Party) made it clear that the Secretary of State would need reserve powers to ensure an adequate supply of teachers. In the words of the Report,

> The establishment of a Teaching Council with unrestricted power to control entry to the profession would mean that an independent body, lacking (through no fault of its own) . . . broader responsibilities and moreover not responsible to Parliament for the public interest, would have the power so to set the qualifications for registration as to make it impossible to staff the public system. Because the government must be responsible to Parliament for securing an efficient education service at reasonable cost, we accept the general principle that it must retain sufficient reserve powers to ensure that in the last resort its purposes were not frustrated by action of the Teaching Council. Similar restrictions apply to other professional bodies.
>
> (DES 1970: 9)

The Weaver recommendation for the setting up of a Teaching Council was not acted upon, mainly but not entirely because of the inability of the teachers' trade unions to agree, but also owing to changing priorities in teacher training in the wake of the 'oil shocks' of the early 1970s and the reorganization of the training institutions as a consequence of demographic downturn and financial exigency (Taylor 1982). As Ross (1990) has pointed out, there was another factor. Attitudes to the idea of professionalism were shifting. Free-market economists were drawing attention to the way in which professions act 'in restraint of trade' and constitute a producers' monopoly that works against the interests of consumers.

During the 1970s and 1980s approaches to ministers produced statements that, although not opposed to the idea of a GTC, suggested that either the time was not ripe or there was insufficient evidence of strong backing from all the bodies whose agreement and support would be necessary. Proponents were not deterred. By 1988 they had signed up seventeen educational associations. Over the next three years the number of bodies in support had risen to thirty.

In 1990, a report from the Education and Science Committee of the House of Commons also lent backing. It stated:

26. The General Teaching Council is not a new idea: there has already been 'a century of aspiration followed by a generation of disappointed initiatives' as a discussion document on the GTC put it. . . . We recognise that establishing a GTC would involve reconsideration of other policies and bodies, including a further review of CATE [the Council for the Accreditation of Teacher Education]. However, we believe that the positive effect on morale from a properly constituted and effective council warrants such effort. To move forward on this we consider that a lead from central government is essential and we therefore recommend that the Government create a General Teaching Council to work for the enhancement of the profession.

In response to the House of Commons Committee recommendation, the Government averred that there was no need for such a body in England and Wales. No action was taken.

A company limited by guarantee, GTC (England and Wales) Ltd, had been established to promote activities that would further the cause and in the event of success to act as a transitional body. Prior to the 1992 general election, the Labour Party, then in opposition, stated that if elected it would take the necessary steps (Labour Party 1991). Labour was not elected.

During 1992, GTC (England and Wales) Ltd returned to the attack. Editors and journalists penned leaders and articles in support. In April and again in September, GTC officers wrote to the new Secretary of State recapitulating the case for professional self-government. On the second occasion they provided a copy of a 50-page set of proposals that had been worked out for the constitution and operation of the Council. It would maintain a register of teachers, and decide on 'what standards of education and training and what levels of competence and conduct should be required of new entrants to the profession' (GTC 1992: 17). Funds would be derived from payment of individual registration fees by teachers. The Council would assume responsibility for determining the criteria under which bodies such as CATE operated and would be free to comment on the advice that they offered. The GTC would be responsible for professional discipline.

These proposals could hardly have come at a worse time. The Government already had its agenda for teacher education. It allowed no room for interventions of the kind that, given its representative character, would almost certainly emanate from a GTC. It was unsurprising, therefore, that both in June and in September, ministers showed themselves to be unsympathetic to the case being advanced. To introduce a new education body with statutory powers would bring about changes in relationships and lines of communication that needed a stronger justification than had been provided. No encouragement was provided for further effort.

Yet such effort continues. In its November 1992 Newsletter, GTC (England and Wales) Ltd, records ongoing approaches to Members of Parliament, participation in professional conferences and meetings, the submission of responses to official consultation documents and a variety of other activities. In January 1993 the National Commission on Education produced a briefing paper on the GTC by Stuart Maclure, formerly Editor of the *Times Educational Supplement*. While acknowledging contemporary realities (Ministerial power 'over teacher training and supply is not an element in the exercise of . . . central control which any political party will readily relinquish') the paper also suggested that there 'could still be an important if limited role for such a body, starting with responsibility for professional discipline' and that 'with modest expectations, a start could be made'. The ideal of professional self-government has a long and honourable history. Despite recent disappointments, it is unlikely to go away.

The case for a GTC is between a rock and a hard place. The politicization of educational policy over the past quarter-century has created problems to the left as much as to the right. No one doubts the concern, commitment and motives of those who back greater professional self-government by means of a GTC. But the political saliency of education, its importance for the economy and for the outcomes of elections, make this a bad time to ask governments to give up powers to the exercise of which they have now become accustomed.

Conclusion

The reform of secondary teacher education introduced by Circular 9/92 (Welsh Office Circular 35/92) has three main thrusts. It requires that training should be school-based. It specifies the competencies that students should be able to demonstrate at the end of their initial training. And it replaces course approval by institutional accreditation, based on five-year institutional plans. In the months immediately after its publication, discussion and action focused on the development of the partnerships between institutions and schools that the Circular required should be established as a condition of subsequent accreditation, and on the resources that would be available for this purpose.

The Government had found six million pounds of new money to be distributed by the Higher Education Funding Councils to 'meet net extra costs incurred during the transition to the new criteria'. No allowance has been made for the possibility that school-based training might be inherently more expensive than the system it replaced, or to meet the costs of the contributions that schools had hitherto made to initial training through the supervision of school practice. There were some complaints about the scale of the top-slicing for central costs that universities and colleges were applying to the per capita grant they received from the HEFC for education students, and the inadequacy of the sums being offered to partnership schools (Berrill 1992) but in many places it appeared that mutually acceptable agreements were being struck that would enable the new system to be operated without fatal effects on the viability of the university faculties of education or the higher education colleges in which training is carried out.

At some of the conferences and meetings at which teacher education was discussed during the summer and autumn of 1992, there were suggestions that institutional size was a factor in the ability to create workable school-based partnerships, and doubts were expressed about the long-term future of some of the smaller institutions. Uncertainty was increased by press speculation at the end of October that the new arrangements merely represented a 'holding statement'. Ministers were reputed to be considering more radical possibilities, such as schools being funded for training, buying courses in 'educational theory' for their trainees from nearby institutions (Hughes 1992). And so it proved. A 'spearhead initiative' was launched in 1993 whereby consortia of schools could bid to be funded for training, with or without an input from a higher education institution. By mid-year there were rumours of even more radical changes in the offing.

It was clear that the Government intended to maintain its initiatives in education, and that teacher education remained high on its agenda. Given the theme of the present volume, it may be appropriate to end with a reference to the introduction into Parliament on 30 October 1992 of a 200-page Education Bill, longer and more wide-ranging than any of its predecessors, which, despite doubts about the centralizing powers being taken, a *Times* leading article justified in the following words:

> If this Bill seems to have conflicting motives – centralizing control of the curriculum where it preaches greater diversity, for example – it is because the political manoeuvring of the education establishment has left little alternative. The interlocking influences of the schools inspectorate, the colleges of education, the teaching unions and the council education officers who dominate the staffing of state schools, present a skilful variety of different faces when threatened with change. ... It is not altogether surprising that in tackling this hydra-headed beast, even the well-intentioned reformer ties himself in knots.
>
> (*The Times* 1992)

This is a very different perception of the role of the education professions from that which characterizes their own self-advocacy. It would be a mistake to believe that it is a perception which lacks political and public support. Teacher educators need to recognize that the debate on professionalization has moved on. Neither the language nor the agenda are those of the 1970s. The ways in which individuals and groups come to terms with these changes depend on personal and political preferences. Those who pin their hopes on an eventual change in the political climate must reckon with the possibility that both the language and the agenda have changed in ways that are irreversible. Organizations such as the Society for Research into Higher Education have an important part to play in stimulating discussion of these issues, and in working towards agreement on an approach to professionalism consistent with the political, economic and social conditions of the twenty-first century.

References

Aldrich, R. (1990) 'The evolution of teacher education', in N.J. Graves (ed.) *Initial Teacher Education: Policies and Progress*. London, Kogan Page.

Aronowitz, S. and Giroux, H.A. (1991) *Post-Modern Education: Politics, Culture and Social Criticism*. Oxford, University of Minneapolis Press.

Avis, J. (1991) 'Educational practice, professionalism and social relations', in Education Group II *Education Limited: Schooling, Training and the New Right in England since 1979*. London, Unwin Hyman.

Beardon, T., Booth, M., Hargreaves, D., and Reiss, M. (1992) *School-led Teacher Training: The Way Forward*. Cambridge, University of Cambridge Department of Education.

Berrill, M. (1992) 'Ready, steady, stop', *Times Educational Supplement*, 16 October.

Blake, D. (1990) 'The teacher training debate: some parallels from health and social work', *Journal of Educational Policy*, 5, 4.

Bone, T.R. and McCall, J. (1990) *Teacher Education in Europe: The Challenges Ahead*. Glasgow, Jordanhill College.

Burbules, N.C. and Densmore, K. (1991a) 'The limits of making teaching a profession', *Educational Policy*, March, 5, 1.

Burbules, N.C. and Densmore, K. (1991b) 'The persistence of professionalism: "Breakin' up is hard to do"', *Educational Policy*, June, 5, 2.

Dent, H.C. (1977) *The Training of Teachers in England and Wales 1800–1975*. London, Hodder and Stoughton.

Department of Education and Science (1970) *A Teaching Council for England and Wales: Report of a Working Party appointed by the Secretary of State for Education and Science*. London, HMSO.

Downie, R.S. (1990) 'Professions and professionalism', *Journal of Philosophy of Education*, 24, 2.

Easthope, C., Maclean, R. and Easthope, G. (1992) *The Practice of Teaching: A Sociology of Education*. London, Allen and Unwin.

Fowler, F.C. (1991) 'The shocking ideological integrity of Chubb and Moe', *Journal of Education*, 173, 3.

Gaziel, H.H. and Taub, D. (1992) 'Teachers' unions and educational reform – a comparative perspective: the cases of France and Israel', *Educational Policy*, March, 6, 1.

General Teaching Council (England and Wales) (1992) *Proposals for a Statutory General Teaching Council for England and Wales*. London, GTC.

Gilroy, D.P. (1992) 'The political rape of teacher education in England and Wales: a JET rebuttal', *Journal of Education for Teaching*, 18, 1.

Hillgate Group (1989) *Learning to Teach*. London, Claridge Press.

Hughes, C. (1992) 'Teacher training could be switched to the schools', *The Independent*, 26 October.

Jackson, J.A. (ed.) (1970) *Professions and Professionalization*. London, Cambridge University Press

JET (1992) 'Mindless imperatives and the moral profession' (Editorial), *Journal of Education for Teaching*, 18, 2.

Labour Party (1991) *Investing in Quality: Labour's Plans to Reform Teacher Education and Training*. London, Labour Party.

Lawlor, S. (1990) *Teachers Mistaught*. London, Centre for Policy Studies.

Lawton, D. (1989) 'The future of teacher education', in N.J. Graves (ed.) *Initial Teacher Education: Policies and Progress*. London, Kogan Page

Leggatt, T. (1970) 'Teaching as a profession', in J.A. Jackson (ed.) *Professions and Professionalization*. London, Cambridge University Press.

McIntyre, G. (1991) *Accreditation of Teacher Education: the Story of CATE 1984–1989*. Brighton, Falmer Press.

Metzger, W.P. (1987) 'A spectre is haunting American scholars: the spectre of "professionism" ', *Educational Researcher*, August/September.

O'Hear, A. (1988) *Who Teaches the Teachers?* London, Social Affairs Unit.

O'Keeffe, D. (1990) *The Wayward Elite: a Critique of British Teacher Education*. London, Adam Smith Institute.

Perry, P. (1989) 'Teacher awareness of the economic foundations of a free society', in V.P. Varma and V.A. McClelland (eds) *Advances in Teacher Education*. London, Routledge.

Political Quarterly (1992) 'Commentary', *PQ*, April/June, 63, 2.

Pratte, R. and Rury, J.L. (1991) 'Teachers, professionalism and craft', *Teachers College Record*, Fall, 93, 1.

Ross, A. (1990) 'A General Teaching Council for England and Wales', in N.J. Graves (ed.) *Initial Teacher Training: Policies and Progress*. London, Kogan Page.

Ross, A. (1991) 'The control of teacher education', in G.E. Jones (ed.) *Education, Culture and Society*. Cardiff, University of Wales Press.

Schon, D.A. (1983) *The Reflective Practitioner*. London, Temple Smith.

Sykes, G. (1991) 'In defense of teacher professionalism as a policy choice', *Educational Policy*, 5, 2.

Taylor, W. (1969) *Society and the Education of Teachers*. London, Faber.

Taylor, W. (1978) *Research and Reform in Teacher Education*. Windsor, NFER Publishing Company.

Taylor, W. (1982) 'Changing priorities in teacher education', in R. Goodings, M. Byram and M. McPartland (eds) *Changing Priorities in Teacher Education*. London, Croom Helm.

Taylor, W. (1984) 'The national context', in R.J. Alexander, M. Craft and J. Lynch (eds) *Change in Teacher Education; Context and Provision since Robbins*. London, Holt, Rinehart and Winston.

Taylor, W. (1989) 'The control of teacher education: the Council for the Accreditation of Teacher Education', in N.J. Graves (ed.) *Initial Teacher Education: Policies and Progress*. London, Kogan Page.

Taylor, W. (1990) 'Education', in F.M.L. Thompson (ed.) *The University of London and the World of Learning 1836–1986*. London, Hambledon Press.

Turner, C. and Hodge, M.N. (1970) 'Occupations and professions', in J.A. Jackson (ed.) *Professions and Professionalism*. London, Cambridge University Press.

Wilkin, M. (ed.) (1992) *Mentoring in Schools*. London, Kogan Page.

4

The Case of Medicine

Johannes Vang

Introduction

In every society collective knowledge is an important resource. The wise
and humane use of this resource is the basis for the success, prosperity and
development of society. The creation and sharing of knowledge is therefore
an important part of every government's strategy for social development.

The health of the public is also a resource. To develop a society free from
disease and with a positively healthy population has become an ambition
and responsibility of governments and a high priority in most developed
countries. The creation of the World Health Organisation in 1948, with its
slogan 'Health for all', reflects this ambition. In modern welfare states the
establishment of equitable and effective health care systems, in tandem with
equitable and effective educational systems, has been a centrepiece of social
construction.

Accordingly, the education of professionals within the fields of health
and disease has become an important matter for governments. Medical
schools and medical faculties have taken a central place in higher education.

The structural power of formal knowledge and the pace of knowledge development

Because knowledge is an asset in society, the possession of knowledge con-
fers a privilege and is to varying degrees combined with power. Formal
knowledge has consequently been used to structure society and to safeguard
privileges (Etzioni 1968). This is clearly the case in relation to medicine
and the caring sciences. These professions are in most countries ranked
hierarchically according to formal educational characteristics. Formal
education within this field has in the past been useful not only in ensuring
the necessary knowledge on the part of those who were to apply medical
skills in society, but also – through rules and regulations – in creating and
maintaining social structures within the health care system. This use of

formal education has at times been a decisive factor in holding back knowledge development and reducing the effectiveness of health services.

Where knowledge development is slow, the structural power of knowledge ownership will only be effective if that ownership is preserved through
rules, regulations and authorizations. The sharing of knowledge becomes a
privileged activity and the organizations that dispense it become structured
and hierarchical. But where knowledge develops rapidly, the sharing of
knowledge becomes difficult to control, even across major social barriers.
Sharing itself becomes a driving force for knowledge development, and the
exchange of knowledge becomes an instrument for success. Hierarchies are
broken down and organizations 'deconstructed'.

From a governmental perspective, the forces that promote knowledge
development may be beneficial for economic advance. But they may also
give rise to new values and novel views on social life and human conditions,
which have an unwanted destabilizing effect on society. There are in consequence forces that strive to hold back progress on the grounds that rapidly developing knowledge may threaten the stability of established social
structures, such as health service provision. The dichotomy between rapid
knowledge development and the sharing of knowledge, on the one hand,
and restricted, regulated and privileged knowledge sharing and knowledge
development on the other, is evident in comparing different political systems and different countries. In some countries ideologies or religious
cultures hold back free knowledge-sharing. Even in very similar cultures,
such as those in Europe, many small and subtle differences in the structure
and organization of education and in attitudes towards knowledge sharing
create substantial differences in economic development and the quality and
effectiveness of social services, including health care. It is the government's
attitude to, and policy on, knowledge formation and knowledge dissemination that is the most fundamental factor governing the development of
such services.

Some specific characteristics of education and health care

In discussing the interaction between government and medical faculties in
the European perspective it seems necessary first to consider the precon-
ditions for this interaction. This can be done by analysing the development
over time of the relationship and by elucidating its basic structures.

One has first to bear in mind the dual responsibilities of the medical
faculties and the balance between their two main tasks: that of searching for
new knowledge – the research facet – and that of educating young people
to take up a professional role in society. The weight given to these two
different tasks varies over time and across different value systems and social
structures.

A particular feature of medicine and the caring sciences in general is their close relationship to fundamental human experiences such as birth, death and suffering. This adds an extra dimension of both power and responsibility to the educational process and the research activities carried out within medical faculties. There is an ethical dualism specific to the relationship between medicine and the caring sciences on the one hand and society at large on the other. While the medical profession addresses the problems of the individual from a duty-ethical perspective, its relationship with society is expected to be within a framework of utilitarian ethics.

Another fundamental challenge to the medical profession arises from the fact that human bodies and their physiology are more or less alike all over the world. The basics of human biology are therefore universal, and medicine has in some of its aspects become an international discipline. However, the diseases the profession has to treat are to a large extent a function of local and cultural circumstances, deeply rooted in socioeconomic and behavioural traditions. This transforms the art of medicine into a geographically limited, localized pursuit. I shall develop this point further below.

In order to look at medical training and its role, how this role seems likely to develop and how it might be affected by governmental action of one kind or another, we shall need to make some analysis of past and present experiences and of future trends, bearing in mind the varied pattern of development in different European countries. The sequence of events to be described may not have been completed in all countries: national characteristics and social structures may have modified responses to universal pressures and common trends. I shall begin by considering the concept of health and health care as a determinant for government action.

The university hospital and its culture

From an educational standpoint, the main concern is to enable medical students to function effectively within the existing health care system; that is, in practice, within the frame of reference of a particular form of organization and in accordance with the values of that organization's present culture. The government's concern is with the extent to which this culture reflects social values, and perhaps also the political values of the government itself. This is a point at which the duty ethics of health care may conflict with the utilitarian ethics of the government and where the values inherent in medical education come strongly into play.

Over the past fifty years the culture of medical education – and indeed the culture of the health services as a whole – has been progressively dominated by the university hospitals. These institutions developed from teaching hospitals at the time of the French revolution, as hospitals which should ideally have a patient population reflecting as closely as possible the epidemiology in society. However, as technology developed and medicine became more and more specialized, the university hospitals came to deal with the unusual rather than the typical cases, with the sophisticated rather than the simple. They developed into 'centres of excellence'. They became concerned with research rather than teaching, with an emphasis on disease rather than health. Their main aspiration was consistent with the concept, inherited from the Renaissance, of diseases as a mechanical disturbance of bodily functions. This concept internationalizes medicine, in that it eliminates social and cultural factors in explaining the genesis of illness. It focuses medical concern on problems that can be dealt with by reductive, 'mechanistic' thinking and tends to apply mechanistic solutions to diseases or illness that are not of that nature.

Donor organizations which support medical research do so at 'centres of excellence' all over the world. This has led people to believe that the 'art and science' of medicine has a general validity. However, most tasks of medicine concern illnesses closely related to culture-governed behaviour patterns and to socioeconomic circumstances that vary from country to country, from region to region, and from province to province. The objective of the health care system is to create health and ameliorate pain and suffering. The rapidly increasing knowledge of the biology of the human body, although of great value in itself, is only of limited use in societies in which unemployment, violence, food deprivation and environmental deterioration are the main causes of illness and suffering. Biology makes medicine international, but the actual pattern of illness makes it local. Notwithstanding this, medical education has during the past fifty years placed its main emphasis on the biology and function of the human body.

From a governmental vantage point this approach is too limited. While the government has to make provision for the care of citizens who are ill, its main commitment is to ensure the general health of the population. It does not have the same obligation to the individual ill person as does the physician or hospital department. In recent years governments have therefore tried to reorient medical education towards primary health care, rather than towards hospitals and disease. At a superficial economic level, this change may be thought to alleviate the financial burdens of public hospital systems. More fundamentally, however, it implies a revolution in contemporary attitudes.

The disease-oriented view is that sound health is a general condition, but that individuals may occasionally catch a disease that can then be submitted to treatment by an appropriate expert. The health-oriented view is that people are not healthy in general, but succumb to ailments and illnesses increasingly often during their lifetime, and almost continuously when they become older, with increasing loss of function towards the end of their lives. Health care in this context is about how to cope with ailments and illness and how actively to delay the loss of function (Antonovsky 1987). Health is not 'natural': it has to be actively pursued by the individual in his or her lifestyle and by society through policies for promoting health. This approach deprofessionalizes some aspects of care and changes the role of health professionals in other aspects. Above all it alters the previous balance of power between the health services and the citizen. It gives the citizen an active responsibility for his or her own health, and broadens governmental responsibility towards health, which now becomes an undertaking not only for ministries of health but also for ministries of industry.

This health-oriented view is currently gaining political strength, going hand-in-hand with ecological movements and post-modernistic ideas. Governments are in consequence under political pressure to reshape medical studies in the direction of a greater emphasis on community health. The strongest resistance to this change is to be found in university hospitals and medical faculties, long embedded as they have been in disease-oriented thinking and reductive scientific philosophy. The result is often a polarization between 'progressive' utilitarian forces and the more conservative 'bio-medical traditionalists'. Governments, because they are more sensitive than medical faculties to the climate of the times and the mood of the public, and because they operate within a utilitarian frame of reference, tend to support the progressives. However, they may run into problems in overcoming the inertia of entrenched interests and their own conservative inclinations.

The role of the physician and the health care system in the welfare state

The present health care systems in most European countries came into being after the Second World War. At that point it seemed natural for governments to consider establishing health care as part of the social security offered to citizens in the emerging European welfare states. Particularly in Northern and Eastern European countries, there emerged a strong belief in science, in centralized hierarchical organization and in Keynesian economy. It was the prevailing view that diseases were well-defined entities existing in the world, and that overcoming them was only a matter of resources and organization. People were generally healthy, and the occasional lapse from this state could best be dealt with by a competent health service. Developing such a service therefore became the objective of governmental actions, with medical education and research as its cornerstones. Keynesian thinking had convinced politicians and decision-makers that society had the means to control the economy and to make provision for the necessary expansion of health services, financed and administered by central or regional authorities. The education of physicians, and the expansion of health care to include a wide range of other caring personnel, became the established governmental strategy for improving public health throughout the 1950s and 1960s (Vang 1992).

The 'shortage or surplus' of physicians

The almost explosive development of health care systems in some of the welfare states, particularly the richer ones in Europe, could not at the outset be matched by a corresponding expansion in the number of physicians, because of the time-lag involved in the process of medical education. The shortage of physicians was in most countries exacerbated by the fact that medicine is a privileged profession and people who do not have the necessary formal qualifications may not carry out the kind of work that is considered as the proper province of medical practice. Most governments were unable or unwilling to relinquish some of the laws and regulatory systems, sometimes old and outdated, that protected medical activities. Formal medical education was still seen as the best safeguard of patients' interests. Moreover, the established health care systems had created territories of power and privilege for politicians, administrators and doctors alike, who acted in concert to maintain the status quo. For those reluctant to change the regulations or the conceptions of what was a doctor and what was a disease, the only available recourse was to expand medical education on the existing pattern (Freddi and Björkman 1989).

The demand for such expansion put considerable strain on universities at the time. The medical curriculum was changed to emphasize a more biological orientation, a change further enforced by the rapid technological development that followed the Second World War. The highly positive view of science occasioned by substantial breakthroughs in physics and chemistry, and particularly in nuclear physics, embedded reductive scientific thinking into medicine and further emphasized the science of the measurable. Aspects of medical research became part of the specialist postgraduate curriculum. The rapid development of antibiotics moved the focus of attention from infectious diseases to degenerative diseases. As there was a lack of basic knowledge of underlying causes, these could only be dealt with by deploying complicated medical technology. Cardiovascular surgery, neurosurgery, laboratory medicine and intensive care, leaning heavily on the sciences of physiology and biochemistry, came into fashion. The consequence was a shortage of physicians in primary care, and especially in rural areas, while the established 'centres of excellence' dealing with tertiary care were intensively staffed.

The shortage of physicians resulted in an increase in their salaries in many countries, particularly those with mixed economies that were not subject to state-governed economic planning. Medicine had become a high-status profession in these countries, winning a large share of well-qualified applicants to medical schools. Even allowing for the perceived need for more doctors, there were limitations on the available teaching facilities and on the levels of investment governments were willing to make. Different governments used different strategies for coping with the problem. Some limited the number of students allowed to study medicine, accepting only those with high marks in mathematics, physics and chemistry, which were considered as providing a particularly good background for 'scientific' medicine. Others instituted a sorting examination after a year or two to select the members of the total student body who seemed most fitted for medical studies: generally those with particular abilities in subjects judged important for the further study of biology, physiology and biochemistry.

Development along these lines was not universal in Europe. In some countries medical education remained more accessible, and physicians were educated without any consideration of likely future demand. Such countries later had to face costly over-establishment or even unemployment among physicians. In Eastern and Central European countries the medical profession never attained as high a social standing as it did in Western Europe. In the Soviet Union the status of a physician was lower than that of an industrial engineer, and medicine was to a large extent a profession for women. Even so, the status of the physician was considerably above that of a nurse, with a salary four or five times as high.

Small is beautiful and the 'greying' societies

At around the end of the 1960s and the beginning of the 1970s, there was a change of attitude in some countries towards the health care system and its objectives. The biological and mechanical disease model was challenged, along with the hierarchical structure of society. Small became beautiful, and within health care community orientation and primary care came into prominence. In some of the affluent welfare states the epidemiology had changed considerably, and caring for the aged emerged more prominently as a central issue. Within a greying society, characterized by high mobility of the younger generation and a weak family structure, the care of the elderly was no longer accepted as a task for the family and coping with ageing acquired a new dimension. This change brought such issues as the caring process, ethics and the humanization of medicine back into focus. A growing scepticism about technology gave rise to the technology assessment movement, while inter-sectoral or trans-sectoral approaches involving teamwork created new professional groupings and brought people from the social sciences into health care. Nursing was translated into caring science, and the traditional hierarchy within medicine was flattened. However, relatively little development of this kind took place in the Southern, Eastern and Central European countries, where the mechanistic view of humanity was maintained alongside a 'steam age' tradition of hierarchical organization.

The effect on education

Although these changes of attitude began to make an impact on medical education, it took some time for them to become recognizable in the curriculum. The shift from a narrowly biological perspective towards a more community-oriented humanistic view of medicine was not accepted by the profession in general, particularly as those in dominating positions had been educated within the biomedical reductionist tradition. Neither was there any established body of research within medical faculties which could enhance the prestige of the community and primary health care oriented doctors, let alone the emergent caring sciences. In the event it was the politicians who intervened. Following the Alma Ata meeting of the World Health Organisation, most governments committed themselves to a health system based on primary care, adapting rules and regulations, and in some cases creating economic incentives, to attract doctors to primary care.

Within this new context, some health researchers abandoned the Kelvinian doctrine: 'When you cannot express it in numbers, your knowledge is meagre and unsatisfactory.' The study of non-quantifiable or not easily quantifiable parameters and the employment of semi-quantitative or qualitative methods more closely related to the methodology used by sociology, psychology and other social sciences became acceptable. A holistic approach was used in place of a reductionist approach. But even though it was adopted mainly in clinical research and the daily clinical activities in medicine, the change imposed a substantial strain on medical faculties and medical schools. Many teachers took the view that it was imposed by political forces, and this revived the familiar discussion about the freedom of research and the role of the teacher. Few of the senior medical academics, who had grown up with a different research paradigm, knew much about the methodology of research using qualitative data, and found themselves deskilled when dealing with this approach, which was now termed health science and which was genuinely new and different, rather than a mere semantic or cosmetic change. Some medical faculties changed their names to become health faculties or faculties of health sciences. A new research genre evolved that, in traditional scientific reductionist terms, appeared highly questionable.

In the dichotomy between searching for new knowledge and making existing knowledge known, education had during the post-war years up to about 1970 been overshadowed by research. In the new situation, with its changing frame of reference, education began to regain authority while medical research underwent an identity crisis occasioned by its removal from the centre of the stage. An additional consideration was that pure basic science had not developed as rapidly as had been hoped. It was the applied sciences that had most evidently gained ground during the years up to 1970. Putting a man on the moon within a decade did not prove a major problem, given the necessary basic knowledge and the opportunity and resources to apply it. It was much more difficult to solve the enigma of cancer: in the absence of the fundamental understanding required, the problem was not merely one of application. In spite of the enormous growth of knowledge, there was a lack of the right kind. The evident need was to return to basic science and to play down technological medicine. It was frustration at the ineffectiveness and cost of the existing applications of medical knowledge, especially to the growing problems of the diseases of the elderly, that opened the path for technology assessment, quality assurance and the move away from biological medicine.

There was at the same time a rising dissatisfaction with the health services in Europe, which were confronting what became known as the 'medical paradox': namely that the more resources that were invested in health care, the more people became ill. The prevalent view among the public, moreover, was that the new physicians had been recruited on the wrong criteria and had been taught the wrong things. The new generation of physicians did not listen, did not know how to communicate, did not know enough about ordinary people's lives and lacked a sense of commitment. In other words, they did not adequately solve their patients' problems.

The restructuring of the curriculum in some medical schools occasioned by these changes led to the introduction of problem-based learning and multi-professional education. Problem-based learning was also justified in terms of the amount of knowledge required within the biomedical frame of reference, which had by this time reached a critical mass. Sub-specialization had remorselessly expanded the demands on the curriculum. Time used in providing basic data that the student could extract from other sources was time wasted. Moreover, much of the information taught had a very short half-life in consequence of the rapid development of new knowledge. There was a feeling, too, that members of the profession were being taught how to reshape patients' problems to fit into their own specialities, in a variant of Cinderella's shoe problem. The curriculum simply could not hold any more specific items.

Concurrent development in informatics made it evident that data and facts could be dealt with in different ways from those previously adopted, perhaps involving the use of computers, videotapes and self-study materials as a complement to traditional teaching and the library. The abilities to communicate with patients and other members of the care team, to identify problems in their broader social context and to orient solutions towards these problems were seen to be important, particularly when dealing with the illness of and support for the elderly population. Communication skills and observational ability had to be taught. It also became more obvious that health care required teamwork, and in particular that it was essential to be able to work collaboratively with people having a different frame of reference, such as social workers and psychologists. These new considerations gave rise to a review of the medical curriculum in some of the more progressive universities, but were in general rejected by universities in countries with a strong medico-technical culture.

While these changes of paradigm were taking effect, the rising numbers of students and teachers, together with the increased demands on teachers' time and consequent union activities, gave rise to administrative problems. The requirements of a growing central bureaucracy interfered with both education and research, resulting in an increasing volume of paperwork being filtered down the teaching hierarchy and an increasing number of new regulations and demands for restructuring. The resulting constraints were felt in all countries, but particularly in those in which powers of decision were shared between different groups of teachers and students. The weakening of academic leadership and the fragmentation of decision-making gave rise to a feeling of powerlessness on the part of all those concerned. Where the power to decide was illusory, because not in practice delegated by government or the central university administration, the result was a sense of frustration and of valuable time wasted.

Entering the 1990s, Europe finds itself faced not only with economic recession, but also with a multitude of other problems related to health care. They include increasing unemployment among health professionals, the development of the caring sciences in competition with medicine, a change of emphasis from disease-orientation towards health-orientation, a shift of health care systems away from state administration towards contracted arrangements which may have different priorities, and a departure from the previous epidemiology of mixed infectious degenerative diseases towards degenerative diseases and social diseases such as violence, drug abuse and behavioural problems. The incidence of social ills is heightened in an increasingly dense and increasingly multicultural population that may include diverse groups of refugees, some of them severely damaged by war or traumatized by experiences of torture.

The free movement of people within the European Community during the current decade can be expected to make the exchange of health professionals more commonplace than it is today. There has for the past twenty years or so been no major constraint on the mobility of doctors and nurses within the European Community, but the opportunity has had little practical consequence, in large part because of language barriers, but also because of the lack of harmonization of medical education (Braad *et al.* 1991). Both these inhibiting factors can be expected to diminish in importance and even perhaps to disappear towards the end of the decade. Several programmes within the EC, such as the Erasmus scheme, and the agreement between EFTA and EC countries, are likely to promote this development.

Governments' political goals and universities' teaching objectives

Every government sees in its universities a means of fulfilling its policies. Its primary requirement for the medical faculty is to educate safe and skilful physicians. Governments are not usually concerned with the quality of medical education in more than a very general way. They may demand a certain minimum standard, but are for the most part concerned with quantity in relation to what they consider to be the national need, and with the achievement of a regional balance of provision to ensure an acceptable level of access to health care in all parts of the country. Governments are, in other words, concerned to avoid any significant under- or overproduction of physicians, and to see that medical education is geographically well distributed.

Another main governmental interest lies in overseeing research and development. While initial medical training is more or less left in the hands of the university, within varying degrees of overall legal or regulatory control, governments will often take a fairly direct interest in research and development, attempting to manipulate this through economic incentives and disincentives. The concept, deeply rooted in universities, of freedom of thought has left its mark on the concept of freedom of research. But medical research, unlike, say, research in philosophy, is heavily dependent on resources: equipment, laboratories, research assistance and the like. It is therefore highly responsive to economic incentives. Clinical research and development in their turn often take place within the context of public hospitals, where unauthorized research on patients is not only unethical, but in many instances subject to criminal law, even though there may be a fuzzy border defining acceptable clinical methods. In consequence, basic biomedical research is relatively easy for a government to control through economic means, provided that it acts as the main financing authority. Clinical research is more difficult to influence by economic procedures, and is usually controlled through legal and regulatory measures in combination with social control, the latter being exercised by the health care system rather than the university.

From a governmental perspective it is in some respects convenient to keep education distinct from research, since it is then easier to vary the dimensions and direction of education independently from those of research and development. In some countries – for instance those in Scandinavia – there is a sharp separation of the two. In others in which they are not separated, separate research institutes may be set up independently of universities, empowered in some cases to make their own provision for teaching and research. While this may promote healthy competition, it may undermine the universities in terms of both recruitment and the unquantifiable support that research gives to the content and quality of education (SOU 1992).

The gap between research and teaching

Research, and particularly biomedical research, has enjoyed a high status since the Second World War. Professorships have in the main been awarded to those who could offer the longest list of scientific publications. Teaching ability, particularly at the level of initial medical training, has been a secondary consideration and more recently a tertiary one, overtaken in importance by administrative capabilities. The first encounters of students with teachers tend as a result to involve the most junior teachers. The effect is similar to that arising from the previously mentioned division between research and education, in that mature research experience may contribute too little to the content and quality of teaching.

It is possible in addition to discern a historical reason for this disjunction within medicine. From the outset, the teaching of the physician-to-be was a process of apprenticeship. The young apprentice would follow a senior physician in his work, learning from him and copying him in his attitudes, beliefs and actions. The extent of formal knowledge was limited and in

large part medicine was more art than science. Tacit knowledge was important; that is, the intuitive kind of knowledge that does not lend itself to
verbal formulation and systematic tuition, resembling 'know-how' rather
than formal knowledge. But as medical practice began increasingly to depend on biology, and on what came somewhat figuratively to be called
'scientific' medicine, the education of practitioners moved progressively
away from apprenticeship towards formal courses, embodying lectures,
laboratory classes and the like. As biological knowledge increased, these
courses expanded further, and as biology penetrated into clinical activities
(such as surgery, in terms of the physiology of surgery and the like), apprenticeship came to take a correspondingly smaller place in initial medical
training, and was virtually confined to postgraduate training. Since the mid-
1960s even postgraduate training has been in the process of being formal-
ized into regular courses. As a result of the knowledge explosion, there is
now much talk of lifelong learning, the major problem being to strike a
balance between what constitutes basic facts to be learned on the one hand,
and the essential skills of learning and problem solving on the other.

In having to deal with an unmanageably large amount of knowledge with
a very rapid turnover, medical education is in a certain sense beginning to
revert to the apprentice system through the medium of problem-based
learning. In problem-based learning the students themselves have to take
responsibility for their knowledge development. They are, in other words,
self-taught in terms of basic facts. In modern universities the process can
be strongly supported by interactive computer programs, videos and the
like. A further aspect of problem-based learning relates to problem definition
and solution. This is a form of activity in which problems are presented,
delineated and analysed. As before, the students have to undertake much
of the work, and in particular the initial information search, but with more
detailed individual support from the teacher in the process of problem
analysis. This part of the activity is strongly influenced by research methodology, and underlines the importance of the teachers' research experience.
The third main element in problem-based learning relates to group work
on evaluation, involving a form of feedback that reviews and assesses the
other two components of the process.

Although problem-based learning has been relatively slow to establish
itself, it is now being taken up more rapidly in different universities in
Europe. Insofar as it becomes a common approach, it might enhance the
harmonization of teaching in European countries. If governments decide
to promote this development, which the rapid growth and obsolescence of
knowledge seems to necessitate, they will also need to encourage a closer
interaction between research and teaching. One might remark that, in
seeking a balance between the quest for new knowledge on behalf of society
and the quest for new knowledge on behalf of the individual learner, there
is common methodological ground that serves to enhance the early development of the students' research potential.

It seems, then, that governments will need to provide for a better integration of education and research in the years to come, perhaps particularly by supporting the development of methodology and the study of the educational process itself.

Quality and quality control

There is an old saying that at the beginning of your career it is important what you have studied, while towards the end of your career it is important where you have studied. This may be defensible at the individual level, but at the societal or political level different universities ought to have an equal opportunity to fulfil the required political objectives. From a governmental perspective this provides a strong argument for centralized control.

What society and governments expect from universities in exchange for financial support is accountability for the content and quality of education and for the effective use of funding. The current internationalization of education, particularly within the European Community, has further emphasized the need for some form of accreditation of universities closely linked to accountability. The traditional approach to quality control has been heavily research-oriented, as exemplified in the control of applications for research grants and in the requirement for applicants to academic posts to register their scientific publications and citations. The quality of teaching tends to be assessed in terms of students' results and their subsequent careers. It is unusual to monitor the actual process of teaching. However, if education is to benefit from the teachers' academic research, it may be desirable to develop better measures of teaching performance and to highlight the results in performance reviews. Such reviews should contribute to institutional performance assessments so as to emphasize the responsibility of institutions and their faculties for the quality of the teaching they provide.

From a governmental standpoint it is the total educational performance of the medical school or faculty that is important. More detailed specifications concerning the curriculum or teaching performance can be covered in the requirements for accreditation. The accreditation of universities might reasonably include assurance about internal quality control relating to the amount and quality of teaching. The implementation of agreed accreditation procedures would be the ultimate responsibility of the deans and the institutional heads.

Government and deregulation

A new conception of the role of government is gradually replacing the postwar view. In most European countries the administration of universities has until recently been somewhat rigid and centralized. As in the case of health care, this centralization has led to a good deal of frustration and has generated a feeling of powerlessness among teachers and students. Universities and their medical schools are 'knowledge organizations' whose product cannot be easily measured, and the nature and quality of whose activities in large part depend on their teaching staff. The administration itself can do little to enhance the outcome of the educational process, though it may well impair it by adopting a heavy-handed approach.

A quickly changing world does not allow time or space for a hierarchical bureaucracy. Although hierarchies and bureaucracies may offer security and predictability, and some scope for ambition and achievement, they also tend to promote a culture of stultification, oppression and inequality. In recognition of this, many governments are now entering an era of what might be called post-hierarchical politics, in which they are searching for alternative social constructs. A common strategy seems to be deregulation, in pursuit of which universities, alongside other social institutions, are given more autonomy and also more responsibility. To be effective, deregulation has to carry with it the forms of institution-wide accountability that have already been mentioned. Effective procedures for such accountability have not yet been developed, but are likely to evolve within the next few years. One problematic consequence may be a greater range of variation between universities and between individual medical schools. However, this variation could be viewed constructively in terms of differing profiles rather than negatively in terms of the uneven quality of education. If the need for better integration between research and teaching is considered alongside that for deregulation and greater institutional autonomy, the issue of accreditation and accountability may be seen as sufficiently crucial to merit not only control by individual governments but possibly also some form of supranational involvement.

Internationalization

Some degree of internationalization of initial medical education in Europe is currently seen as an important step towards the free movement of professionally qualified people between the European countries, and particularly those within the European Community. If the ambition to create an enlarged European Community is sustained throughout the coming decade, the governments concerned may be expected collectively to promote a harmonization of the content and the quality of education as well as to set aside substantial funds for exchange programmes. An internationalization of student programmes would accord even greater importance to accountability and to making public the outcome of evaluation programmes.

It is important in this context to consider the potentialities of the distance education process developed by a number of universities, the best known of which is perhaps the Open University in the UK. If problem-based learning is seen as an alternative to traditional teaching, it is possible to envisage a distance education system interleaved with problem-based learning and case studies at any one of a network of universities that have harmonized their curricula. The most effective contributions from governments to such a development would be the accreditation of the network, the endorsement of their curricula and financial support for teacher and student exchange.

Summary and conclusions

The developments in medical education and in the actions taken by governments that have been described here are by no means identical in all European countries. Some have not yet completed the whole sequence; others are moving beyond it into uncharted territory, where terms such as primary, secondary and tertiary care no longer have a clear meaning, where health care is integrated and hospitals are ceasing to exist in their present form, where hospital departments are participants in networks alongside social institutions and a variety of educational institutions committed to knowledge development and knowledge sharing, and where the deregulation of universities and health care organizations is linked with responsibility and accountability. In this emergent world, international networking provides a strong incentive for the development of new ideas and for mutual learning.

There will inevitably be differences between European countries in terms of the governmental actions to be taken within the next decade. Even so, pressures for deregulation and accountability are likely to impinge on most medical schools, strengthening the leadership role of heads of institutions and deans, but at the same time placing new and different demands on them. They may have a more limited period of office, and the basis for their recruitment may change. The scope may also be increased for national and international networking, but there may at the same time be a tendency towards greater national competition. There is a risk that internationalization will be slow to develop, given that language barriers are still substantial in those countries in which second and third languages are not an integral part of college education. Medical education will allow students more autonomy in terms of knowledge and the acquisition of data but will also demand a heavier teaching commitment in terms of helping with analysis and problem definition. Small-scale research activities may be included in the curriculum. Governmental involvement in medical education will be through publicly accessible accreditation procedures, reviews and quality control programmes.

References

Antonovsky, A. (1987) *Unravelling the Mystery of Health*. San Francisco, Jossey-Bass.
Braad, P.M. *et al.* (1991) *Sunhedsvaesenet og EF*. Copenhagen, Dansk Sygehus Institut.
Etzioni, A. (1968) *The Active Society*. New York, Free Press.

Freddi, G. and Björkman, J.W. (eds) (1989) *Controlling Medical Professionals: the Comparative Politics of Health Governance.* London, Sage.

SOU (1992) *Frihet, Ansvar, Kompetens.* Stockholm, Allmänna Förlaget.

Vang, J. (1992) 'Health policy', in M. Hawkesworth and M. Kogan (eds) *Encyclopedia of Government and Politics*, Vol. 2. London and New York, Routledge.

5

Governmental and Professional Power and Influence in Legal Education in Europe

Julian Lonbay

Introduction

Law is a nationally based topic. An important attribute and aspect of statehood is reflected through the existence of separate legal orders. Indeed this is one of the matters guaranteed to Scotland by the Act of Union 1707. There are of course common features in the national legal orders in Europe resulting from historical connections between countries. Thus the Irish system is primarily a common law system for historical reasons. There are also, for example, strong similarities between the Swedish and Finnish systems, and those of France and Belgium. The similarities resulting from historical links have naturally eroded over time, as states can exert and display their independence and internal control through adaptations to their panoplies of legal rules.

The advent of a 'new legal order' for the member states of the European Communities, coupled with the gradual emergence of supranational political structures at the European level, has caused some convergence of individual legal rules and adoption of many common legal rules (Lonbay and Spedding 1992). This factor of diminishing national statehood is having repercussions on the national provision of legal education. For example, the overlay of Community law has been recognized as requiring an increase in legal training in this area by the Law Society in the UK (Lonbay 1992b; Law Society 1992) and elsewhere. The European Communities have also passed laws that affect educational provision for lawyers, at least indirectly.

The educational needs of lawyers and their organization

In all the member states of the European Communities except Denmark the legal professions are divided. However, the functional allocation of tasks to the separate national legal professions is different in each member state. The difference is reflected not just in the common law professions but also in the civil law professions. In the common law world, the division of functions between solicitor and barrister allocates different tasks to these professions than is the case with the classical continental division of tasks between advocates and notaries. Not surprisingly, notarial education is different from that of *avocat* in most continental countries.

The educational requirements of lawyers across Europe will therefore vary according to both country and profession. One method of dealing with this variation has been to establish professional education courses suited to particular professions, independently of university courses. The training of lawyers has both academic and professional aspects (Lonbay *et al.* 1990). The professional input into the university sector, at least from one point of view, need not be too great, if the profession can insist on its own educational and other requirements after the university law degree has been passed.

The professional or vocational training stage has wide varieties between the different member states. There is currently no mandatory professional training in Spain, for example. There is a *stage* in some countries, in others there is a *stage* plus exam and in some countries after having passed and qualified as a full professional one is subject to post-admission training requirements, as in England and Wales for solicitors.

The length of university and professional training of lawyers

The duration of law degrees in the member states is set out in Table 5.1, which details each country separately. One can see a fairly wide variation from three years in the UK and Ireland to five years in Belgium, Denmark, Portugal and Spain. The durations given, it must be emphasized, are the minimum duration in years. In Germany, where three and a half years is the minimum, it frequently takes up to a further year and a half or longer to fulfil the complete university legal study requirements.

Post-university training comprises vocational education, often in formal educational institutions and *stages*, the *stages* being designed to introduce the student to the practical application of knowledge he or she has acquired, in the appropriate legal office or other environment. When one looks at the total legal education process, one gets the results set out in Table 5.2. For the UK, for example, one must add a further three years to the training programme, making six years in all; that is the minimum length of time before qualification as a lawyer. In Germany a further two and a half years minimum are added, making at least seven years to become a *Rechtsanwält*. In Spain there is no requirement for professional training, so after five years of legal education at university it is possible to become a member of the legal profession on enrolment in the appropriate *colegio*. In Denmark a further three years is required, leaving it, with Belgium, as having

Table 5.1   Duration and names of law degrees in the EC member states

Country	Title of law degree	Duration of law degree (years)
Belgium	licence en droit	5
Denmark	cand. jur.	5
France	maîtrise	4
Germany	referendarexamen	3.5
Greece	law degree	4
Ireland	law degree	3
Italy	laurea in giurisprudenza	4
Luxembourg	—	—
Netherlands	Meester in de Rechten	4
Portugal	lic. em direito	5
Spain	lic. en derecho	5
United Kingdom[a]	law degree	3

[a] There is no legally set minimum number of years; thus the University of Buckingham, the only private university in England, runs a two-year law degree.

Table 5.2   Duration of professional training in the EC member states

Country	Duration of professional training	Minimum total duration of training (years)
Belgium	3	8
Denmark	3	8
France	3	7
Germany	2.5	7
Greece	1.5	5.5
Ireland	2+	5+
Italy	2	6
Luxembourg	3	7–8
Netherlands	3	7
Portugal	1.5	6.5
Spain	0	5
United Kingdom	3	6

formally the most long-winded process of training within the European Communities.

Clearly the length of degree and length of overall training is in fact a major difference in education between the member states. One can clearly teach a far wider range of subjects in a five-year degree than one can in three years. At the post-university qualification stage of training, the existence or not of formal exams and courses and the length and requirement of the *stages* will vary considerably in the different member states, thus having a strong impact on the overall professional training of would-be lawyers.

The autonomy of the universities as regards legal education

The educational role of the state is another important manifestation of sovereignty, and is exercised in varying degrees of centralization across Europe as regards legal education. What is the capacity of the university law schools to react to changes and to control their own curriculum alone, and what is the extent of governmental, parliamentary or professional power to control the curriculum? As might be expected, the answer is different in the various countries.

The independence of the educational process will clearly affect its ability to react to change. Funding plays a key role here and the existence or not of private education institutions alongside the public sector universities is another variable. This chapter does not discuss these issues, important though they are. They affect all higher education and not simply legal studies. At the International Congress of Comparative Law in 1990 nearly all the national reports expressed concern at state control of research and teaching through its funding powers. However, even with those factors taken into account there is still considerable variation in the autonomy of institutions in curriculum matters as regards legal education. The question of who determines the topics to be studied varies from state to state. In most member states of the European Communities it is the government, or to be more precise the parliament, that establishes the basic minimum curriculum.

In many of the countries there is a relatively strong degree of governmental control over the contents of the academic stage. In Denmark the contents and structure of the law degree have been recently reformed (in 1987) and are set out in law (Lonbay *et al.* 1990: Chapter 3 and Appendices B1 and B2). In Austria too the central authorities have traditionally set out in detail curriculum requirements for law studies, through the framework law (*Allgemeines Hochschulstudien – Gesetz AHStG*) and the *Bundesgesetz über das Studium der Rechtswissenschaften* (as implemented). In Norway the King in Council determines which degrees a university can grant (under the University Act 1989), and the Ministry of Education decides on the main topics for the degree courses, leaving the universities through their boards (*Det Akademiske Kollegium*) to decide on the details. In Iceland, although the Government in fact regulates the legal curriculum, *de facto* the Ministry accepts amendments suggested by the University of Iceland Law Faculty. In Italy the Constitution guarantees freedom of teaching and the principle of university autonomy (article 33) (de Vergottini 1990). This still permits private universities which can follow a particular ideological bent (Constitutional Court no. 195, 29 December 1972; de Vergottini 1990: 13). The state nevertheless issues very detailed curricula through the Ministry of Public Instruction (e.g. Decree no. 1652 (30 September 1938) as amended; Lonbay *et al.* 1990, Chapter 8 and Appendix G1).

However, the extent of state control has been weakening, partially as a result of the late 1960s student agitations. In Italy prior to 1969 there were eighteen obligatory topics set out in law and students were only permitted to choose three options. Now it is more like a free-for-all, with law faculties making suggestions to students (Lonbay *et al.* 1990: Appendix G2), and the legal profession exercising *de facto* control through admission requirements (Olgiati and Pocar 1988: 345). A reform law on universities, granting them greater autonomy, has been awaited for some time (Moratto 1987, generally; Ricciardi 1990, on legal education).

In the Netherlands, under the University Education Act (Koekkoek 1990: 9) the *Academisch Statuut* in articles 72 and 82–95 sets out the subjects to be studied for the basic law degrees (e.g. Dutch law, notarial law, fiscal law, Antillian law, etc.). (Lonbay *et al.* 1990: Chapter 10 and Appendices I1, I2 and I3.) Within this general framework the universities can decide which degree courses to offer, and exactly how the contents will be presented. Nevertheless, they cannot totally deviate from the structure set out by the law. The law itself can permit exceptions. For example, the university of Limburg Law School has a specialized law curriculum (de Groot 1992: 20; Lonbay *et al.* 1990: Appendix I4). The law is under review to allow universities more freedom, but as de Groot (1992) points out, the law on lawyers has similar requirements to the *Academisch Statuut*, which would also have to be altered before law schools would actually feel free to alter their curricula. Should the legal profession allow the alteration of the law on lawyers in the sense suggested, it may be that they would exert pressure on the law schools to maintain the teaching of subjects they felt were important, as happened in Italy after the curriculum reforms of 1969 (Lonbay 1992a: 80). Thus the contents of Dutch legal education at the university stage are structured from outside the university itself.

In Germany each *Land* has autonomy in principle (articles 91 (a) and (b), Basic Law) in the sphere of higher education though, there is a Federal Higher Education Framework Law (*Hochschulrahmengesetz*) and the Federal Government pays for 50 per cent of university buildings costs (Lorenz 1990: 4; Karpen 1990: 9). The *Länder* mostly set out only the broad content required, leaving it to professors to determine the finer details (Lonbay *et al.* 1990: Chapter 4 and Appendix C1). Professors themselves are guaranteed academic freedom in research and teaching (article 5(3) Basic Law; Lorenz 1990: 13). However, the examination system is strictly under the control of the *Land* examining bodies in which professors are a minority. Law schools engaging in curricular frolics of their own are likely to see their students fail the final university 'state exam'. The existence of the private tutors (*repetitors*) which are used by many German law students to help them pass the state examination (Blankenburg and Schultz 1988: 131) indicates the difficulty of the test. Thus the methods of teaching law are freely chosen but the ultimate degree content is state (*Land*) mandated (but see Bund 1988, *contra*).

Decentralization or democratization are also factors in giving universities more autonomy over their degree courses. In both Spain (Ferreiro *et al.* 1987; Lonbay *et al.* 1990: Chapter 12; Lonbay 1990a) and Portugal (Lonbay *et al.*

1990: Chapter 11) the extent of governmental control, which had been very great under fascism, is currently being diminished (the universities being granted more autonomy), and there are likely to be some significant changes to the content of the law degree. Spain, for example, is moving from the Francoist model of twenty-five courses (legally mandated in great detail) over five years to a system that will allow a four-year law degree and a choice of topics for students, as well as more practical exercises (*Consejo de Universidades* 1988). The new Catalan University of Pompeu Fabra in Barcelona follows a newly agreed four-year model, and is an example of the increased autonomy in the university sector in Spain. The university is also able to develop its own courses and has done so with a series of diplomas in law (for example, a diploma in urban and property law).

The rigidities introduced by governmentally mandated courses are to some extent mitigated by practical considerations. In Spain, for example, the old-fashioned 'legal' curriculum has been altered ahead of changes in the formal legal regime by professors using their powers of discretion. If this were not so, European Community law would have difficulty in finding a place on the formal legal curriculum there, and Spanish participation in the Erasmus programme, at least for law studies, would have been out of the question.

Where the state does not lay down the foundation courses (mainly in the UK, Ireland and, latterly, Italy) the legal professions have, *de facto*, exerted a strong influence. For example, the 'core topics' required in the UK for a law degree in order to provide the student with exemption from some of the professional examinations take up a considerable proportion of the available space within the curriculum. The current proposals for reform of the academic stage of legal education by the Law Society (Law Society 1992) are being resisted partly on grounds of their over-inclusive nature (Birks 1992).

In Scotland, where the Joint Standing Committee on Legal Education (composed of representatives of the Law Society, the Faculty of Advocates and the Deans of the five Scottish Law Schools) helps to decide many curriculum matters, the mandatory inclusion of European Community law into academic studies was seemingly relatively easily agreed upon (Lonbay *et al.* 1990: Chapter 13 and Appendices L9 and L10). (See Paterson 1988: 77–85 for a historical overview of the interaction of the state, legal profession and university law schools in Scotland.)

In the British model it seems that the legal professions have more influence and power (*de facto*) than the Government over details of legal curricula. The Lord Chancellor's Advisory Committee on Legal Education and Conduct established by the Courts and Legal Services Act 1990 is currently undertaking a review of legal education that is set to last three years.

Moving beyond the member states of the European Communities one can observe that in Sweden the state has traditionally played a large role in controlling universities (through the National Board of Universities and Colleges (UHÄ); UHÄ 1989). Prior to the decree of 1958 setting out the legal curricula it had been heavily criticized for its emphasis on rote learning (Ginsburg and Bruzelius 1965). The first laws regulating the university sector were adopted in 1977, and further reform to the law degree followed (Bogdan 1981: 138). Prior to that, Royal Ordinances had regulated the sector (Petrén 1990). Although research is not directed, the legal curriculum was set out in a framework fashion by the UHÄ and, at the four universities that taught the law degree, by the university board. But it must be noted that examinations are controlled by the university professors themselves, thus assuring local autonomy.

In 1991 the Swedish universities were granted further autonomy in curricula matters, and from 1 July 1993 they will be free to make changes to the law degree. The legal profession in Sweden has no monopoly over the giving of legal advice, but access to the formal title of *advokat* is normally via a special training programme, admission to which is controlled by the *Domstolsverket*, which is likely to insist on maintaining most of the old curriculum, thus pressuring the universities to maintain a 'practitioner-approved' syllabus. In Australia too there has been a devolution from governmental quangos (Commonwealth Tertiary Education Commission) to the state and territory authorities (Chipman 1990: 9). (More fully and generally on Australian legal education see Weisbrodt 1988.)

The 'European' influence

One can say that, within Europe, and probably elsewhere, legal education transmits national cultures. This is overt in the case of content (primarily based on national legal rules) but it is also part of the hidden curriculum of the overall training package of lawyers (Lonbay 1992a: 82). To what extent is this breaking down under the European influence? The legal professions have used universities and other 'professional' entry requirements to regulate access to their professions (the 'gatekeeping' function) (Abel 1988: 13 *et seq.*). The advent of European Community law, in which lawyers play a very important role (Ehlermann 1992), has led to an increasing contact and mutual cooperation of legal practitioners across national borders, evidenced *inter alia* by the spate of 'alliances', 'groupings' and so on. These are recorded in new journals set up to service the growing market, such as *Lawyers in Europe*. Although the European Communities have no direct competence in the educational sphere (de Witte 1989; Lonbay 1989; Commission of the European Communities 1991), they are nevertheless slowly influencing legal training (and more so legal practice), in both its structure and its content.

Directive 89/48/EEC on the mutual recognition of professional qualifications (OJ L 19/16 (1989)) will ultimately give rise to new national 'examinations' in legal training, not just for migrants but also for nationals. This is so even where traditionally there was no professional law exam (or in some cases training) prior to its adoption. I believe that it is a likely

Table 5.3 Duration of training in the EFTA states

Country	Minimum Duration of Law Degree (years)	Minimum Duration of Professional Training (years)	Minimum Total Duration of Training (years)
Austria	4 } 5	7 } 6	11
Finland	4	4	8
Iceland	5	3[a]	8
Liechtenstein	—	2	5+
Norway	5–6[b]	2	7+
Sweden	4.5	5	10
Switzerland	3–5	1–3	2[c]

[a] A lawyer who wants to become an advocate (to the district courts) must either have shown by pleading four cases that he or she is fit to be an advocate or undertake the three-year *stage*.
[b] No minimum set, but the period stated is usual.
[c] As education is a cantonal matter, the requirements for legal training vary considerably in the 26 cantons and it is not sensible to rely on a global figure.

outcome in Spain, Portugal and Denmark. This effect will spread to the EFTA states (except Switzerland, following its referendum rejection of the EEA on 6 December 1992) as a result of the EEA Agreement, which adopts the EC rules in this field. Thus the structure of professional legal training is affected. In those countries where the content of legal education is mandated by the state authorities, reform is in the air. I have mentioned the changes occurring in Spain, Portugal, Sweden and the Netherlands to grant universities more autonomy. Competitive pressures might lead countries with longer formal training periods for the legal professions to make them less lengthy. The EFTA countries have noticeably longer periods of legal education (see Table 5.3) and I would predict contractions within two or three years of the EC–EFTA treaty coming into force.

The directive allows for much easier interaction between the legal professions of the member states (it being easier to transmute between professions), and an increasing exchange of professional functional allocation (i.e. interprofessional mobility) is likely. Thus, for example, under the English Transfer Regulations, Irish barristers can become English solicitors, and even English barristers are becoming English solicitors with much greater ease than hitherto.

The European Communities are unlikely (and unable) to make detailed inroads in legal educational curricula in the way national, regional and professional authorities have in the member states. The effect is indirect, being exercised primarily through pressure from the profession in the UK, for example. Where national quangos, or state authorities, regulate content, they too will be under pressure to update the curriculum. But perhaps the strongest pressure is from students (and staff) of the universities. They, funded by the European Communities' Erasmus and Tempus programmes, have increasingly developed cross-border links and courses. Thus the old trick of 'paying' for influence is clearly at work and having a significant impact on the content of legal education received by law students throughout Europe.

It can be observed that the trend appears to be for governments to play a less direct role in the setting of the legal curriculum than before. The universities, though subject to professional pressure, are gaining an increased control over their own curriculum. This is particularly so where they have control over their own examining and evaluation processes. The European influence, like that of the legal professions, is brought to bear indirectly rather than by prescription.

Acknowledgements

This chapter draws extensively on a paper presented at a conference in Limburg in 1991 (Lonbay 1992a).

References

Abel, R. (1988) 'Lawyers in the civil law world', in R. Abel and P. Lewis (eds) *Lawyers in Society: the Civil Law World.* Berkeley, University of California Press.

Birks, P. (1992) 'Honorary Secretary's column', *SPTL Reporter*, Winter.

Blankenburg, E. and Schultz, U. (1988) 'German advocates: a highly regulated profession', in R. Abel and P. Lewis (eds) *Lawyers in Society: the Civil Law World.* Berkeley, University of California Press.

Bogdan, M. (1981) 'Sweden', *Comparative Law Yearbook*, 5, 137.

Bund, E. (1988) 'The study of law and the first national law examination in the Federal Republic of Germany', in J. Grant *et al.* (eds) *Legal Education: 2000.* London, Avebury.

Chipman, J. (1990) 'State control of education: Australia', paper presented at 13th International Congress of Comparative Law, Montreal.

Commission of the European Communities (1991) *Memorandum on Higher Education in the European Community.* Luxembourg, EC.

Consejo de Universidades (1988) *Reforma de las enseñanzas universitarius: licenciado en derecho.* Madrid, Consejo de Universidades.

de Groot, R. (1992) 'European legal education in the 21st century', in B. de Witte and C. Forder (eds) *The Common Law of Europe and the Future of Legal Education.* Dordrecht, Kluwer.

de Vergottini, G. (1990) 'State control of education: Italy', paper presented at 13th International Congress of Comparative Law, Montreal.

de Witte, B. (ed.) (1989) *European Community Law of Education.* Nomos.

Ehlermann, C.-D. (1992) 'The European Community: its law and lawyers', *CML Review*, 29, 213.

Ferreiro, J. *et al.* (1987) *La enseñanza del derecho en España.* Barcelona, Tecnos.

Ginsburg, R. and Bruzelius, A. (1965) *Civil Procedure in Sweden.* Dordrecht, Martinus Nijhoff.

Karpen, U. (1990) 'State control of education', general report, 13th International Congress of Comparative Law, Montreal.

Koekkoek, A. (1990) 'State control of education: the Netherlands', paper presented at 13th International Congress of Comparative Law, Montreal.

Law Society (1992) 'Review of the academic stage of legal education', consultation paper.

Lonbay, J. (1989) 'Education and law: the Community context', *European Law Review*, 14, 363.

Lonbay, J. (1990a) 'Spanish legal training', *Lawyers in Europe*, 1(5), 22.

Lonbay, J. (1990b) 'State control of education', in *UK Law in the 1990s*. London, UKNCCL.

Lonbay, J. (1992a) 'Differences in the legal education in the member states of the European Community', in B. de Witte and C. Forder (eds) *The Common Law of Europe and the Future of Legal Education*. Dordrecht, Kluwer.

Lonbay, J. (1992b) *The Training Needs of Solicitors: New Opportunities in the Single Market and in Central and Eastern Europe*. London, Law Society.

Lonbay, J. and Spedding, L. (1992) *International Professional Practice*. Chichester, Chancery Law/Wiley.

Lonbay, J. *et al.* (1990) *Training Lawyers in the European Community*. London, Law Society.

Lorenz, D. (1990) 'State control of education: the Federal Republic of Germany', paper presented at 13th International Congress of Comparative Law, Montreal.

Moratto, G. (1987) *Elementi di legislazione universitaria*. Napoli, Simone.

Olgiati, V. and Pocar, V. (1988) 'The Italian legal profession: an institutional dilemma', in R. Abel and P. Lewis (eds) *Lawyers in Society: the Civil Law World*. Berkeley, University of California Press.

Paterson, A. (1988) 'The legal profession in Scotland', in R. Abel and P. Lewis (eds) *Lawyers in Society: the Civil Law World*. Berkeley, University of California Press.

Petrén, G. (1990) 'State control of education: Sweden', paper presented at 13th International Congress of Comparative Law, Montreal.

Ricciardi, E. (1990) *Lineamenti dell'ordinamento professionale forense*. Milano, Giuffre.

UHÄ (1989) 'Higher education in Sweden on the eve of the year 2000', in *UHÄ Report 17*. Stockholm, UHÄ.

Weisbrot, D. (1988) 'The Australian legal profession', in R. Abel and P. Lewis (eds) *Lawyers in Society: the Civil Law World*. Berkeley, University of California Press.

6

Social Work: an Incorrigibly Marginal Profession?

Mary Henkel

Introduction

Of all the occupational groups that claim the status of profession, social work is *prima facie* the most open to government intervention in its internal workings. The identity and boundaries of social work, and thus of social work education, are contested within and across national frontiers. At the same time, social work is deeply implicated in the social policies of nations with widely differing conceptions of the welfare state. It fulfils functions that are important to governments with varying agendas who may seek to control and shape it. However, it has also been argued that 'a profession placed socially and politically on the boundaries between so many divisions' in societies should be in a position to take a lead in conceptualizing and facilitating the crossing of new frontiers in a period of major change (Lorenz 1991).

The strength of these contentions will be explored in this chapter, primarily in the British context, where social work has, arguably, a peculiarly marginal status as compared with other European countries, and where government interventionism, at a number of levels, has been particularly marked during the past five years.

The impacts of direct and indirect government actions on social work education will be the primary focus. After a period of not so benign neglect by central government during the 1970s, British social work education found itself subject to government action that was apparently catastrophic for the professional identity of social work. Direct intervention into its educational plans meant that social work in Britain lost any chance, at least in the immediate future, of meeting the definition of a profession formulated in the European Community Directive of 1989 (89/48 EEC). But this action can be located in a set of wider-ranging government strategies: for fundamentally restructuring the health and social services; for radical change in the relationships between tertiary education, the labour market and the economy, and in the role of professionals in the public sector; and for a cultural revolution across the public sector, notably in the requirement to address outcome, output and performance rather than the inputs and processes of work.

The impact of all these strategies upon social work education can be seen in a major reframing of requirements for course design, a trend towards de-academization and a realignment of authority patterns. However, it will be suggested here that they could be seen not simply as setbacks in the search for a place in the professional sun but also as opportunities to throw aside some disabling traditions. But as the nature of social work and its location on the professional map are essential to the analysis of these impacts, that is where it will begin.

The professional identity of social work: a comparative perspective

When Brauns and Kramer undertook their comprehensive descriptive study of social work education in twenty-one European countries in the 1980s they were unable to state how many schools of social work there were in Europe because of the problem of definition (Brauns and Kramer 1986, 1991). The International Association of Schools of Social Work (IASSW) defines eligibility for membership of the organization by reference to countries' own national guidelines on what constitutes social work practice.

Social work is concerned with individuals' and groups' capacities to function in societies and the social processes and institutions that facilitate and inhibit those capacities. Thus its knowledge base, definitions of value priorities and practice orientation are inherently susceptible to shifts in dominant ideologies. Ambiguity between the functions of social control and promoting individual development, between social care and the pursuit of individual rights and between focus on public troubles and on private issues is integral to its identity. The requirement to negotiate between government and citizen, individual and family, service provider and service receiver and various interest groups in communities is built into its working. However, social workers' confidence in their authority and capacity to manage these ambiguities and negotiations varies widely according to the kind of systems in which they practice and the recognition they are accorded within them.

In 1980 there was legal protection of the title 'social worker' in five member states of the European Community (EC): the Federal Republic of Germany (FRG), Belgium, Denmark, the Netherlands and Luxembourg. 'Protection of title did not, however, . . . ensure protection of function' (Barr 1990). Only three states in the now enlarged EC license social workers (Germany, Greece and Luxembourg), although in France only those holding a recognized qualification in social work may hold social work posts (Malherbe 1982).

In 1991, the EC general directive (89/48 EEC) outlining a system for Community-wide recognition and mobility of professions came into force. It lays down the level and minimum period of training (three years) and the modes of regulation required for an occupation to be recognized as a regulated profession: its activities must be 'subject by law, regulation or administrative provision to the possession of a [higher education] diploma' (Barr 1990) or it must be pursued by the members of an association, whose purpose is to promote professional standards and that is 'recognized in a special form' by the member state.

As far as social work was concerned, all member states except the UK met the minimum training period condition and nine met the regulatory conditions. Again the UK was not among the nine.

A unified professional association (the British Association of Social Workers, BASW) was formed in 1970. Its foundation was to coincide with the launching of the new unified local authority social services departments that were to be the major, indeed almost monopoly, employers of social workers. But the association was born in a climate of emergent hostility to professionalization. It was set up in the face of fierce internal critique (*Social Work Today* 1970, vol. 1, no. 1). The egalitarian and anti-intellectualist lobby in British social work that was to prove such a powerful internal force in the 1970s was already at work.

In 1992, BASW commanded only minority support among employed social workers in the UK. Social work in the UK remains without an authoritative body (independent or state) for the accreditation and registration of professionals or the regulation of professional practice. The most recent national committee charged to define the role and tasks of social work was deeply divided on the issue of establishing an independent regulatory body and rejected the idea on the grounds of limited support for it among either social workers or the public (Barclay Report: National Institute for Social Work 1982). However, ten years on the position has changed. Proposals for a General Social Services Council (a broader-based conception than a General Social Work Council) have been prepared by a high-level action group and based on a commissioned study (Parker 1990).

The employment base of social workers is an important influence on their professional identity and autonomy. In Britain and Scandinavia, the overwhelming majority of social workers are employed by the state. In other countries, such as the Netherlands and Germany, voluntary organizations are important sources of employment and the functions of statutory and non-statutory social work are highly differentiated. In several states social workers administer social security benefits; in Germany state-employed social workers are said to be 'caught up in a process of increasing legalisation' (Lorenz 1991) and their rights of discretion are tightly defined. Professional autonomy is far easier to sustain by the large numbers of social workers employed in voluntary organizations.

If, as in the UK, the state is the major employer in a highly integrated system, social work may, on the face of it, have substantial power. However, it is suggested that integration attracts more blame and allows less scope for innovation and different conceptions of practice than a more fragmented employment system (Lorenz 1991).

Certainly in Britain integration has meant an organizational model in which local authority directors of social services are managers of large-scale systems for service delivery and increasingly control social work practitioners through managerial lines of accountability and detailed administrative guidelines. The boundaries between social work and the range of social services provided by social services departments are sources of ambiguity and friction that are particularly strongly reflected in social work education · in the UK.

Social work practice is substantially defined by the pressures upon adjacent and more influential policy sectors, such as health, by the law (Howe 1986) and by the courts. A recent Anglo-French comparative study of child protection reveals how much more powerfully the practice of British social workers is defined by the law than that of their French counterparts (Cooper *et al.* 1992).

Social work education and its governance: a period of *laissez-faire*

The reorganization of social work and the personal social services at the beginning of the 1970s meant that the existing system for the regulation of social work training had to be replaced. In consequence, the Central Council for Education and Training in Social Work (CCETSW) was established in 1971.

In opting to maintain state regulation, Britain was in line with most other European countries, although the model of state regulation is unique to it and (until recently) Ireland, which made use of the British system. The most detailed control is administered by France, Denmark and Spain, where curricula and examinations are subject to legislation. In Germany, regulation is in the hands of the *Länder* governments, who, however, have jurisdiction over only the final year of social work courses (Barr 1990). In 1971, two main options were considered in Britain. The first was direct regulation by a central government department, as in Sweden, the Netherlands, Belgium, Austria and Norway. The second, the option chosen, was regulation on the basis of semi-independence from central government.

CCETSW is a non-departmental public body established by statute to operate at arm's length from the (now) Department of Health, although it is funded from the departmental vote (Greenwood and Wilson 1989). In practice, such an arrangement gives scope for wide variations of involvement and control on the part of central government, as has proved to be the case in social work.

CCETSW's remit is to promote and to regulate training in social work, and to attract recruits to that training. It establishes the framework for national qualifying awards through making rules that may specify subjects to be included in courses and must lay down the conditions for admission to and the successful completion of courses leading to Council awards. The Social Work Education and Training Rules are subject to government approval.

The linked issues that have dominated social work education in the UK since 1971 have been those of differentiation in the nature and levels of practice and qualification, whether to establish social work as a graduate profession, and how to install a framework for progressive qualification in social work and the personal social services that would begin to address the low level of training in the workforce as a whole and provide an adequate level of post-qualification education.

The story of CCETSW's attempts to grapple with these issues and the role in it of government falls into two main periods. The first, from 1971 to 1987, was one when central government remained at arm's length from the governance of social work education. In the event this meant that CCETSW fell prey to a pluralism in which social work educators were the weakest participants and local government ultimately emerged as the most powerful force. The second period, from 1987 onwards, has seen decisive moves by central government to assert its authority in social work education.

The first attempt to establish two levels of qualification in social work in the UK had been the institution in further education colleges of the Certificate in Social Work courses following the Younghusband Report (Ministry of Health 1959). These courses were designed to equip staff in health and welfare settings working at a lower level of complexity than existing qualified practitioners who were trained in universities. But their content and output were hard to distinguish from existing forms of training and the qualifications were amalgamated into one, the Certificate of Qualification in Social Work (CQSW), in 1971.

CCETSW then set about the task of expanding the trained workforce, particularly in residential care. Proposals for a second level of training below that of the CQSW were, however, aborted in 1973, amidst objections about elitism and inequality. Instead, in 1975, the Certificate in Social Service (CSS) was established as a 'separate but equal' qualification for workers in the personal social services who were not engaged in social work. Initially, employers interpreted this as meaning residential workers. Later, some saw it as a preferable option to the CQSW for fieldworkers too.

The CSS training was structured closely around students' current roles and was under stronger employer control. At the same time, it incorporated a good deal of knowledge taught on CQSW courses. CQSW courses were committed to a generic concept of social work (posing problems of transferability for newly qualified recruits to social services departments (SSDs)) and to an independent set of values and theories, some of which encouraged radical critique of SSDs. But CQSW courses were themselves vulnerable to criticisms of lack of rigour in student assessment, a disregard for the more technical aspects of social work, such as knowledge of the law, and a failure to enable students to combine theoretical understanding with practical competence. (It should, however, be noted that perceived mismatch between social work education and the demands of employment is by no means unique to the UK. The German system of regulation of courses by their own *Länder* governments does not avoid it.)

By 1981 the original distinctions between the two types of course were felt to have broken down and CCETSW put in train a major review of qualifying training. The problems of gaining a working consensus between interested parties were such that the review was not converted into a firm proposal to government until 1987. The final outcome, after the rejection by government of these proposals, was the replacement of both certificate courses, this time by the Diploma in Social Work, which will come fully on stream in the year 1994–5.

One consequence of these problems of differentiation has been the huge variety of qualifying courses in social work in the further and higher education system, all of which will lead to one award. Social workers can qualify: through two-year (or three-year part-time) non-graduate CQSW courses; through four-year undergraduate degree programmes carrying a dual academic and professional award (although these degrees are now rapidly being overtaken by three-year programmes comprising a combined Diploma in Higher Education and Diploma in Social Work plus one year's study); through two-year full-time postgraduate diploma courses; and through two-year full-time Master's degree courses. The phasing out of one-year postgraduate diploma courses for graduates with 'relevant' social science degrees began only in 1990. Finally, since 1987, CSS courses taken part-time over a minimum of two years while students continue in employment have been recognized by CCETSW as qualifying courses in social work (CCETSW 1989a).

While social work training in the UK has longer associations with universities than that anywhere else in Europe (Barr 1990; Brauns and Kramer 1991), this has not resulted in the establishment of social work as a graduate profession in the UK. Rather it has led to a position where there is no hard and fast distinction between the role of the universities, old and new, colleges or institutes of higher education and colleges of further education. Qualifying training courses in social work can be found in all of them.

How is the failure of CCETSW to impose more rationality on social work education in the first sixteen years of its work best explained? It is suggested here that the problems were political and institutional, but also conceptual and historical.

The regulatory system established for social work education lacked the institutional authority to tackle the issues. In the circumstances in which CCETSW was to operate during its first decade, it had little chance of achieving decisive governance. Pressure for the rapid development of social work training was high in the 1970s (see Birch Report: DHSS 1976). There was no institutionalized profession with which standards and criteria could be established or from which the staff of the new Council could derive political or professional support. The Council was required to reach a largely negotiated order with interests – higher education, local government, public sector unions – whose power was generally on the increase. The forum was the Council itself, whose membership was based on the representation of the main stakeholders. Of the sixty members, twelve were personal appointments of the Minister; the rest were appointed on the nomination of the various constituent bodies. Higher education did not need to be persuaded to enlarge its commitment to this form of training – there were financial incentives to do so, in the form of earmarked funding – and some institutions saw it as a contribution to the strengthening of the welfare state as well as to their own expansion.

CCETSW had to deal with two rather different parties: the universities, who could see no reason why such a body should impinge on their independence, and the public sector of tertiary education, which was subject to its own system of external regulation, the Council for National Academic Awards (CNAA), with which CCETSW had increasingly to collaborate (inevitably as a junior specialist partner) as social work degrees took hold in the polytechnics. The CNAA had its own agenda, to impose academic values and standards. This tended to perpetuate the view that the educational institutions' role only marginally impinged on the practical component of social work training: their real job was academic.

Meanwhile, social services departments were growing at a rapid rate. In the 1970s, it was the power of local, rather than central, government that weighed most heavily with CCETSW. As public sector services became more radicalized, this was manifested through the public sector unions, as well as local government politicians and management.

Social workers became an increasingly high profile target for public criticism and attack from more established professions. This was partly an inevitable consequence of the growth of SSDs and unrealistic expectations engendered, not least by social workers themselves. But more seriously they were at the centre of the child protection scandals that erupted in the early 1970s.

Among the consequences were increased distance and distrust between practitioners and managers in the personal social services, which further undermined any claim to a unified profession. Social workers now saw unionization as a more potent force for them. Meanwhile, employers perceived an academic drift in social work education that, in their eyes, rendered it less able to produce competent practitioners. The tension between their interests and goals and those of higher education sharpened into conflict, which had substantial repercussions on social work education by the end of the 1970s.

The problems were also conceptual and historical. They were exacerbated by the fact that the UK had set up an integrated system of employment in the personal social services that was in no way underpinned by a coherent model of practice or an authoritative definition of professional boundaries. In the British context the boundaries between social services and social work and between social care and social work have proved most contentious.

Ambiguity about the boundaries of social work was built into social services departments in 1971. In Scotland these were social work departments; in England and Wales they were social services departments. Whether social work encompassed the collection of activities of those departments or was only one of a number of services contributing to them was fudged. CCETSW's statutory remit remains to this day 'to promote training in relevant social work', but the definition of that remit has been extended incrementally to include relevant training needs of the entire workforce in the personal social services (including that of the private sector).

That workforce has always been numerically dominated by those whose work is defined as social care: staff in residential homes, day care for adults and children and domiciliary care. Historically, their work was classed as either unskilled or semi-skilled, and although residential work was categorized as social work by CCETSW in 1973, this view has never taken root, either in reward systems or in social work, or, indeed, among residential workers themselves, whose professional association firmly grounds its identity in social care (Social Care Association). This history goes some way to account for the egalitarianism and anti-intellectualism that dogged attempts in Britain to establish differentiation in definitions of work and in education and training in the personal social services.

In continental Europe a quite different professional tradition had developed: the pedagogic. Pedagogic practice is associated with residential work, day centres, youth work and community education. It early established an intellectual base, in Germany at least, in university education departments. It has a reputation for progressive thinking and a quite different public persona from residential care or even youth and community work in Britain and Ireland, offering a strong and prestigious counterpoint to the casework tradition.

By the end of the 1970s it was clear that many of the fundamental problems besetting social work education and its contribution to the personal social services in the UK had not been solved within an arm's length relationship with government. The 1980s were to see a quite different government approach brought to bear upon them.

Government and the reframing of social work education in the 1980s

Like other quangos, CCETSW was slimmed down in the early 1980s and its Council reduced to a membership of twenty-six. Although the majority of these members were appointed following nomination by key stakeholders, all were there in a personal capacity. But the Government took no more decisive action on its structure and governance until 1988. That year saw the institution of the Government's annual departmental review for non-departmental public bodies. In October 1988, CCETSW had its first annual meeting with the Minister and the Department of Health to review the past year, consider future strategy and determine action plans to meet agreed strategic objectives. Annual reports are now structured around those objectives.

The change in the governance of social work education is not just a matter of tighter control by central government. It is part of a significant shift in the framing of CCETSW's work. Its objectives are explicitly linked with the government's strategy for the personal social services (CCETSW 1990b, 1992). And, for the first time, the idea that CCETSW's remit could be converted into a coherent system of training has been given tangible force, even if the conceptual and political problems of the relationship between social care and social work have not been overcome. A framework has been proposed that incorporates awards in social care, a qualifying award in social work, a post-qualifying award and an advanced award. It allows for progression from the lowest to the highest levels of award.

A significant factor in this development was the founding of the National Council for Vocational Qualifications (NCVQ) in 1986. Since then, CCETSW has played an active role in the development of national vocational qualifications (NVQs) in welfare and related services through the Care Sector Consortium, a cross-sector (health, criminal justice and the personal social services) initiative directed towards the establishment of joint awards, at least at the lower levels of NVQ.

The NVQ system is significant for two further reasons. The NCVQ has embarked on a programme to incorporate all vocational and professional training within five levels of complexity. It is thus challenging conceptual boundaries, for example between technical and professional education, that are deeply entrenched in the tertiary education system. But the involvement of CCETSW in NVQ symbolizes something more: social work training as part of a broader government policy objective to ensure a more extensively trained national workforce. It suggests that social work training is located in a frame where its connections with employment and social policies are being strengthened, perhaps at the expense of those within the education system.

The strength of this proposition can be tested by a closer examination of key changes at the qualifying and post-qualifying levels of social work training.

In 1988, the government made its most public and direct intervention into social work training policies, when it rejected CCETSW's proposals for a new unified qualification in social work based on a minimum of three (instead of two) years' training. This was a particularly heavy blow, not simply in view of the huge obstacles that had had to be overcome to achieve a broad consensus on the way ahead. It seemed to end any hope that social work would be classed as a profession under the terms of the EC directive that was to be finalized in 1989. The three-year training scheme would have cost £40 million to introduce. Instead the Government provided £1 million to plug gaps in post-qualifying training under the Department of Health

Training Support Programme. And it invited CCETSW to submit a five-year development plan to improve practice learning and extend one-year social work courses for postgraduates with relevant degrees to two years.

Soon afterwards, the Minister convened a working party on post-qualifying training to develop a framework for systematic provision, an important initiative in view of the changing and intensifying demands upon qualified social workers, and the paucity of post-qualifying training available to them. Out of forty-eight post-qualifying courses (minimum sixty days' duration) approved by CCETSW, forty-two recruited students in 1988–9. One hundred and sixty-six social workers successfully completed such programmes in 1988 (CCETSW 1990a). In effect, post-qualifying courses were catering for only about 0.2 per cent of the eligible population.

The schemes that emerged from these two points of departure, the new Diploma in Social Work (CCETSW 1989b) and the framework for post-qualifying training (CCETSW 1990c), have important common features that give clear indicators about the future role of higher education in social work training. They also set up structures within which the concepts and theories underpinning that training could radically change in the 1990s.

First, in both cases, exhortations to education institutions to collaborate with employing agencies have been replaced by mandatory joint sponsorship and provision. Consortia of education institutions and agencies must be formed for these purposes. Agencies and agency-based practice teachers are accredited by CCETSW for student training and student assessment boards must incorporate practice teacher representatives. Second, the emphasis in regulation has switched from the content and structure of courses to the outcome or acquired competence. Moreover, CCETSW now appoints all social work external examiners who sit on student assessment boards, thus impinging on the authority of higher education in a quite new way. Third, the patterns of professional and post-qualifying training have been deregulated. Until the acceptance of the CSS as a professional qualification, a cardinal principle of professional social work training was that it should be full-time (breached only in the development in the 1970s of three-year part-time programmes for women with family responsibilities) on the grounds that a concentrated college-based programme was required for the shifts in learning and personal development that were required for professional qualification.

The new Diploma in Social Work regulations open up the field for part-time programmes, modularization, credit accumulation and transfer and distance learning. Work-based, as well as college-based, training programmes are encouraged. But the move away from the course or the integrated curriculum as pivotal structures for social work training is far more pronounced in the new framework for post-qualifying training. Here accreditation of prior learning is allowed for and the individual candidate (together with his or her line manager and work-based mentor) is in many ways the programme architect and integrator of the curriculum. The requirement is the accumulation of credits for an award, evidence for which will be presented by candidates in portfolios to assessment boards and within assessment arrangements determined by the newly established consortia.

The combination of change in the ownership of programmes and freedom to experiment with structures, patterns and forms of learning represents a substantial shift of power from the higher education sector. Together with the regulatory emphasis on outcome and assessment rather than input and process they might provide a catalyst for changes in the conceptual, as well as the institutional, boundaries within which social work training operates. It is implied that a variety of institutional arrangements, frames of reference, modes of learning and mixes of responsibility might produce satisfactory forms of learning – as opposed to the relatively restricted range of arrangements operating until now.

Competence and the continuing role of higher education in social work training

The concept of competence holds a central place in contemporary social work education policy. At one level, its adoption by CCETSW as the organizing concept in the assessment of professional and post-professional awards in social work signifies a clear movement away from the world of higher education into that of employment. It means that social work training is being absorbed into a framework developed by the NCVQ, a body grounded in the needs for a national training strategy but also seeking to reduce the distinctions between vocational and professional training.

It is argued that the concept of competence developed by NCVQ is reductionist and atomistic and denies holistic and reflective conceptions of practice; that it reduces the significance of theory, knowledge and understanding in social work education in favour of practice, skills and decision-making. Thus, it is said, it strengthens the claims of those who would make higher education a subsidiary or even redundant partner in the development and delivery of social work training.

There is, however, a substantial body of argument that competence can and does incorporate a range of complexities including those of professional practice. The Department of Employment's Training Agency (later the Training, Education and Enterprise Directorate) asserted that:

> Competence . . . embodies the ability to transfer skills and knowledge to new situations within the occupational area. It encompasses organization and planning of work, innovation and coping with non-routine activities. It includes those qualities of personal effectiveness that are required in the workplace to deal with co-workers, managers and customers.
>
> (TA Guidance Notes, quoted by Winter 1991)

Vernon *et al.* (1990) find that, within the competence literature developed under the auspices of NCVQ, approaches have differed according to the levels of work under examination: from a 'task-oriented' approach to a 'knowledge-driven' approach at a level of work where the requirement is for conceptualization and transfer of learning and for 'core knowledge to infuse the specific tasks'.

CCETSW (1991), in its statement of requirements for both the Diploma in Social Work and advanced and post-qualifying awards, declares that 'competence in social work practice is the product of knowledge, values and skills'. Winter's (1991) ideas about competences are developed within a model of professional work comprising 'interdependent elements of a unified process which links professional practice and professional under-standing, skill, commitments and self-knowledge'. The moral underpinnings of professional social work practice are strongly emphasized, as are its essential uncertainties. For that reason such practice must always be col-laborative and its judgements open to question.

These ideas challenge the view that competence is too mechanistic a concept to incorporate professional practice. They also cut the ground from under the feet of those who think that competence will provide an easy solution to the problems of deciding what is good enough in the assessment of qualifying social workers.

Certainly, the adoption of competence undermines the separation of theory and practice, knowledge and skills, understanding and action. It thus attacks the long-lingering dualistic thinking in higher education that has created problems for social work educators. That dualism has sometimes weakened the aspiration to find more creative forms of collaboration between educational institution and agency, to enable students to integrate theory and practice and at the same time demonstrate the intellectual challenge of that integrative task. An example is afforded by a decision made by the CNAA about undergraduate social work degrees. Students on these courses had only to complete their social work placements in order to be awarded a degree. The requirement to pass this practice component was made only for the combined qualification of a degree and a CQSW. The placement was not an integral part of the learning expected in the degree programme.

Several commentators have noted how social workers in the past have fought to incorporate *education and training* into, for example, CCETSW's own title, in order to safeguard its claims to professional status (Cooper 1983; Harris 1988; Bamford 1990). But some have also argued that in doing so they have perpetuated a mode of thought that undermines the signifi-cance of the intellectual contribution to practice. Harris suggests that 'to talk about education and training is to marginalise both: education is marginalised because the real job is about being able to do it; and training because the existence of the notion of education reduces it to a mere technicist set of practices and procedures' (Harris 1988). He has long ar-gued for encouraging a reflexive approach to practice and for helping students to understand that practice is developed through the acquisition of knowledge, theoretical perspectives and intellectual skills (Harris 1983, 1987). Meanwhile, Howe has contended that a deep immersion in practice is the source of the quality of imagination that he regards as essential in social work but also that imagination should be exercised within a framework, problem-solving, that is strongly cognitive (Howe 1983).

This kind of thinking may nevertheless accommodate arguments that, at least at some levels, higher education should play no more than a service role in professional education. An interesting example from the competence literature is the scheme developed by Winter and Maisch and their colleagues. Adapted from a pre-professional training and assessment scheme, it is based on the assumption that professional knowledge, insight and practice expertise are honed by 'the continuous intellectual, moral and emotional challenge of professional practice itself'. The training is located in the workplace and 'does not necessarily involve any attendance at a formal course' (Winter and Maisch 1991). Training modules each comprise a unit of competence, constructed from a functional analysis of social work practice competences described by groups of practitioners. Learning agreements are negotiated with individual candidates. They include how assessment criteria are to be met and how specified competences will be acquired on the job.

Resolving the issues: from the margin to the leading edge?

Decisive influences on the resolution of these issues will be extrinsic and intrinsic. Extrinsic factors are the developing balance of power between higher education and the employers of social workers and the strength of incentives for the continued involvement of higher education in social work training. Intrinsic factors include the level of intellectual endeavour required to make the new training requirements work.

The implications of these requirements are being worked out simultaneously with the major organizational challenge presented to local authorities by the NHS and Community Care Act 1990 in a financially hostile environment. Local authorities are required to take the lead role in implementing an enlarged policy of community care but as enabling authorities. This means among other things the division of SSDs (along with health services) into purchasers and providers to constitute a quasi-market.

In this context, the strategies pursued for the development and management of training will depend on how local government (assuming that it survives in a recognizable form) interprets the concept of the enabling authority, how far it decides to relinquish direct provision and how fragmented and variegated the provider organizations become. If local authorities develop a more strategic role in social and other public services, they might wish to be proactive in shaping training provision. Large provider bodies might have similar aspirations. In these cases, or where there is an alliance between providers and purchasers, the balance of power in training consortia would be expected to be with employers. Where provision is more dispersed or authorities are not able or willing to take an active strategic role, training consortia might be more independent bodies and educational institutions more influential in them.

In either case, however, the employer voice is unlikely to fade. And employers will surely wish to retain control of post-professional training, so that it can be tailored to their changing needs. The ground is laid for them to do so, by virtue of the financial arrangements, the framing of post-qualifying and advanced training around the collation of individual portfolios, and the requirement that candidates give evidence of advanced professional competence that is defined more widely than advanced academic achievement. Indeed, in the context of financial constraint combined with the current shortfall of personnel with any formal post-professional training, the likelihood of the third level of advanced awards getting institutionalized must remain in doubt.

In these circumstances, what is the incentive for higher education institutions to invest in social work training? On the face of it the attractions would be overwhelmingly for institutions weighted towards teaching, whose traditions and practice were strongly grounded in vocationally oriented qualifications. Educational institutions have lost formal control of the syllabus; there is heavier emphasis (whatever the outcomes of the arguments surrounding the concept of competence) on performance in the workplace. The increased expenditure of time on collaboration is likely even further to reduce the time that social work educators can devote to research. And there is already evidence that social work is declining in popularity among the graduate population (although this is not a phenomenon unique to the UK) (Brauns and Kramer 1991; Pinker 1991). At the post-professional level, the requirement is likely to be to formulate and market modules that can be incorporated into individual portfolios, or at most integrated degree programmes framed by employer demand. Pure and taught research degree programmes will have little financial support in the personal social services.

In the face of these phenomena, what can be said about intrinsic rewards for academics to retain an interest in social work training? The developments described are not taking place in isolation but in the context of a revolution in ideas about the role of higher education in society and in the theories of knowledge that underpin such ideas. The developments in social work education reflect shifting conceptions of student needs and changes in governance that have been taking place throughout higher education in the past decade.

These changes, brought about by the closer encounter with government, reflect the conceptions of knowledge that inform policy development. Within advanced capitalist societies, now commonly characterized as knowledge societies, knowledge is regarded as the primary social and economic force and the motor of exponential change (e.g. Bell 1973; Bohme and Stehr 1986). Within such a context knowledge is obviously perceived as useful if not uncompromisingly for use.

Changes in conceptions of human action forged in a whole range of modern philosophical traditions have all been given practical expression in policy: analytic philosophy as shaped by Wittgenstein, the dialectical encounter of Marx with Hegel and the concepts of theoria and praxis, Popper's critical rationalism and the pragmatist philosophy developed in the USA by Peirce. A practical shift has been made from a conception of the human subject grounded in the Cartesian view of philosophy (the separation of mind from body, thought from action and the 'myth of the given' or the idea of reality pre-existent to and independent of the human subject, of which that subject can have direct intuitive and certain knowledge).

Bernstein (1971) characterized what was happening in philosophy as a move from 'an incorrigibly contemplative conception of knowledge' (quoting Anscombe) to recognition of 'the need to understand man as an agent, as an active being engaged in various forms of practice'. Both Peirce and Popper brought together the idea of man as agent and man as inquirer. For Peirce, 'the concept of self-controlled conduct provides the mediating link between the traditional dichotomies of theory and practice, thought and action. Man as knower or inquirer is viewed as an agent who . . . can control his habits and is not a passive spectator of reality.' Both Peirce and Popper were, of course, scientists and their conceptions of human action are that it is fundamentally scientific. Scientific inquiry is a refined form of normal human action. For Popper, whose theories of knowledge are embedded in theories of evolution, the primal human activity is problem solving, his paradigm of scientific inquiry. Like Polanyi (1958), both Peirce and Popper have highly normative theories of scientific behaviour, in which personal morality and scientific excellence are integrally linked.

These are some of the frames of reference underlying the internal and external expectations of academics throughout higher education. They are being required to rethink how to characterize what their students are learning in terms of skills as well as knowledge, to review their conception of what counts as evidence of learning, to widen their educational responsibilities to include enhancing students' personal effectiveness as well as their cognitive abilities, and to change the way they and their students perceive the relationship between the university and the world of work or between education for life and education for work – so that they are no longer distinct but two dimensions of the same thing.

Against that background, the requirements of those in social work education within the new context become less distinctive. There is a shared need to reconceptualize the relationship between pure and applied knowledge and to understand what is involved in the transfer of learning (an idea which social work educators were tackling early in the 1980s). But there are also particular needs, not only to identify ways of expressing what constitutes professional practice but also to develop understanding of how reflective practice or problem-solving in social work can be learnt. This task involves hard intellectual work, grounded in a deep understanding of practice, together with the imagination, flexibility and critical rigour to collaborate with practitioners, as well as disciplinary and education specialists.

It is difficult to see how that task can be undertaken unless those whose full-time job is in social work education (and scholarship and research) take the lead.

Thus the need for the involvement of higher education in social work training persists. Further, the intrinsic rewards for so doing are high. Not only are the intellectual demands rigorous but current shifts in policy, at one level an attack on the intellectuals, could create an environment in which social work educators could come in from the cold. They might be seen as partners with other academics, as well as with other professionals in tackling a common set of challenges.

Conclusion

At present, then, there is some strength in the argument that a profession on the margins of traditional assumptions and values, as far as function, institutional authority and educational practice are concerned, could make a significant contribution in the contemporary environment. Critiques of traditional forms of professionalism are an international phenomenon, even if the political will to make effective inroads into them have been more evident in the UK than elsewhere in the Western world. The combined forces of managerialism, market philosophies, consumerism, technological and concomitant social change seem likely to force a reappraisal of occupational categories, roles and power.

However, it would be naive to ignore the political weakness of the marginal professions. In the case of social work and social work education in the UK, the most likely outcome is that they will be forced into new peripheral positions or, at worst, positions in which they become the instruments of others' visions of the future of the public services. Three things have made social work education in the UK more vulnerable to external intervention and control than most of its counterparts in Europe: the almost wholesale integration of social work into larger state welfare delivery systems; the inability to resolve the problems of differentiation; and the failure to establish a clear rationale or a rigorous intellectual base for the profession.

References

Bamford, T. (1990) *The Future of Social Work*. Basingstoke and London, Macmillan.

Barr, H. (1990) *In Europe: 1. Social Work Education and 1992*. London, CCETSW.

Bell, D. (1973) *The Coming of Post-Industrial Society: a Venture in Social Forecasting*. New York, Basic Books.

Bernstein, R. (1972) *Praxis and Action*. London, Duckworth.

Bohme, G. and Stehr, N. (1986) 'The growing impact of scientific knowledge on social relations', in G. Bohme and N. Stehr (eds) *The Knowledge Society*. Dordrecht, Reidel.

Brauns, H.-J. and Kramer, D. (1986) *Social Work Education in Europe. A Comprehensive Description of Social Work Education in 21 Countries*. Frankfurt-am-Main, Eigenverlag des Deutschen Vereins fur offentliche und private Fursorge.

Brauns H.-J. and Kramer, D. (1991) 'Social work education and professional development', in M. Hill (ed.) *Social Work and the European Community: the Social Policy and Practice Contexts.* London, Jessica Kingsley.

CCETSW (1989a) *Annual Report, 1987–88.* London, CCETSW.

CCETSW (1989b) *DipSW: Rules and Requirements for the Diploma in Social Work.* London, CCETSW.

CCETSW (1990a) *Annual Report, 1988–89.* London, CCETSW.

CCETSW (1990b) *Annual Report, 1989–90.* London, CCETSW.

CCETSW (1990c) *The Requirements for Post-qualifying Training in the Personal Social Services.* London, CCETSW.

CCETSW (1991) *DipSW: Rules and Requirements for the Diploma in Social Work*, 2nd edn. London, CCETSW.

CCETSW (1992) *Annual Report, 1990–91.* London, CCETSW.

Cooper, A., Freund, V., Grevot, A., Hetherington, R. and Pitts, J. (1992) *The Social Work Role in Child Protection: an Anglo-French Comparison.* Beauvais, JCLT/London, West London Institute for Higher Education.

Cooper, J. (1983) *The Creation of the British Personal Social Services 1962–74.* London, Heinemann Educational Books.

Department of Health and Social Security (1976) *Working Party on Manpower and Training for the Social Services* (Birch Report). London, HMSO.

Greenwood, J. and Wilson, D. (1989) *Public Administration in Britain Today*, 2nd edn. London, Unwin Hyman.

Harris, R. (1983) 'Social work education and the transfer of learning', *Issues in Social Work Education*, 3(2).

Harris, R. (1987) 'Problem solving as a vehicle for the development of core intellectual skills in social work students', *Issues in Social Work Education*, 7(2).

Harris, R. (1988) 'Education and training – what is the balance?', in A. James and D. Scott (eds) *Partnership in Probation Education and Training.* London, CCETSW.

Howe, D. (1983) 'The social work imagination in practice and education', *Issues in Social Work Education*, 3(2).

Howe, D. (1986) *Social Workers and Their Practice in Welfare Bureaucracies.* Aldershot, Gower.

Lorenz, W. (1991) 'Social work practice in Europe', in M. Hill (ed.) *Social Work and the European Community.* London, Jessica Kingsley.

Malherbe, M. (1982) *Accreditation in Social Work (CCETSW Study 4).* London, CCETSW.

Ministry of Health and Department of Health for Scotland (1959) *Report of the Working Party on Social Workers in Local Authority Health and Welfare Services* (The Younghusband Report). London, HMSO.

National Institute for Social Work (1982) *Social Workers: Their Role and Tasks* (Barclay Report). London, Bedford Square Press.

Parker, R. (1990) *Safeguarding Standards: on the Desirability and Feasibility of Establishing a United Kingdom Independent Body to Regulate and Promote Good Practice in Social Work and Social Service.* London, NISW.

Pinker, R. (1991) 'A downward spiral?', Community Care Inside: the Crisis in Social Work Training, 25 April.

Polanyi, M. (1958) *Personal Knowledge: Towards a Post-Critical Philosophy.* London, Routledge and Kegan Paul.

Vernon, S., Harris, R. and Ball, C. (1990) *Towards Social Work Law: Legally Competent Professional Practice.* London, CCETSW.

Winter, R. (1991) 'Outline of a general theory of professional competence', in R. Winter and M. Maisch, *The ASSET Programme*. Chelmsford, Essex County Council Social Services Department and Anglia Higher Education College.

Winter, R. and Maisch, M. (1991) *Professionalism and Competence*. Chelmsford, Anglia HE College and Essex County Council Social Services.

Part 2

National Perspectives

7

External Scrutiny, US Style: Multiple Actors, Overlapping Roles

Elaine El-Khawas

In the United States, external scrutiny of professional education follows a distinctively American style of governance, one that is based on multiple actors, each with a specific role. The result may be characterized as offering a web of many separate strands, each contributing to a larger, combined purpose. Several general features are readily apparent:

- both public and private agencies are involved;
- the federal government has a limited role;
- state governments have substantial involvement;
- many private, voluntary agencies play a part.

Most review mechanisms, whether sponsored by the state or by private agencies, focus on the academic programmes that offer preparation for the professions (e.g. law, medicine, dentistry, nursing, engineering, radiological technology or social work). Others look to the skills of individuals, either as students or as graduates of programmes, who wish to enter professional fields.

Different combinations of these general features are found when one examines particular academic programmes. In medicine, for example, state governments play a dominant role: they approve programmes and also certify individuals wishing to enter active practice. A private, voluntary accrediting agency also enforces its own regulations for all aspects of medical training.

Detailed, multiple-actor scrutiny of this type is found within almost all programmes that offer preparation for the professions. Most professions have their own accrediting agency. There is, for example, a National Architecture Accrediting Board and an American Council on Pharmaceutical Education. Sometimes various combinations of professional bodies are involved; for example, the Committee on Allied Health Education and Accreditation (part of the American Medical Association) is a single umbrella agency with sixteen review committees representing thirty-nine professional organizations and programme areas.

In contrast, much less external scrutiny is directed to the general programmes of study that universities and colleges offer (e.g. in history, economics or Asian literature). Thus, academic programmes that offer foreign-language training are subject to very little scrutiny; however, closely related programmes that prepare students to be teachers of foreign languages are subject to extensive scrutiny.

The rationale for outside forms of scrutiny rests with the need for protecting the public: for persons who will work in areas affecting the health and safety of the public, the state declares an interest and a responsibility for offering safeguards that appropriate standards of training have been met. The involvement of private agencies in setting and enforcing standards is based partly in historical precedent but it also derives from the technical detail and expertise that is required in the process of setting standards (Glidden 1983: 200).

It is generally thought that a workable division of labour exists among the various partners, one that has been in place for decades. State governments are thought to provide the basic framework, stipulating minimum requirements to be met in order for the state to approve the operation of a programme and, later, for the graduate to enter the profession (see Bender 1983: 270–88). In turn, the specialized accrediting agency is thought to focus on how the programmes operate, especially offering scrutiny with regard to quality assurance and quality improvement. Each college or university, of course, is the partner in this arrangement that carries out the academic programme itself.

One of the long-standing if often unstated agreements in this division of labour is the belief that state governments should not interfere in substantive academic matters; another groundrule is that both the state and the private accrediting agencies should leave many matters to the discretion of the universities and colleges. However, a number of recent issues and controversies suggest that the respective roles of the partners are subject to considerable ambiguity. For example, there is now some concern about limited employment prospects in some professional fields and a sense of frustration that no agency takes responsibility for trying to match supply and demand. Some state policy-makers, responding to such public concerns, have pushed for enrolment limits in certain fields, including engineering and law. Traditionally, decisions about enrolment numbers and, consequently, likely numbers of graduates in such fields have been left to the universities. As another recent issue, many state governments have questioned whether academic programmes in teacher education are of sufficient quality; in response, a good many states have introduced new teacher education requirements that are intended to raise standards.

Universities have various complaints of their own about the external scrutiny they face. They object to sometimes detailed accrediting requirements that seem designed primarily to protect the 'guild-like' interests of the practitioner community. Many universities feel hamstrung by a tangle of regulations they must comply with, from both state and private agencies.

They also contend that the number of specialized accrediting agencies is proliferating beyond what is necessary and, at the same time, that some state governments are expanding their own forms of programme scrutiny in unwarranted ways (Bender 1983: 280; Larson 1983: 335).

These issues are symptomatic of the ambiguities that surround the working arrangements for external scrutiny of college-level academic programmes in the United States. In theory, these arrangements offer a system of checks and balances, with no strong central force and with each partner playing a limited role. How well this works is another question. Much depends on whether each actor has the capability to carry out the assigned role, on how well defined the boundaries are among the partners, and on the extent to which the entire arrangement is responsive to public needs under changing circumstances.

This chapter reviews the forms of external scrutiny that affect programmes of professional education in the United States. It describes the major forms of scrutiny, governmental and non-governmental, and then takes a closer look at the requirements in one field, teacher education. This discussion of teacher education programmes illustrates the overlapping demands of state and private agencies and describes a type of external involvement that looks closely to the curricular components of academic preparation. It also illustrates the way that the state's interest in protecting the public can be interpreted quite broadly in a period when many parties are calling for substantial reform of the schools and schooling available to American children. The chapter concludes with a brief discussion of several continuing tensions within the current system of external scrutiny of programmes to prepare professionals.

The main forms of external scrutiny

Table 7.1, which forms the basis for this section of the chapter, shows the main forms of external involvement that may affect academic programmes in the United States. It indicates the agent involved and the type of external action imposed. As is noted, most of these review mechanisms are limited to programmes of professional preparation but some also affect a college or university's other academic programmes, e.g. in history, economics, music, physics or other fields that do not lead to a profession.

All these forms of scrutiny are in force currently. Among them, the two most significant mechanisms – judged by their ability to influence the shape of an academic programme – are the state power to approve programmes and the private mechanism of granting accreditation status to specialized programmes. Generally, state authority for approval is limited to professional programmes in which the health or safety of the public is at stake; specialized accreditation casts a wider net, based on an expanded definition of public needs (Glidden 1983). Specialized accreditation is found in such

Table 7.1   Mechanisms of external scrutiny in the United States

Mechanism	Extent of coverage
State governments	
Programme approval	Specific professional fields
Licence or certification	Persons entering specific professions
Programme review	All academic programmes; in most states
State-mandated assessment processes	All academic programmes; in most states
Federal government	
Eligibility for veterans' programmes	All institutions of higher education
Eligibility for federal student aid programmes	All institutions of higher education
Non-governmental agencies	
Regional accreditation	All institutions of higher education
Specialized accreditation	Specific professional fields

fields as nursing, medicine, law, engineering, architecture, physical therapy and social work; however, it also extends to theological studies, home economics, journalism, landscape architecture, interior design, librarianship, music and art and design (see Wade 1992: 692, for a full list of recognized accrediting agencies).

Governmental involvement in academic programmes

As Table 7.1 indicates, governmental bodies – in this context, mainly state government – have various tools available to them for reviewing academic programmes at universities. Most such tools focus on entire programmes, whether by stipulating minimum requirements that they must follow or by requiring some form of external review of them, usually on a periodic basis. Governmental powers are also used to test the professional knowledge and skills of individuals wishing to enter employment in specific areas; such licensing tests are found especially in the professions. Both programme approval and certification are long-standing and widely accepted forms of state governmental control over academic programmes.

It should be noted that the powers of the purse – state control of academic programmes by requirements tied to funding – are not given attention here because, generally, scrutiny of academic programmes is not directly tied to the budgetary process. Most state universities receive state funding on the basis of a formula linked to enrolment numbers, sometimes with adjustments for the ratio of undergraduate to graduate students or similar adjustments. These formulae only rarely take into account the specific fields in which students are enrolled; dentistry and veterinary programmes are an exception, where states often offer funding for a certain number of students.

Private universities and colleges generally operate with a form of incremental budgeting, in which each year's budget reflects the previous year's budget adjusted for necessary changes. It is not part of current practice to tie budget funding to any judgemental facts about programmes, e.g. completion rates, percentage of graduates passing a certification examination, etc.

The primary device for state involvement is programme approval, in which the state government requires that persons wishing to enter a specific professional field must have completed studies in a state-approved programme. Generally, this also means that the state government has issued regulations that specify the characteristics of a university programme that must be present in order to be approved by the state. Often, there is a state-appointed board or commission (made up of both professional practitioners in the field and general citizens) that advises the state government on what should be included in an acceptable programme.

In most professions, a licence or certification is another state-imposed requirement, directed to individuals wishing to enter professional employment. Frequently, a licence is granted solely on the basis of completion of a state-approved programme. Sometimes other requirements are involved: for instance, a certain amount of practical experience, personal recommendations and, even, evidence of no prior criminal conduct. Often, too, a licence or certification is awarded on the basis of an individual taking and passing a certifying examination. In law, for example, each state offers an examination on that state's laws that must be passed in order to practise in that state. In the past, a person could study for the bar on a private basis, with the advice and assistance of a practising lawyer, and did not need to complete a structured academic programme. Today, this option remains available in a number of states although general practice has evolved so that almost all persons preparing to become lawyers do so by enrolling in three-year academic programmes.

Two other mechanisms are sometimes used by state governments to restrict individual entry into a profession, namely minimum requirements for entrance into academic programmes and, later, specific requirements for continuing to work in the profession. Entrance requirements, which often exist for nursing and other health-related professions, typically involve a minimum attainment level in high-school study (e.g. attaining a certain grade average). Requirements for continuing certification, for persons already employed in a professional field, are not as common. They generally stipulate that the individual show evidence of having engaged in some amount of continuing professional study or training in addition to having professional work experience.

More recently, other forms of state oversight have developed. The usual pattern of evolution for such new forms is that state legislatures or governors raise concerns that appear not to be met satisfactorily by present methods and that these concerns continue to be voiced over time. With sufficient pressure and growing consensus that 'something is needed', proposed reforms are suggested, sometimes by state officials and at other times by university officials, seeking to control the shape of the inevitable change. Typically, the response is to create new procedures that respond to the specific concerns being voiced at the time.

This process led to the development of state-based procedures called 'programme reviews' during the 1960s and 1970s and, during the 1980s, to procedures for 'assessment' of student learning. This means that, for some programmes and some universities, state-level involvement in oversight of academic programmes now includes four mechanisms: regulations for programme approval; certification requirements for each graduate; programme review; and assessment requirements.

Programme review is the term used for a process in which an academic department or other unit undertakes a review of its programme. Typically, this review includes an internal component – assembling and interpreting available evidence on the programme's strengths, accomplishments and weaknesses – and an external component – in which a visiting team of scholars with appropriate credentials examines the programme and offers judgement about it. In most state universities, a system is in place that schedules each programme for review every five years and, over the course of a five-year period, all programmes thus undergo such a review. Most private institutions have also established programme review procedures that follow this model, although it is more flexibly administered – perhaps done on a less regular basis, for example. Notably, this process of programme review applies to all academic programmes, not just to preparation in professional fields.

Assessment, the most recent entrant, includes additional, somewhat different, forms of scrutiny. It requires that universities develop new analytic techniques for assessing what students have learned during their studies. Typically, this means that students are tested after several years of study on certain broad areas of expected achievement, e.g. on writing and analytical skills, or on their level of knowledge in a subject area.

There was a great deal of assessment activity by state governments in the early and mid-1980s (Hutchings and Marchese 1990: 16). Some states developed new assessment tests to be administered to all college-level students in the state. Others developed incentive schemes that awarded special funds to state universities that initiated new assessment programmes of their own. Still others called on all universities to develop new assessment procedures.

By 1990, about two-thirds of the state governments in the United States required all their state-supported colleges and universities to have assessment procedures. It should be noted, however, that most states do not specify what form the assessment procedures should take; they mandate that each university should have student assessment procedures but leave it to university officials to design appropriate ways of meeting this requirement. Florida and Georgia are notable exceptions: both mandate that universities administer an assessment test, focused especially on writing skills, to all students after two years of study.

As Table 7.1 indicated, two mechanisms of federal involvement should be mentioned. Both are indirect mechanisms, tied to the federal government's responsibility for conducting two of its own financial aid programmes. The first mechanism, tied to veterans' benefits, is a programme approval mechanism based on state-administered criteria; it extends financial assistance to military veterans who study in approved academic programmes. This federal programme, quite substantial in size during the past three decades, is largely phased out today. The second mechanism of federal involvement is tied to current federal programmes of student financial assistance. Under these programmes, a condition of eligibility for students to receive federal grants or loans is that they enrol for college-level study in an accredited institution of higher education. The federal government has an advisory board that recognizes accrediting organizations whose procedures are deemed to be appropriate for this purpose (Chambers 1983: 233–69). In effect, the federal government thus defers to the judgements of private accrediting bodies in determining what are worthy institutions, at least for purposes of allowing students of those institutions to apply for federal financial assistance. This mechanism, which has been in place for several decades, has normally meant that all institutions of higher education that are accredited by private, voluntary accrediting bodies are also eligible for participation in federal financial aid programmes.

Non-governmental involvement

The requirements of accreditation agencies affect both public and private universities and colleges in the United States. Accreditation, as defined in the American context, is a system of non-governmental scrutiny of the academic programmes and overall institutional effectiveness of universities and colleges. It is a voluntary arrangement, in that a university chooses whether or not to submit its programmes to the accreditation process. It is a self-regulatory arrangement, in that the standards and procedures that accrediting agencies follow are developed and revised by commissions made up of university officials, with other representatives in some instances (El-Khawas 1983: 54–70).

Although accreditation is, technically, a privately controlled process, its decisions are widely accepted and, in the absence of strong governmental oversight, accreditation decisions have taken on semi-public functions. As one report notes, 'while accreditation is basically a private, voluntary process, accrediting decisions are used as a consideration in many formal actions – by governmental funding agencies, scholarship commissions, foundations, employers, counselors, and potential students' (Harris 1986: 438). Accreditation is a widely accepted process, respected and followed by almost all universities and colleges in the United States.

As Table 7.1 indicated, two distinctive forms of accreditation exist. The first, institutional accreditation, is the responsibility of six regionally organized associations that accredit most higher education institutions, along with five nationwide associations that accredit specialized types of institutions (e.g. Bible colleges, trade schools). The second form, called specialized accreditation, involves scrutiny of professional or occupational programmes in such fields as business, dentistry, engineering, law and medical technology. Nationally organized associations in each professional field have developed accreditation procedures, each with their own distinctive definitions of eligibility, evaluation criteria and procedural guidelines.

Both forms of accreditation follow similar general procedures. The first step is taken by a specific university or department, which makes a request to have a review of its activities, with the aim of gaining accreditation by the accrediting organization. Generally, the institution or department then develops a schedule involving a self-study – a quite comprehensive review and description of its operations and accomplishments – that follows detailed guidelines provided by the accrediting agency. The resulting report, normally prepared by a sizeable number of the university's or department's faculty and encompassing 200 or more pages, is submitted to the accrediting agency and becomes the basis for the next review stage, which involves external review. The accrediting agency then schedules a several-day visit to the university. The site visit team, made up of educators with expertise appropriate to the university or department being examined, prepares its own report and recommendations. The university or department has the opportunity to review the report for factual accuracy. Once the report is accepted as accurate, it becomes the basis for the accrediting agency's decision about whether the department or university warrants accredited status.

Once accreditation is granted, a university or department undergoes a re-accreditation review, following much the same procedures, at regular intervals. Regional accrediting bodies, for example, may review a new institution's programmes several times over the course of a five-year period but, once an institution receives accreditation, it is scheduled for another full review, including site visit, only after ten years. There is, however, a shorter interim report expected after five years. Some specialized accreditation agencies require yearly reports.

Notably, accreditation reports are not made public. This reflects the prevailing view among accrediting organizations about their purposes. They acknowledge a limited responsibility to the public – to potential students, to employers and to the community – but give greater emphasis to their role in promoting standards of excellence among universities. In their view, their public responsibility is met by their decision to accredit or not. This decision is made public. However, because the specific recommendations of the visiting team are meant primarily to foster improvement in academic programmes, recommendations are not made public. The report and its recommendations – sometimes quite direct, in other situations only pointing to areas of weakness – do exert pressure on the university to improve those areas because the accrediting organization asks for progress reports with respect to such areas and makes it clear that improvement is expected, at least by the time of the next report. Normally, a visiting team has been apprised of the specific weaknesses that were pinpointed in the previous visit to each institution.

External scrutiny: scope and sanctions

The mix of governmental and non-governmental forms of external scrutiny creates a complex web of external influence on academic programmes in the United States. Most universities and colleges face multiple forms of scrutiny, as Table 7.2 helps to demonstrate. Virtually all institutions of higher education are regionally accredited, based on a review of the institution's overall effectiveness, and almost all offer programmes that come under the jurisdiction of specialized accrediting agencies; at public universities (where enrolments generally range between 10,000 and 30,000) an average of twelve programmes are covered by specialized accrediting reviews. At private universities and colleges (where enrolments generally range from 1000 to 10,000) an average of four academic programmes are subject to specialized accrediting reviews (El-Khawas 1992: 41). At the same time, a majority of institutions, public and private, conduct regular programme reviews. Most public universities and colleges face requirements from their state government related to programme approval. Regional accrediting status is important, and institutions would not want to operate without it, for two separate reasons. First, it is a widely accepted badge of respectability, and questions would be quickly raised if any institution was not accredited or lost its accreditation. The second reason is currently very important: institutions must be accredited in order for their students to be eligible for federally sponsored student financial assistance. Apart from this federal-aid eligibility, a good many institutions of higher education today might well question whether regional accrediting status is worth their trouble. Many feel that it is a cumbersome process, yet one that is not detailed enough to provide a good review of an entire institution, particularly for very large, complex universities. And, as critics note, because it is rare for an institution to lose its accreditation status, there is a sense that accreditation offers little information about the quality of an institution's academic programmes.

It should not be surprising that most university and college administrators feel that accreditation is bothersome. At the same time, it is also true that many consider it a worthwhile process. Table 7.2, which summarizes information from a recent survey of campus administrators (El-Khawas 1992: 40), shows that specialized accrediting procedures and programme reviews are the most popular. Even so, barely one-half of administrators describe these mechanisms as very useful. Most university administrators feel that the external review requirements of accrediting agencies offer a useful impetus for review and change in programmes and, certainly, offer a basis for keeping up with changing views on good academic practice.

Table 7.2 Use of external review mechanisms in the United States

	Public universities	Private universities
Percentage of institutions that have:		
Regional accreditation	100	100
Specialized accrediting	96	97
Programme review	60	74
State-mandated assessment	91	—
Number of specialized accrediting bodies at each institution (mean):	12.3	4.4
Ratings (%) among institutions that have each review mechanism:		
Regional accreditation		
Very useful	47	38
Somewhat useful	50	61
Not useful	3	1
Specialized accreditation		
Very useful	53	41
Somewhat useful	46	56
Not useful	1	3
Programme review		
Very useful	54	76
Somewhat useful	44	23
Not useful	2	1
State-mandated assessment		
Very useful	25	—
Somewhat useful	66	—
Not useful	9	—

Source: El-Khawas 1992: 41–2.

Complaints from campus administrators point to the often detailed requirements set out by specialized accrediting agencies. Recently, for example, institutions have complained about the requirement by the accrediting agency for business programmes, the American Assembly of Collegiate Schools of Business, that a large proportion of teaching faculty in business administration programmes must have doctoral degrees in business. Administrators argue that this requirement unduly restricts the programmes because appropriate instructors can also be found with doctoral degrees in related areas, including economics, mathematics or the social sciences.

In terms of sanctions, the state approval process is the most potent. If the state withheld its approval of a university's dentistry programme, for example, individuals in that programme would not be allowed to enter the profession. Obviously, the university would then have no basis for offering a programme. In contrast, the sanction power available to specialized accrediting agencies has more variable impact on institutions. In some situations, universities rely on their programme approval from the state and operate successful programmes without the added status of being accredited by a specialized accrediting body. This has occurred, recently, for many institutions offering business administration programmes. It has also occurred with respect to teacher education programmes.

Teacher education: extensive external review

Teacher education programmes offer a good illustration of the interplay among various mechanisms of external scrutiny. These programmes are subject to both state and specialized accrediting requirements; their graduates must be certified by the state, often based on passing scores on a nationally standardized test, and must submit to further certification requirements in order to continue in the profession. Considerable overlap exists in the various requirements that academic programmes must meet, especially in the requirements set out by state approval agencies and by specialized accrediting bodies. Furthermore, over the past decade, teacher education programmes have been subject to changing requirements as part of a general move throughout the United States towards tougher standards for classroom teachers.

External scrutiny of teacher education programmes begins with the public's need to have qualified teachers in the schools. Historically, this has been achieved by requiring teachers to participate in approved academic programmes. Approval is organized on a state-by-state basis, with most approval procedures requiring that a college or university must document the course of study it offers in teacher education and allow a state-sponsored site visit to inspect the programme.

The state's authority is considerable: the only persons certified to teach in each state are those who completed their studies in approved programmes. Many states participate in a reciprocal agreement that gives recognition to the graduates of academic programmes approved by other states that are part of the inter-state agreement.

A second important actor influencing teacher education programmes is the specialized accrediting agency responsible for oversight of academic programmes that prepare teachers and others (e.g. school counsellors, school librarians or school principals) for careers in the schools. NCATE, the National Council for Accreditation of Teacher Education, provides accrediting standards and procedures for the education programmes that prepare teachers and other professionals for employment in both elementary and secondary education.

In some states, completion of a state-approved academic programme is a sufficient basis for obtaining a teaching licence or certificate. In other states, additional requirements exist, sometimes including a requirement for a passing score on the National Teachers Examination, a standardized test of subject knowledge and teaching competency.

As part of the programme approval process, some states impose minimum entrance requirements for persons wishing to enrol in teacher education programmes or stipulate minimum exit requirements that go beyond completion of an approved programme. In Missouri, for example, programme entrants must have a composite score of at least 800 on the SAT test, a nationally standardized aptitude test taken by high school seniors. To graduate from a teacher education programme, individuals must complete an approved programme with an overall grade average of at least 2.5 on a 4.0 scale, must demonstrate oral proficiency, must complete mathematics and general education requirements, and must gain a passing score on an appropriate NTE subject exam.

Most state approval agencies offer detailed guidelines for what constitutes an acceptable teacher education programme. In Massachusetts, for example, both institutional standards and teacher standards must be met. Recently revised institutional standards in Massachusetts, thirteen in number, among other things call for evidence that a university or college: publicizes its requirements; allocates funds, space and professional and support staff adequate to carry out the programme; conducts an ongoing assessment of students in teacher education programmes; and makes every effort to recruit, admit and retain students of diverse economic, racial and cultural backgrounds. Teacher standards under the new Massachusetts regulations include both common standards, applicable to all persons preparing to enter education professions, and additional standards appropriate to particular certificates (e.g. elementary teacher or teacher of mathematics). The seven common standards call for: demonstrated knowledge in the subject field; effective communication skills; knowledge of human development and principles of curriculum development and instructional technique; ability to use various evaluative procedures to assess and modify one's teaching; analytical and critical thinking skills; ability to deal equitably and responsibly with all learners; and an understanding of the legal and moral responsibilities of the teaching profession (Massachusetts Board of Education 1991: 7–8). These 'common' standards are supplemented in mathematics, for example, by standards that specify areas in mathematics that must be taken in one's courses, including instruction in use of computers in mathematics, and that also specify certain pedagogical competencies, e.g. the ability to use a variety of techniques in teaching mathematics and to 'teach students to transfer the knowledge of mathematics to situations that are typical of everyday life'.

A similar specification is found in the curriculum guidelines issued by NCATE, the private accrediting agency for teacher education programmes. NCATE has eighteen standards and ninety-four criteria that must be met by academic programmes seeking accreditation (NCATE 1992: 45–60). The NCATE criteria offer detailed standards with respect to the curriculum; clinical and field-based experiences; student admissions, advising, progress and completion of studies; faculty qualifications, teaching load and evaluation; personnel, funding and physical facilities; and library support. With respect to the curriculum, the NCATE criteria call for programmes to be well-planned, reflective of best practice and research, and based on 'a rigorous, professional quality instructional quality control mechanism' (NCATE 1992: 47–8). Programmes are to include a general education component, including studies in communications, mathematics, science, history, philosophy, literature and the arts. NCATE criteria also specify key components of the professional training offered as part of an academic programme, including characteristics of student-teaching experiences.

As can be seen, the requirements of the state for programme approval, and of NCATE for specialized accreditation status, are quite detailed and impose serious constraints on the ability of a university or college to design its academic programme in teacher education. Universities and colleges have voiced complaints about the burden such requirements represent, sometimes pointing to specific criteria that appear to be unduly constraining and at other times bemoaning the overall burden created by multiple sources of external scrutiny. Specific criteria that cause problems do get discussed by various NCATE bodies and, to be sure, NCATE offers appeals procedures for institutions that wish to challenge the way in which the criteria have been applied to their programmes.

The external review bodies have also responded to complaints by developing forms of collaboration intended to reduce the burden. Thus, for instance, NCATE has made provisions for a representative of the state education department to join the NCATE-established team making an on-site visit. At times, too, certain states have developed joint protocols with NCATE which are the basis for joint state–NCATE evaluation visits. Other collaborative agreements have been reached to allow NCATE accreditation to be recognized as a form of programme approval for purposes of certifying graduates to enter teaching; similarly, NCATE accreditation is often the basis for certification of graduates who complete a programme in one state and then wish to apply for a teaching certificate in another state.

Teacher education: review mechanisms serving reform

The past decade has seen considerable change in expectations for teacher education, part of a larger national debate directed towards improving schooling for American children. One of the most widely quoted reports shaping this debate, issued in 1986, was titled *A Nation Prepared: Teachers for the Twenty-first Century* (Task Force on Teaching as a Profession 1986). It called for nationwide efforts to improve the schools and, among its priorities, supported efforts to raise standards for teachers. Specifically, it proposed that all aspiring teachers should complete a master's degree in teaching, based on an undergraduate baccalaureate programme in the arts and sciences. This would replace the existing system, in which a baccalaureate degree in education was the most typical preparation for beginning teachers. The Task Force also called for the creation of a National Board for Professional Teaching Standards, intended to 'establish high standards for what teachers need to know and be able to do, and to certify teachers who meet that standard' (Task Force 1986: 55).

As part of this debate, concern has been raised that the nation is likely to face a shortage of teachers and, in particular, that serious shortfalls will occur in the availability of teachers from minority backgrounds. The Task Force (1986: 32) predicted 'a steep increase in demand for teachers' and 'a particularly acute need for minority teachers', arguing that the nation 'cannot tolerate a future in which both white and minority children are confronted with almost exclusively white authority figures in the schools'.

This larger debate has had substantial impact on both state approval agencies and NCATE, the specialized accrediting agency, with respect to their standards for teacher education programmes. Many states have, for example, revised their programme approval and certification standards to stipulate that baccalaureate-level programmes must be completed in a subject field in the arts and sciences and that teacher training is to be concentrated in a master's level degree. Other states have introduced entrance requirements for students wishing to enrol in teacher education programmes. Many states have also adopted special initiatives for minority teacher recruitment (AACTE 1991).

New requirements facing universities in Massachusetts provide an illustration of this change. Regulations announced recently by the Massachusetts Department of Education stipulate a two-stage teacher certification process: provisional and full certification. The first stage requires a bachelor's degree with a liberal arts, science or interdisciplinary major, and completion of education coursework leading to a provisional certification. The second stage necessitates the completion of a master's degree, including education coursework and supervised classroom teaching, leading to full certification.

Concern for increased recruiting of minority teachers is reflected in a Statewide Committee that Massachusetts organized with respect to the recruitment of minority teachers. The Committee issued a report in March 1990, for which a follow-up plan is being developed. The broader concern, for teachers to be able to work effectively with minority children, is reflected in the new standards that Massachusetts has adopted as a basis for programme approval. In their institutional standards, for example, approved programmes are required to show that they 'make every effort to recruit and retain minority faculty' and 'to recruit, admit, and retain students of diverse economic, racial and cultural background' to their programmes. Similarly, in their common standards for certification, it is stipulated that programmes must demonstrate that they train prospective teachers to be able to 'make curricular content relevant to the experiences of students from diverse racial, socio-economic, linguistic, and cultural backgrounds' (Massachusetts Board of Education 1991).

Concluding remarks

The general picture conveyed by this description of external review mechanisms that affect professional education programmes is undoubtedly a complex one. Various mechanisms are in place to specify requirements that individuals must meet to prepare for a profession. At the same time, administrators and faculty who are part of the academic programmes designed to provide professional preparation face a lengthy list of requirements, usually from both state and private agencies. The illustrations in this chapter focused primarily on teacher education programmes; much the same pattern of detail would be found if other professional programmes had been described.

As 'is clear, the programme approval and specialized accreditation functions offer substantially overlapping requirements about the nature of the academic programme which have to be met for external approval. This has not always been the case because, for many states, programme approval offered quite minimal specifications. The recent trend, however, has been one of increasing specificity in state requirements.

Is the level of external review burdensome? Unfair? Overreaching? Supporters of the accrediting agencies and the state approval agencies would not think so. In defending such agencies, supporters would note that agency requirements are often couched in general language, typically describing goals or objectives rather than specific procedural demands. They would point out, too, that the actual evaluations of a programme occur infrequently, with substantial advance notice and advice about what is to be evaluated, and in visits that last only a few days. So, no, the burden is not too great, especially in view of the public protections that external review provides.

Critics of such external review, however, argue that the overall picture is both burdensome and harmful to good educational practice. The sum total of such requirements, they contend, must be seen from the perspective of the individual academic programme of each university or college. From this vantage point, external review seems to be omnipresent, involving several different agencies with different schedules and different requirements that typically change in a way that causes programmes to make frequent changes with little ability to fashion those changes in ways that the faculty in the programme would consider educationally sound.

Debates of this sort are heard regularly in the United States, both within universities and at various meetings and conferences of professionals involved with the academic programmes that are subject to state approval or accreditation. In fact, recognition and discussion of these inevitable tensions are generally seen as part of a process by which excesses are curbed, whether excessive neglect or omission of important issues or, at the other extreme, excessive regulation of programmes. From time to time, a consensus develops that certain external review procedures need to be changed and reforms are put into place. In ideal terms, this is a self-correcting process, one that allows for opinions and criticisms to be freely expressed and also one that spurs change only when a considerable press of opinion consolidates around a problem. It is certainly not a neat and orderly process; however, most long-term observers argue that, as with democracy itself, it is a poor system except when considered against the alternatives. Accreditation and state approval are likely to have a very long lifespan in American higher education.

References

American Association of Colleges for Teacher Education (AACTE) (1991) *Teacher Education Policy in the States: a 50-state Survey of Legislative and Administrative Actions.* Washington, DC, AACTE.

Bender, L.W. (1983) 'States and accreditation', in K.E. Young *et al.* (eds) *Understanding Accreditation.* San Francisco, Jossey Bass.

Chambers, C.M. (1983) 'Federal government and accreditation', in K.E. Young *et al.* (eds) *Understanding Accreditation.* San Francisco, Jossey Bass.

El-Khawas, E. (1983) 'Accreditation as self-regulation', in K.E. Young *et al.* (eds) *Understanding Accreditation.* San Francisco, Jossey Bass.

El-Khawas, E. (1992) *Campus Trends, 1992.* Washington, DC, American Council on Education.

Glidden, R. (1983) 'Specialized accreditation', in K.E. Young *et al.* (eds) *Understanding Accreditation.* San Francisco, Jossey Bass.

Harris, S.S. (1986) *Accredited Institutions of Postsecondary Education, 1985–86.* Washington, DC, American Council on Education.

Hutchings, P. and Marchese, T. (1990) 'Watching assessment – questions, stories, prospects', *Change,* Sept.–Oct., 12–38.

Larson, C.W. (1983) 'Trends in the regulation of professions', in K.E. Young *et al.* (eds) *Understanding Accreditation.* San Francisco, Jossey Bass.

Massachusetts Board of Education (1991) *Amended Regulations for The Certification of Educational Personnel, Effective October 1, 1994.* Boston, Massachusetts Department of Education, Division of Educational Personnel.

National Council for Accreditation of Teacher Education (NCATE) (1992) *Standards, Procedures, and Policies for the Accreditation of Professional Education Units.* Washington, DC, NCATE.

Task Force on Teaching as a Profession (1986) *A Nation Prepared: Teachers for the 21st Century.* New York, Carnegie Forum on Education and the Economy.

Wade, W.A. (1992) *Accredited Institutions of Postsecondary Education, 1991–92.* Washington, DC, American Council on Education.

8

Governmental Control and Professional Education in Sweden

Lennart G. Svensson

Introduction

The welfare state is in considerable flux in Sweden, as it is in many other Western societies. Participants at different levels are, in various fields, involved in decentralization, deregulation and privatization, affecting education for most of the professions as well as their practice.

In order to control rising entry with allegedly low pass rates in the 1960s, centrally determined study programmes became an important government means of steering the social demand for higher education. This changed again in the all-embracing 1970s reforms, when the objectives became equal opportunity irrespective of gender or class, vocationalization, regionalization and recurrent education.

Since 1977 the number of student places has been decided by Parliament, following Government recommendations. A total *numerus clausus* for higher education, together with the number for the general study programmes, was set by Parliament in 1977, based upon manpower forecasts and predictions of social demand commissioned by the Government. In 1988 the Government required the National Board for Universities and Colleges to develop totally new forecasts in advance of the budgeting process in consultation with the Swedish Central Bureau of Statistics, the National Board of Education and the National Swedish Labour Market Board. At that time higher education was assumed to be levelling off, but this was exaggerated (NBUC Report 1989: 17; Trolle 1989). (The total annual number of new students in full study programmes was about 45,000 until the end of the 1980s.)

There was restricted admission to professional education at the colleges for a long time before 1977, although some credit was given for work experience in order to admit students from the less privileged social strata. Many study programmes still have their number of places restricted; the universities and professional colleges are only allowed to make small adjustments. In the case of other study programmes, Parliament has allocated funding for a group of programmes at a given institution, indicating only a planned number of admissions to each programme. It is then for the institution itself to decide what number to allocate to each. A recent policy proposal for funding higher education is to base it upon places actually taken up, rather than planned numbers; this is one step towards account-ability (SOU 1992b; UbU 1992/3).

When selection of applicants is necessary, it is based on school grades for only half of the places, while for the other half it is based on the university standard aptitude test and post-secondary education. Credits for work exper-ience may be added to this test result, but from 1992 half the places set aside for tested applicants are to be designated for those lacking work experience. It is for individual universities or colleges to decide what selection procedure to adopt, and it is proposed that from 1993 admission policies for study programmes should also be a matter of only local concern.

Since 1977 central study programmes have had progressively less influence, and two-thirds of the central study programmes were abolished in 1988. Programmes were maintained for teaching and for health, the two principal fields for government steering in higher education, and for some other programmes directed towards vocations that require public certification (forty-eight programmes in total).

In 1992, ideas of 'freedom, responsibility and competence' led the Government to propose a large number of changes in the higher education system, intended to reinforce the autonomy of the academic profession, the disciplines and the students (SOU 1992a, b; Ds 1992; Government Bill 1992/3). Thus, from 1993, there will be no central study programmes al-though there will be certain exceptions in the case of some prescribed degrees (Government Bill 1990/1a, b, 1992/3; Ds 1992). The organization of study programmes will be of local concern only. The Government retains the authority to make provision and to prescribe which degrees can be awarded and what requirements should be stipulated. Thirty-seven vocational or professional degrees are proposed in addition to the four general higher education degrees. These include the six considered below.

Competence and quality are much discussed. For teachers in higher education competence is primarily secured through postgraduate education and research, but new proposals include further pedagogic education, peer review, external examination and evaluation (SOU 1991; NBUC Report 1992b). Local evaluations would be combined with various kinds of national evaluation undertaken by various independent institutions and *ad hoc* groups.

A specified educational budgetary commission is to be given to each university and college during the three-year budget cycle, to include quantified proposals as well as programmes for securing quality. The main subsidy is to be allocated in accordance with the number of places filled, with a subsequent rendering of account before the next budget period.

These proposals have contributed to decentralization and deregulation, continuing the reinforcement of the academic professions and disciplines, and are to some extent based on theories of professions and organizations. As in all professional organizations, the intention lying behind the proposals is to exercise *ante hoc* influence by ensuring staff competence. But the changes also represent a major switch from control through the formulation of rules and regulations in advance to control through the evaluation of results. How this will affect the different professions is naturally of great concern, one important issue being accountability as against professional autonomy (Bauer 1988; Kogan 1988; Neave 1988; van Vught 1988; Björklund 1992: 15).

With some simplification it is possible to discern three periods of government control of higher education, with associated forms of internal management: before 1977, government control exercised through rules and regulations, with collegial management; after 1977, government by objectives with management through democratic representation within corporations; as proposed in 1992, government through evaluation and management by a combination of collegial bodies and hierarchical corporate authorities. Within the last changes, although less explicitly than in the proposals described earlier, an interest orientation is detectable, with 'management' following market forces.

Different forms of professional education will have to relate to new forms of governance and management, as well as to new forms of market control. At the moment it is very difficult to evaluate how this will develop. The breadth and speed of the changes happening in Swedish education have already been matters for serious criticism by some international experts (OECD 1992).

Six professional fields

Six professional groups and their education are here compared in terms of governance. Medicine, law and education are traditional fields for higher education; social work, psychology and architecture are more recent additions. They all differ in size and status and in the way they are controlled, and their selection is intended to introduce some of the major issues raised by changes in the governance of professional education in Sweden. The discussion will focus on education as such, and will exclude comparable issues about research and professional practice. (For the concept and history of professions see Burrage and Torstendahl 1990; Torstendahl and Burrage 1990).

Medical education has been certified by the National Swedish Board of Health and Welfare. Psychologists were granted a comparable certificate in 1978, supplemented by a certificate in psychotherapy from 1985, also open to non-psychologists.

Court lawyers should by the code of court be members of the Swedish Bar Association, which requires basic law education, three years' practice in a law office and two years' court experience. These posts are allocated in close competition by a governmental board. However, a court career has become less attractive, and other legal work has, in recent decades, had to compete with various other specialisms, a process that has been characterized as marginalization (Bertilsson 1987).

The other professional groups have no required certification. The question of a certificate for teachers has been postponed. In 1990 the employment of teachers was fully transferred to the municipalities, and responsibility for the rules of qualification for teaching posts from central government to the local authorities. Related to that reform was a much criticized proposal to introduce a certificate based upon an evaluation of teaching practice made by the headmaster at the employing school.

Social workers have had various educational backgrounds. They are now on the road to professional status, but have not yet achieved certification. This issue is once again on the agenda, and will be covered by a current government review of social work.

The number of architects with higher education is increasing. However, only a fraction of all architectural work is as yet undertaken by those with education as architects, and they compete with engineers of various kinds. In the last review of planning and building laws, the educational requirement was abolished, even for city architects. Members of the Swedish National Association of Architects (SAR) can be expected to have a higher level of education in architecture, but no certificate is involved.

Except for teachers, the professions have agreed codes of ethics stipulated by their professional organizations. Boards of ethics serve as a control upon members, as well as an assurance for clients and the general public. The Swedish Association of Headteachers and Principals consented to a code of ethics in 1991, and work on such a code for teachers is in progress. The public control of lawyers is through membership in and an ethical examination by the Bar Association. For medicine and psychology, there are governmental as well as professional controls. For architecture, control is exercised both by the local building boards and by the profession. All the main professional organizations representing the groups considered here belong to the Swedish Confederation of Professional Associations (SACO), except for the new organization for compulsory school teachers. This belongs to the Swedish Central Organization for Salaried Employees (TCO).

Medicine is mainly in the public sector, although it has experienced privatization in the past decade. Few social workers or psychologists are employed by private institutions. Since 1992, financial impediments to private schools have considerably diminished, resulting in an increase in the number of privately employed teachers. More than half the architects, and somewhat fewer than half those with a legal education, are working in the private sector (Wadensjö 1991). Thus most of those under consideration are working in professional bureaucracies, and many are working as street-level bureaucrats in a close relationship with clients (Lipsky 1980; Mintzberg 1983; Svensson 1991). Swedish psychologists have, however, developed strategies to separate themselves from direct client employment, in order to establish a position distinct from that of those working in health or social work.

All activities – other than in the courts – that have a bearing on the work of these professions have been subjected to, or are currently undergoing, considerable deregulation and decentralization of decision-making, together with more explicit accountability and privatization. Additionally, there have been substantial cutbacks in public spending owing to the change of Government and general financial situation. The changes to the different forms of professional education discussed below need to be set in the context of these broader changes.

All the selected professional groups illustrate a trend towards feminization, to a greater or lesser extent. About two-thirds of medical and architectural students and half the law students come from the upper class, while about half the education and social work students come from the middle class, although we find more from the working class in the latter group. The league table of class origins is more or less matched by relative earnings. Physicians earn far more than other groups, followed by jurists and architects. Teachers, psychologists and social workers earn much the same. For all groups other than teachers, those employed in the private sector earn much more than the others.

All the examples of professional education considered are characterized by a close relationship with the corresponding professional practice. Especially in medicine, law and architecture, practising professionals are recruited as part-time teachers, but this is to some extent also true of the others. There are, however, not enough comparative data, in the case of Sweden, to determine how research, teaching and practice influence one another (Becher 1990).

Medicine

Manpower forecasting for the health services has been separate from that for the rest. From 1978 the Medical Association presented its own rolling manpower plans, the most recent in 1992, which are submitted to the Ministry of Education and Parliament's Committee for Education. The number of physicians tripled between 1960 and 1985, possibly more as a result of what the Government decided was in the public interest than in the profession's interest. The number of first-year places for students of medicine decreased in the mid-1980s from about 1000 to 815. Current forecasts propose that the higher figure be restored by the mid-1990s.

Currently it is recommended that medical studies last for five and a half years, divided into a pre-clinical phase and a clinical phase. The degree should be followed by general practice as a hospital registrar: now examined by the faculty, with the Royal Caroline Institute as coordinator, and no longer by the National Board for Health and Welfare. The latter is, however, still conducting the certificate examinations.

The central study programme was revised and extended after discussions in 1990. These were severely critical of what were alleged to be traditional teaching practices, which reinforced the fragmentation of theoretical sub-jects through the content of lectures being wholly determined by individual teachers. Influenced by international debate, by some new foreign models for medical studies and by the model established at the new medical uni-versity in Linköping in 1986, the Ministry of Education and the Swedish Medical Association have started to work to bring about the important changes in medical education happening elsewhere. This developmental work is being undertaken mainly at the level of the local committees for undergraduate education and is being remitted to the appropriate faculty board.

These new programmes emphasize the abolition of the division between pre-clinical and clinical phases, integration of theory and practice, problem-orientation, group organization, tuition, life-long learning and self-instruction (Swedish Medical Association 1989). Under the local medical faculty boards, boards for undergraduate studies are allowed to develop a local profile without any direct intervention from either the Ministry of Education or the National Board for Health and Welfare (other than the initial specifi-cation of the degree and rules for the certificate). The specification of what is required in order to receive the degree stipulates: knowledge and skills as the basis for medicine, including general practice, as well as the basis for medical research; knowledge of environmental effects on health; knowledge of the economics and organization of the health service, as well as prepara-tion for team-work and collaboration; development of self-knowledge and a holistic perspective, with the ability to develop good social relationships. In all, this specification covers less than half a page (Ds 1992: 95).

The development and control of the undergraduate curriculum is more than ever at the level of the faculty and departments, and this local profiling will create new problems in ensuring common national standards and quality in the practice of medicine in conformity with certificate requirements. At the moment there do not seem to be any developments in train that are intended to meet these problems.

Law

There was open admission to legal studies until 1977, with a very low success rate. In the 1980s there were 1200 to 1400 entrants annually. But the success rate is still extremely low, with less than half the students completing their examinations. About half the graduates gain a position practising in court, an occupation of major importance in the context of the traditional career openings for law graduates, although now decreasing in significance. Law graduates have increasingly entered other fields, including the private sector with its more favourable remuneration. Especially in the late 1980s, this created difficulty in recruiting for the courts. The extension of careers to new fields has emphasized competition with graduates from the social sciences. The traditional faculties of law have been supplemented by special schools for law and administration, directed primarily at private enterprises.

Since 1977 the central study programme has specified four and a half years for education in law (with 80 out of 180 points for basic education in law, which can be used as the first part of the education leading to the master's degree in law). The national study programme has gradually been abandoned to allow for local profiling, although the initial specification of degrees enumerates certain basic subjects. Teaching has become more intense – a major argument in the recent lobbying to raise what is an extremely low level of grant per student compared with other vocational study programmes.

The local profiling and current developments seem to be assessed very differently by the separate groups active in the field of law – the faculties, the judicial courts and the professional organizations. The faculties and departments of law have been developing their teaching to secure integration, problem orientation, teaching on a group basis and extended free choice. The competition for places in court practice, however, produces a 'grades chase' among students, which impedes pedagogic development. This is the crucial problem in evaluating the completed programme. Consequently, proposals to cut grades from three levels to two cannot be realized. The pursuit of grades is also prolonging studies in a way that should be prohibited.

There will be greater variation between degrees, and the courts are already showing a preference for the earlier study programmes. For the Bar Association, on the other hand, profiling will probably not pose the same problems, since consideration of the particular study programme is already part of their procedures for admission to court positions. The Swedish Federation of Lawyers, Economists and Social Scientists (JUSEK) seems ambivalent about the way in which the education provided by the faculties is developing. In its response to the Government proposal for reforms in higher education there is an emphasis upon arguments intended to maintain professional interests (JUSEK 1992). JUSEK is demanding more explicit and complete specification of degree requirements. Certain prerequisites for the practice of law are necessary where legal security is involved. The practice of law is here compared with medical practice, and it is argued that the central specification of compulsory subjects should be reinforced. Although determining the curriculum should be left to local faculties, there should be a similar core of subjects for all faculties. The Master of Law degree is required for judicial careers, and the specifications should be more explicit in order to avoid the Government's office of courts, or the Bar Association, making detailed demands in respect of curricula. According to JUSEK, this would give these bodies unreasonable power over the faculties. The problem of congruence would not be solved by a system of external examiners, which would be too expensive and very difficult to organize, and could militate against local autonomy. Nor would the problem be solved by centrally administered tests, as these would also be inconsistent with local development.

The various law faculties have networks for some coordinated lobbying at the level of deans. However, most of the development of study programmes in law seems to be instigated by local faculties and by committees under them. On the whole there is not the same coordination as in medicine, and the different interest groups are working at a distance from one another. It is possible to suggest some reasons for this. First, there are two very different professional organizations, JUSEK and the Bar Association. Second, these organizations are not at all close to the university faculties. Third, the job market is less favourable in judicial work than in medicine, and there has been a great diversity in the directions taken by careers, increasingly in competition with people with education other than in law. Fourth, the close connection between the requirements for admission to judicial careers and the evaluation of the graduate's education represented by the 'grades chase' allows less scope for new ways of organizing teaching.

Teaching

Teacher education is a vast and heterogeneous field, with, in total, about 10,000 new entrants annually. The education of teachers for the compulsory schools is considered here because a new programme was introduced in 1988, with revisions for 1992 and more in train for 1993. Compulsory schooling used to be subject to very intense central control, but is now being deregulated and decentralized in many respects. Coincidentally, integration is taking place between pre-schools, leisure schools and compulsory schools. The current Government considers teacher education to be of great importance in ensuring uniform quality in schools, alongside the national curriculum programmes (Government Bill 1991/2a). Having a strong vocational orientation, it needs to be steered more explicitly by central government than do other kinds of education, as is emphasized by Parliament's education committee (UbU 1991/2).

The fundamental objectives of the 1988 reform were to strengthen admission requirements, increase the length of the study and include interdisciplinary studies and more teaching theory (Bentley and Persson 1991). By integrating what were formerly distinct programmes into one, the Government and Parliament intended to complete the development of comprehensive schooling for all children of seven to sixteen, and to level out the three stages, thus removing one survival from the system of parallel schooling. Subject-based training and specialization were reinforced for teachers at the lower levels, and weakened or rendered less specialized for teachers at higher levels. The experiential tradition of the teacher training colleges was thereby integrated with the subject-oriented tradition of the universities.

The study programme varies from three and a half years to four and a half years (or 140–180 points). It is regulated by a very detailed national programme in an unusually extensive document, which stipulates 45 to 50 points in compulsory subjects: methodology, pedagogics, practical training and communication. Most of the rest is satisfied through six optional subject programmes for the school years one to seven, and about fifty optional subject programmes for years four to nine. Students can choose to specialize in teaching pupils in grades one to seven or four to nine. The former should be trained to teach all subjects in years one to three and the chosen options in years four to seven. The latter students should be trained to teach a group (or a pair) of subjects in years four to nine. Certain subjects are required to have been studied in detail before, depending upon the options chosen.

Teaching practice is typically undertaken at a large number of schools. A director of practice from the university is responsible for its organization and examination. In collaboration with the school teachers, supervisors at the schools are selected and paid by the universities. This is an instance of frequent contact between the educators of the professionals and those in professional practice. Other examples are regular meetings with all headteachers in the area, and, less frequently, enquiries or surveys.

From 1993, not even teacher training will be regulated by national programmes, except for the specification of what is required for the degree. These initial specifications leave much freedom to local programme committees, and development work is far advanced. The conservative 'salami-strategy' is left behind in favour of a flexible system of modules of 20 points each. This system is supposed to allow for more options and for more efficient teaching, as well as for recurrent education (Government Bill 1991/2a).

National programmes have again been considered to provide fairly strict guidance in the governance of education, although the central allocation of funding has been regarded as the strongest steer. But by far the strongest measure has actually been the changes in the number of first-year entrants; e.g. in the mid-1980s there were 3900 first-year entrants for class teaching, but by the end of the decade as few as 1200. The stricter admission regulations introduced in 1988 for the new programme for compulsory school teachers, which required applicants to have had three rather than two years at upper secondary school, could be one reason for the decline in the number of applicants. Almost half the places were left unfilled at that time, but in 1991 only 7 per cent were empty. The number of entrants will be gradually increased to more than 6000 by the middle of this decade.

The demand for teachers has, in its turn, been influenced by the Government's steering of local schools. Previously the size of school classes determined the number of teachers and a 'chain of steel' was created: 'central allowances – class size – school organization – time schedules – teaching duties' (SOU 1992c: 40). This chain is now broken through de-regulation and decentralization. There is another chain growing through the current reforms: values – educational objectives – teaching aims – results – evaluation. This will be a strong reinforcement for professional responsibility.

The shift towards professionalism and evaluation seems to be very attractive for teacher education. The competence of those who educate the teachers is regarded as decisive for efficient education. Educators with recognized research competence (docents) have been nominated as examiners for courses of 10 points or more. Scientific competence needs to be increased among educators in the practically oriented sections of the curriculum, which would mean more academization. External examination and international peer review seem to have gone further in this area than in the others considered in this chapter.

The professional organizations for classroom and for vocational study teachers were merged as the Swedish Association for Teachers in 1991. As separate organizations they had advocated integrated teacher education, consistent with their wish to bridge the traditional abyss between themselves and subject-trained teachers at the upper level of the compulsory school. They also support integration with nursery and leisure schools. However, they oppose the decentralization of salary negotiations, making teachers almost the last group left defending this aspect of the so-called 'Swedish model'. They are opposed to giving marks in the early school years, and to children starting school at six, as well as to some other policies of the Government. On the whole, the trade union is taken up more with occupational and employment issues than with teacher education.

Social work

The consideration of social workers is limited here to socionomists. This is, in itself, rather a heterogeneous occupational group, but since 1977 there has been comprehensive social work education at six colleges and universities, quite strictly controlled by a national study programme. New study programmes were validated in 1990 after a review undertaken in 1988 by a commission appointed by the National Board for Universities and Colleges (NBUC 1988). The annual number of entrants has been 1200, apart from a decline to about 1000 in the 1980s, and the special requirements for admission are two years of mathematics and social science. The national programme stipulates 140 credits, including 10 for studies in the field and 20 for supervised practice: equivalent to half the time previously devoted to practice. Successful students receive a bachelor of science degree in social work. A professional certificate has been on the agenda since the late 1950s, but with no success. In autumn 1992 four motions on this matter were again submitted to Parliament. There is a preliminary Government proposal to review all education affected by certificates. On this issue, social work is usually compared with the health professions.

During the 1970s and 1980s the discipline of social work became more academic and more scientific, and in the process grew considerably. Postgraduate education and research have developed in conjunction with undergraduate study. Adopting the traditions and organization of higher education, the departments and study programme committees have devoted themselves to issues of teaching as well as vocational practice. In the view of the departments, education in the discipline should be extended, and moved even further in the direction of theory and research. The development work is undertaken by the departments, collaborating across the country through regular meetings. Local profiling is only able to influence the field studies and single-subject courses.

The organization that represents most social workers, the Swedish Association of Socionomists (SSR), seems to be in agreement with the academic interest group in wanting to extend the teaching, making it more theoretical and directing it towards disciplines. Support for this is found in the philosophy of education articulated in the Government proposals. In another respect there is less support. In order to allocate Government funding, some vocational study programmes, such as medicine and psychology, were classified as client-oriented. Social work was not, and this aroused animosity and calls for strong reaction on the part of the SSR and the departments (SOU 1992b: 64).

The SSR makes its views on study programmes and practice known directly to the universities, but is not otherwise involved in examinations or in the supervision of the departments. The SSR was, however, involved in the recent national review of social work and welfare initiated by the Ministry of Health and Welfare. The SSR regularly expresses its opinion of budget proposals through lobbying, sometimes supporting this with its own analysis of education and social work and sometimes supported by teachers and students.

As a professional organization, the SSR has close contact with professional practice and employers as well as with education and the universities. Some social workers now belong to another trade union, which is amalgamated with the national union for service work; this is weakening the profession as a whole. There has been a growing tension between the interests of the practitioners and the interests of the teachers and researchers, who are seeking more control over a distinct discipline. This developing gulf may, however, be bridged by action taken by the SSR, and by the more frequent contacts between teachers and practitioners occurring as part of field studies and periods of practical training.

The Government's control of social work education will continue through the national study programmes, although with an increasing element of local profiling. However, for the moment, central government seems to be exerting its influence chiefly by controlling the cutbacks, and by making changes in the organization of the social service sector.

Psychology

Since 1978 the national study programme for psychology has been followed at five universities. This is a comprehensive programme (revised in 1982) extending over five years. It includes one year of supervised practical training in clinical and other forms of psychology, and is divided into three stages. Successful completion entitles the student to apply for a certificate from the National Board for Health and Welfare. Psychology is one of the programmes in higher education that particularly commands official interest. Uniquely among the examples of professional education considered here, there is a requirement for one year of work experience before entry. This is one reason why these students are somewhat older than others. The basic education also covers two shorter periods of practical training.

A recent peer review of the programme indicates that there are only slight differences in the profiles at the various universities (NBUC Report 1992c). The completion rate is very low, leaving a great deal to be desired. The organization of practical training also needs to be changed, since the finding of placements and supervision depends entirely on the good will of the teachers and informally recruited supervisors. There is a continuing shortage of placements, although this is chiefly so in the vicinity of the universities. Applications are made to the Swedish Psychologists' Association, which allocates placements. The practical year ought arguably to be regulated and organized by the National Board, as is the case for medical practice, leaving more of the control and responsibility in the hands of government authorities.

The number of entrants fell in the early 1980s, and has remained between 150 and 200. The national boards, like the National Association and the university departments, view this with concern. The planning of the programme for 1993 is primarily progressing in the departments and their standing committees, which ensure collaboration, and is taking the recent peer review as one point of departure. Profiling of the various parts of the curriculum will be extended to provide points at given intervals. The departments want their work to supersede the Ministry of Education's formulation of the national programme. However, neither the Association nor the National Board for Health and Welfare is involved in the planning at this stage. There will be problems in evaluating certificate requirements as a result of less regulated and more profiled programmes.

Psychology started from the position of being a theoretical academic discipline, and, in contrast to social work, the process of professionalization has mainly been concerned with how the practice of psychology in the field is organized, and has served to make psychology less theoretical and more directed towards practice. The fact that in the mid-1970s the Swedish Association for Psychology was reorganized according to fields of work rather than continuing to reflect university distinctions indicates how successful this strategy was. But the new distinctions have, in their turn, created tensions between academic specialisms and occupational fields, thus weakening the professional body. In spite of this, the organization has been very successful in monopolizing both the academic discipline and the occupational fields, and soon acquired a Government certificate (1978).

Architecture

Basic architectural education has, since the late nineteenth century, been provided at technical colleges in three cities. This education has comprised four years of study. There is only a tenuous relationship between such education and employment that requires architectural skills, and attempts to exercise governmental authority over the profession have failed. Membership of the Swedish Association for Architects (SAR) is limited to those who have competed the basic education and are prepared to submit themselves to the Association's code of ethics.

The number of entrants (180) is comparable with that for psychology. The special requirements for admission are two or three years of previous study of mathematics, physics and chemistry, but an admission test can be used as an alternative for one-third of the places. The teaching is mainly through group projects, a local reform initiated by the departments in the early 1970s. The curriculum at Chalmers Technical College, running ahead of this, was designed at the departmental level in the 1950s and informally negotiated with the Minister of Education by the senior professor.

As a result of differences in the professorial representation of subjects, there are different profiles at each of the three technical universities, although from an international perspective these differences seem negligible. In the absence of a common national programme, current collaboration between the technical universities is aimed at greater uniformity rather than profiling. This solidarity was tested in the late 1970s when, as a result of unemployment, the Government threatened to suspend teaching at Lund. Instead, the number of entrants was reduced at all three universities from a total of 200 to 150. After lobbying, the number was increased again, to 180 in 1992.

A trade union, the Association of Architects (AF), was established in 1975 alongside the SAR, to cover educational and occupational issues. One issue was practical training, which comprises seventeen weeks of the basic education. Attempts have been made to introduce a year of compulsory practice at the beginning or end of the basic education period, as an additional requirement for graduation and for membership of the SAR, the total period thereby matching international standards. Another initiative concerns the status of the work for final examination at the end of the basic education. Many students do not finish this work, which results in both slower and lower rates of graduation. The idea that there would be an increasing demand for architects was supported by the National Board for Universities and Colleges in 1989, but in 1992 the profession was again hit by unemployment, completely changing the planning assumptions.

Study programme committees no longer exist, and decisions regarding the general curriculum are taken by the board for the architecture area. Once again, this leaves more of the curriculum decisions to the departments, and in these terms they have considerable autonomy. There are external interests represented on the boards, but only very rarely do they put forward any strong opinions. External control is mainly exercised by central government, but this largely concerns the number of entrants and the associated funding. The special enquiry instigated by the National Board for Universities and Colleges in 1983 did not have a significant effect on departments, despite many proposals about practice and the length of study being supported by the union and the departments (NBUC 1983). However, in the recently proposed specifications for degrees architecture is to be extended to 180 points.

Conclusion

The previous Government's *modus operandi* was to structure and regulate the activities of higher education in advance. Among the means used were: a formal decision-making organization; rules of qualification and competence attached to certain posts; control of resource allocations, the size of study programmes and entry figures; admission regulations; centralized specification of study programmes; and specification of conditions for the award of degrees. Generally, there was a contradiction between strict organization and financial control on the one hand and, on the other, lack of control of curricula and the form of examinations. The extensive changes currently in train involve a growing autonomy for the sector and a great swing from governance *ante hoc* to governance *post hoc*, through audit and evaluation. The development of opportunities for cohorts of students to undertake higher education will, in future, be reviewed by the Government but will not be regulated by it (Ds 1992: 37; NBUC 1992a).

There is a universal welcome for more autonomy in all six areas of professional education analysed above. In terms of the procedures for staff appointments, many are asking for more freedom than is now offered by the system of local appointments boards. But growing autonomy in one regard is matched by reduced autonomy in others. Audit would affect law, psychology and architecture the most, owing to the poor efficiency represented by both low and late completion rates. Medicine, education and psychology seem best prepared for evaluation. In education, especially, a system of highly qualified examiners, including external examiners, has been developed.

The proposals for reinforcing the competence of staff would benefit academics on the ground as a whole, but mainly those in departments with poor qualifications on average. If, however, evaluation takes account of existing qualifications, then of course the best qualified departments and areas of professional education will be favoured. What favours the academic profession could be of disadvantage to the position of the practitioners and the power of the associations, in comparison with the power of the faculties. The latter already enjoy significant autonomy in relation to the world of work. This academization seems most in tune with the struggle for professionalization in social work education. But all the academic groups concerned have close and frequent contact in many ways with practitioners and the world of practice, primarily on their own terms, so they would not be very likely to become out of touch with vocational requirements.

Teacher education has been the most regulated, for a number of related reasons, and so is likely to be most affected by the abolition of national study programmes. At the same time schools are being decentralized and deregulated to a very great extent, and teachers find themselves working under quite new conditions locally. Nevertheless, all schools are still, at least notionally, assumed to offer equal opportunities wherever they are, and it is the responsibility of the Government to ensure this. There is a similar problem for medicine and for psychology. Will *post hoc* audit and evaluation satisfy the public's demand for quality? Will this produce another paradox: securing quality and at the same time abandoning the means of exercising influence before the event? In one respect, to be a profession implies the support of government authority exercised through legislation: the possession of a certificate. This dilemma is greater when political and administrative decentralization is taken into account. Would that not call for even more central policy guidelines?

The dilemma of audit is frequently discussed among planners and teachers in the fields we have been considering. How will the quality of degrees be maintained where there is increasing pressure to achieve higher graduation rates in the future? In what ways could that be achieved without a loss of quality?

During the 1970s most professional associations gradually became trade unions, and wage bargaining and other employment issues became their most important activities. Negotiations were with the national boards and the centrally organized employers, as well as with the Government. In many ways the professional associations run the risk of ending up in a vacuum created by the academic educators, strongly supported by the current reforms, on the one hand, and by those they used to negotiate with, who are disappearing in a wave of decentralization, deregulation and privatization, on the other. New and more direct channels for communication with the ministries and central government need to be opened up for efficient lobbying, while for negotiating, bargaining and other important issues, other integrated and less exclusive professional organizations will need to be established at the local level.

References

Bauer, M. (1988) 'Evaluation in Swedish higher education: recent trends and the outline of a model', *European Journal of Higher Education*, 23 (1/2), 25–36.

Becher, T. (1990) 'Professional education in a comparative context', in R. Torstendahl and M. Burrage (eds) *The Formation of Professions*. London, Sage.

Bentley, P.O. and Persson, T. (1991) *Teacher Education for Compulsory Comprehensive Schools in Sweden*. Gothenburg, School of Teacher Education.

138   *Governments and Professional Education*

Bertilsson, M. (1987) 'The legal profession and law in the welfare state', paper presented to National Board for Universities and Colleges Conference, Rosenön, Dalarö.

Björklund, S. (1992) *Leadership and Accountability in the Republic of Scholars.* Stockholm, National Board for Universities and Colleges.

Burrage, M. and Torstendahl, R. (eds) (1990) *Professions in Theory and History.* London, Sage.

Ds (1992) *Autonomous Universities and Colleges* (in Swedish). Stockholm, Ministry Report.

Government Bill (1990/1a) 100 app 9 (in Swedish).

Government Bill (1990/1b) 150 app II:7 (in Swedish).

Government Bill (1991/2) Teacher Education 75 (in Swedish).

Government Bill (1992/3) Universities and Colleges – Autonomy for Quality 1 (in Swedish).

Government Bill (1992/3) Higher Education to Higher Qualification 169 (in Swedish).

JUSEK (1992) *Response to Commission Report Ds 1992: 1* (in Swedish).

Kogan, M. (1988) 'Government and the management of higher education: an introductory review', *International Journal of Institutional Management in Higher Education,* 12 (1), 5–15.

Lipsky, M. (1980) *Street-level Bureaucracy.* New York, Russell Sage Foundation.

Mintzberg, H. (1983) *Structure in Fives.* Englewood Cliffs, NJ, Prentice-Hall.

NBUC (1983) *Architecture. Education and Research* (in Swedish). Stockholm, National Board for Universities and Colleges.

NBUC (1988) *On Social Work* (in Swedish). Stockholm, National Board for Universities and Colleges.

NBUC (1989) *The Forecasting of Higher Education* (in Swedish). Stockholm, National Board for Universities and Colleges.

NBUC (1992a) *Can Higher Education be Decentralized?* (in Swedish). Stockholm, National Board for Universities and Colleges.

NBUC (1992b) *Self-evaluation and External Reviewing* (in Swedish). Stockholm, National Board for Universities and Colleges.

NBUC (1992c) *Evaluation of the Study Programme for Psychology* (in Swedish). Stockholm, National Board for Universities and Colleges.

Neave, G. (1988) 'On the cultivation of quality, efficiency and enterprise: an overview of recent trends in higher education in Western Europe, 1986–1988', *European Journal of Education,* 23 (1/2), 7–23.

OECD (1992) *Review of Education Policy in Sweden.* Paris, OECD.

SOU (1991) *Examination as Quality Control at the University* (in Swedish). Stockholm, Governmental Public Investigation Report.

SOU (1992a) *Freedom, Responsibility, Competence* (in Swedish). Stockholm, Governmental Public Investigation Report.

SOU (1992b) *Resources for Undergraduate Higher Education* (in Swedish). Stockholm, Governmental Public Investigation Report.

SOU (1992c) *Schooling for Cultivation* (in Swedish). Stockholm, Governmental Public Investigation Report.

Svensson, L. (1991) 'The steering of public service work', in S.E. Olsson and G. Therborn (eds) *Vision Encounters Reality. On Social Steering and Virtual Development of Society* (in Swedish). Stockholm, Allhaenna Foerlaget.

Swedish Medical Association (1989) *Life-long Learning. An Educational Policy Program.* Stockholm, Swedish Medical Association.

Torstendahl, R. and Burrage, M. (eds) (1990) *The Formation of Professions.* London, Sage.

Trolle, U. af (1989) *Towards an Internationally Competitive Academic Education* (in Swedish). Lund, Studentlitt.

UbU (1991/2) *Report 20* (in Swedish). Stockholm, Educational Committee in Parliament.

UbU3 (1992/3) *New Law for Higher Education* (in Swedish). Stockholm, Educational Committee in Parliament.

van Vught, F. (1988) 'A new autonomy in European higher education? An exploration and analysis of the strategy of self-regulation in higher education governance', *International Journal of Institutional Management in Higher Education*, 12 (1), 16–26.

Wadensjö, E. (1991) *Higher Education and Earnings* (in Swedish). Stockholm, Governmental Public Investigation Report.

9

Routine and Discreet Relationships: Professional Accreditation and the State in Britain

Michael Burrage

Equality gives way to relevance

Broadly speaking, British educational policy-making since the Second World War has been driven by two great concerns. The first was to expand equality of educational opportunity. This concern was sustained by a considerable body of research that documented the persistent class inequalities in educational opportunity and it long dominated educational policy and debate, especially under Labour Governments. Conservative Governments never embraced the policies that were intended to reduce these inequalities with any enthusiasm but they accepted them as long as they did not threaten the independent schools in any respect.

The second major concern has been the failure of the British educational system to provide industrially relevant skills and qualifications. This concern was bi-partisan, and expressed long before the election of Mrs Thatcher in 1979, but it has over four successive administrations been made the guiding theme of Conservative educational policy, as though they are relieved, at long last, to have found a positive role for the state in British education. It remains in the ascendant, and has totally eclipsed the earlier concern with equality of opportunity.

The Conservatives first addressed this concern with the Technical and Vocational Education Initiative, which was launched experimentally in 1982 and nationally in 1986 and was intended to expand the vocational element of secondary education. Several further measures to lay the foundations of a new system of vocational education were taken in subsequent years. In 1985 a Youth Training Scheme was launched to provide access to some form of vocational training to all young people. In 1986, the de Ville working group recommended national hallmarking and validation of all forms of vocational education, with priority given to manual skills (de Ville 1986).

Later in the same year a National Council for Vocational Qualifications was established to give effect to these recommendations.

Kindred policies have been pursued with similar vigour in higher education. The Thatcher Governments continued the policies of the mid-1970s, to promote 'selectivity' in the distribution of funds to higher education, and left no doubt that this power was to be used to make higher education more vocationally relevant. In April 1987, shortly before Mrs Thatcher's third election triumph, the Government issued a White Paper which insisted that the universities should be 'more responsive to industrial requirements of the country'. It promised that 'the Government and its central funding agencies will do all they can to encourage and reward approaches by higher education institutions which bring them closer to the world of business' (Stewart 1989).

In the Education Reform Act of July 1988 the Government fulfilled this promise by abolishing the University Grants Committee (UGC), which it thought too respectful of academic opinion. In its final year it consisted of sixteen academic members and three senior industrial executives. Its fifteen subject sub-committees were entirely composed of academics. It was replaced by a University Funding Council (UFC), which was to be directly controlled by the central government and evidently to have a larger proportion of members who appeared to the Secretary of State 'to have experience of and to have shown capacity in industrial, commercial or financial matters or the practice of any profession' (Simon 1988).

Analogous reforms in the 'public sector' of higher education led to the replacement of the National Advisory Body, on which local government had been strongly represented, by the Polytechnics and Colleges Funding Council. This was placed under still firmer Department of Education and Science (DES) control than the UFC but in 1992 merged with it to form the Higher Education Funding Council (HEFC). The act also included specific requirements about the composition of polytechnics' governing bodies. At least half their members were to represent 'business, industrial, professional and other employment interests including trade unions'. Only one-fifth of their members could be drawn from local authorities, two from their own academic staff and one from their students.

Doubts about a research base

These policies, and the concern that fuelled them, were supported by a body of research. Influential historical warrants were provided by the work of Weiner (1985), which documented the enduring anti-industrial ethos of British intellectual and political elites, and of Barnett (1986), which showed the failure of British governments before and after the Second World War to ensure that the British labour force had an adequate technical training. The Finniston Committee provided contemporary corroboration for these arguments by supporting engineers' oft repeated complaint that, compared with engineers abroad, they were accorded an extremely low status in both industry and British society at large. Simultaneously, the National Institute of Economic and Social Research (NIESR) began a series of matched-plant comparative studies, which repeatedly showed the lower levels of formal vocational training of manual workers in Britain compared with those in France, Germany and other countries (Prais and Steedman 1985).

This body of research was, however, rather less detailed, persuasive and authoritative than that supporting earlier concerns about equality of educational opportunity. Perhaps it was, in the nature of things, more difficult. Any data that showed that educational access and success did not correspond with the class distribution of the population contributed to the case for more equality. To understand and explain British attitudes towards vocational education, or the indifference of educational institutions towards vocational training and the effects such attitudes may have had at the workplace, required extensive and difficult historical and comparative research.

Only the NIESR studies provided what was required. Weiner not only failed to conduct comparative analyses to show that anti-scientific, anti-entrepreneurial values were distinctively British, but gave no clue as to how the values of a literary and academic elite may have affected school-leavers' educational and career choices, managers' and employers' preferences, or their relationships and behaviour at the workplace. While Barnett scathingly documented the failures of pre- and post-war governments, he made little attempt to understand the views of those most intimately involved in the application of science and technology at the workplace, namely the qualified engineers, technicians and skilled workers themselves. By scolding and berating previous governments, he no doubt encouraged vigorous and positive government action but he could give no precise indications of what national policy should be.

The enquiries and deliberations of the Finniston Committee were not entirely consistent with the historical evidence since they revealed that the most powerful pressure groups with which it had to negotiate and contend were not ivory tower academics but the associations of practising engineers. Its comparative research was superficial and included no survey evidence about the formation of engineers abroad or about their use in the workplace. As a piece of research it was incomplete and unsatisfactory. Later research therefore threw doubt on its conclusions (Van den Berghe 1986: 46, 147–69).

The Government preferred not to wait until the uncertainties and ambiguities in this research were resolved. They drew on major ideas that much research and commentary seemed to support, namely that the root cause of Britain's economic decline was that it had failed to create an adequate system of vocational and professional education and that the main culprits, apart from past governments, were teachers and academics who had always shown themselves to be indifferent to the application of knowledge and who, more than anyone else, had perpetuated the long-standing

British prejudice against vocational education in general and engineering in particular.

Policy then flowed from these starting assumptions. The Government seized control of school curricula from the teachers and made them more vocationally relevant. The funding bodies of universities and polytechnics were reconstituted, presumably in the belief that substantial industrial and professional representation would ensure appropriate financial incentives and sanctions to redirect higher education towards more vocational ends. The newly constituted governing bodies of polytechnics would presumably reinforce this redirection. No effort was made to enlist professional support for any of these policies, since the professions were seen as part of the problem. Policy was therefore based on the belief that academic behaviour could be best changed, or perhaps only changed, by more direction and supervision and control.

Since power and money have often proved to be effective means of changing behaviour, this might be the end of the story, or of a dramatic chapter at least, in British higher education. It only remains to measure the effects of these policies. Universities and industry, however, have a variety of other, more equal, relationships and other ways in which they respond to each other's concerns, such as consultancies, continuing education courses and research contracts. The present analysis is based on the supposition that there is still some value and interest in trying to document and understand these other relationships and in particular the routine, discreet and therefore almost forgotten channel by which practitioners may exercise a continuing influence over the curricula and conduct of academic institutions, namely by accrediting degrees and courses that provide a preliminary qualification for their professional qualification.

This chapter reports preliminary attempts to understand the workings and characteristics of accreditation, or more precisely some variants of it. It is based on a handful of pilot interviews with those involved with accrediting of law, engineering and accountancy degrees, either as panel members or as staff members of the relevant professional bodies. They are not a representative sample and the interviews have not yet included those subject to the authority of accrediting bodies. Obviously, they only allow one to begin to identify some of the characteristics of accreditation of this sort and to raise some questions for future study. First, however, it would seem sensible to make clear the starting assumptions of the inquiry since they differ, in certain respects, from those that seem to have informed recent government policies.

A comparative framework

To identify the peculiarities of the relationship between school-based and practice-based professional education in Britain, or any other society, it is useful to begin by recognizing that there are four interested parties or major players in the generation, reproduction and certification of specialist knowledge. For simplicity's sake, we may label them the practitioners, meaning the practising members of the professions who possess and apply the knowledge, the professors, meaning all the staff of institutions that have some responsibility for providing professional education, the state, meaning those who exercise public authority with respect to the transmission and certification of specialist knowledge, and finally the users, meaning all those who buy, benefit or make use of it, such as customers, patients, clients and the commercial and industrial employers of professionals.

Any system of professional education is a product of the interactions between these four actors. Their resources, as well as their ability and willingness to act, have varied greatly between countries and hence one may begin to understand the peculiarities of Britain, or any other country, by tracing and comparing the interaction of these interested parties (Burrage *et al.* 1990).

The point can be illustrated by reference to the well-documented example of the very active, almost possessive, role of the French state with respect to all kinds of specialist and technical knowledge. From the earliest beginnings of military engineering in the fifteenth and sixteenth centuries, for instance, French kings were at pains to acquire specialists in the techniques of forti- fication and siege warfare from Italy and the Netherlands, then both at the leading edge of these technologies. By the end of the sixteenth century, the French had developed an indigenous expertise in military engineering and 'had become the greatest takers and builders of fortresses . . . a pre- eminence they maintained until the demise of siege warfare at the end of the eighteenth century' (Duffy, 1979: 138). The French state subsequently showed the same interest in many other kinds of engineering knowledge, such as map-making and surveying, road and rail building (Burrage 1992a).

The French state consistently appears to have recognized its dependence on such specialist engineering knowledge and therefore has sought to appropriate and develop it for its own purposes and to support, train, organize and employ the specialists who possessed it and were responsible for transmitting it. It displayed the same interest in the training and cer- tification of legal specialists and organized its own corps of legal specialists, and later took a similar interest in medical training and certification.

By contrast, the British state was content to let private individuals appro- priate and develop such specialist knowledge as they might find useful, and organize their profession as they saw fit. It took essentially the same attitude to the barristers in the thirteenth century, physicians in the sixteenth, so- licitors and surgeons in the eighteenth, and civil engineers and the host of industrially related professions in the nineteenth and twentieth. Its re- sponsibilities and interest extended little beyond granting the representa- tive body of practitioners powers of self-government.

The British state appears to have taken a different attitude only in ex- ceptional circumstances when it perceived itself under some kind of threat, such as the problem of defending India, which propelled it into engineering education and map-making, the rising of the clans in Scotland or the Rebecca riots, which prompted it to begin road-building in Scotland and Wales, or some political or press campaign or wartime emergency, both of which forced it to become interested in the railways. For the most part, however, the development, transmission and certification of specialist knowledge were left to self-governing bodies of practitioners.

The early American state provides some similarities with France, particularly in the establishment of West Point, which was for two or three early decades the main source of formally trained engineering manpower for the new republic. There are further parallels in federal support for technical and vocational education by land grant legislation after the Civil War, by the GI Bill after the Second World War and by various other expenditures subsequently routed to higher education via the Department of Defense. However, since these did not entail direct state control of the transmission and certification of technical and specialist knowledge, the parallels with France become increasingly remote.

Much the most significant state action in the United States was the repeal of virtually all legislation and professional rules restricting access to the legal and medical professions by state governments in the early decades of the nineteenth century. This legislation effectively destroyed the practitioner-controlled and practice-based systems of training which both professions had inherited from England and which their professional associations were beginning to organize and regulate. Henceforth, apprenticeships were purely private arrangements, and, having lost control of entry to their professions, virtually all the practitioner associations in both professions collapsed.

Once the practitioners as an organized force were removed, the universities were able to act like entrepreneurs and devise and sell specialist knowledge. Moreover, since trained practitioners were unable to distinguish themselves from their untrained and self-styled competitors, they welcomed the chance to use their academic credentials for marketing and advertising purposes. Professional schools, both private commercial and public university ones, were therefore the beneficiaries of state government attacks on the practitioner associations, since these enabled them to develop their now familiar entrepreneurial, market-oriented characteristics (Burrage 1992b).

Peculiarities of the British

One might initially summarize the differences between professional education in these three societies by saying that France has been state-led, while Britain has been practitioner-led and the United States has been school-led. No doubt this caricatures the differences between the three countries. No doubt also we ought to distinguish between professions, since they have not all displayed exactly the same configuration. Employers, for instance, seem to have exercised a considerable influence on American engineering schools (Noble 1977). An extended analysis would also note the alliances and axes

of two of the parties against the others. But despite these and other qualifications, this simple framework does direct attention to certain distinctive
characteristics of the British system of professional education, in particular
that it alone developed a system of training and certification that preceded
the development of universities.

This can be simply observed by looking at the relative timing of the
establishment of professional associations and formal professional education
in universities or specialist schools. In Britain, the associations always precede
the schools, while in France and the United States the foundation of
professional schools almost always preceded the development of their
modern practitioner associations (Lundgreen 1990: 36–75). In these
countries therefore, and most others have followed them in this respect,
universities or equivalent institutions of higher learning have naturally assumed responsibility for the generation, dissemination and certification of
professional knowledge, either as agents of the state, as in France or in
their own right, as in the United States.

Britain is therefore exceptional, in that practitioners were able to assume exclusive responsibility for the training and certification of entrants
to the professions. Universities are rather recent claimants to a share of
these rights and responsibilities who have been allowed by the practitioners to offer their degrees as preliminaries to professional qualifications.
This explains the peculiar dual professional qualifications of Britain. There
are also, it is true, some dual qualifications in both the United States and
France. The peculiarity of Britain is that the practitioners' qualification, the
call to the bar, the membership of a royal college, accountancy or engineering institute for long remained the more significant, credible, and
marketable of the two.

The prior development of a practitioner-controlled and practice-based
system of professional education and certification provides a better explanation of why the British universities failed to show much more enthusiasm
or interest in formal professional or technical education than that discerned
by Weiner or Barnett. Britain already had in existence a system of practice-
based professional training that had evidently secured widespread legitimacy
among both employers and entrants to the profession. Creating a new
system of school-based professional training therefore posed quite peculiar
difficulties since it would have been difficult, indeed without strong state or
employer support impossible, to dislodge the existing system. Since this
support was not forthcoming the universities and other higher education
institutions had to work with the practitioners' associations, agree a division
of labour and reconcile their respective contributions to the education of
the professionals.

Recognition of this prior practitioner-controlled and practice-based system of professional education tempers one's judgements of the earlier
generations. No doubt one might still criticize universities for being excessively deferential to the practitioners by not seizing control of professional
education; and one might still blame governments for failing to grasp

opportunities to develop and expand technical education. However, in the light of the history of practitioner self-government in Britain such criticisms lose much of their sting. One might just as well criticize employers, or even entrants to the professions, for long preferring the established practitioner-controlled system.

It also prompts some reconsideration of recent government reforms. In a sense, it vindicates them as a belated attempt to assert an appropriate role for the state in arrangements in which it had previously taken a peripheral, almost ceremonial, part. However, it raises a number of questions. For instance, it is not clear why giving employers power over educational policy should be seen as a cure for Britain's problems, since employers long had the opportunity to express their preference for university-trained technical manpower but never did so. In fact they appear to have taken little interest in the content and certification of technical education, or any other kind of education for that matter. Nor is it clear why practitioners' associations were not included in the reforms, since they have shaped professional education in Britain far more than universities have ever done.

The present argument, however, is not concerned with the mechanisms of control and surveillance by which the Government hopes to force change on the universities but rather with examining what might be seen as their participatory or consensual alternatives. Accreditation is a part of the long process of adaptation and reconciliation between practitioners and professors. It entails a working relationship between professors and practitioners and is a means by which they may respond to each other's concerns.

Historical roots of accreditation

The initial problem in trying to study accreditation as an institution is that it has no written history, and is barely visible in the history of either professional or educational institutions. In Britain at least, there is no directory of accrediting bodies and there are no quantitative analyses of its frequency and scope. Initially, therefore, one has to retrieve the real life of the institution from the files of educational and professional bureaucracies and thereby try to identify its basic characteristics.

The first well-documented case of accreditation was that organized after the Flexner Report on American medical education by an alliance of elite medical schools, the Carnegie Foundation, state boards of medical examiners and the American Medical Association (Woodworth 1973). It may be, therefore, that accreditation is an American import that has been slowly, thoroughly and imperceptibly anglicized. There cannot be any certainty on the matter, however, since the Law Society was doing something very like accreditation when it first started lectures for students taking its examinations at the end of the nineteenth century and then when it started to allow the universities to teach towards its examinations in 1902.

In the United States the Council on Medical Education used its powers with devastating effect to cut the number of medical schools. Accreditation was then adopted, with rather less success, by the American Bar Association. Both these examples suggest that it was primarily used to regulate a rapidly growing and fiercely competitive market in professional credentials. Britain has never faced such a problem and accrediting was never used for this purpose. Accrediting developed in response to the recognition that formal schooling was an essential part of a professional training and that, since professional bodies were unable to provide for the growing numbers of those wishing to enter the profession directly, they had to monitor those private and public institutions to whom they had subcontracted their professional teaching responsibilities. Accrediting was a means of monitoring these 'subcontractors'.

As university degrees have become in many professions an essential preliminary requirement for a professional qualification, the procedure was extended from courses preparing students for the professional bodies' own examinations to the universities' own courses and degrees, though the problems of accrediting these two stages are rather different. In the United States, where the freedom to grant diplomas and degrees was readily available, accrediting was a means of dealing with an already overcrowded educational market. In Britain, since the state had exercised more control over who might grant degrees, and professional bodies over who might teach their courses, it was more preventive, to determine who might enter the market.

No doubt one could trace other roots of accrediting in Britain, from, for example, the work of Her Majesty's Inspectorate of Schools. However, the state seems to have extensively encouraged accrediting as part of its efforts to expand educational provision, most notably by the Council for National Academic Awards established in 1964, which accredited polytechnics and other institutions that might teach courses leading to the award of one of the Council's degrees. The state subsequently extended the use of accreditation with the creation of the Business and Technical Education Council in 1983, which built on accrediting precedents provided by its two predecessor councils as well as the City and Guilds Institute and the Royal Society of Arts. Indirectly, the state also encouraged the use of accrediting by chartering the Engineering Council in 1981, which was given responsibility for approving the training arrangements of forty-four professional bodies. Before the creation of this council, the professions granted exemption for degrees but accreditation procedures seem to have been uneven and inadequate, often no more than *post hoc* accrediting by professional examination results.

The most recent and most ambitious state intervention was the creation of the National Council for Vocational Qualifications (NCVQ), established in 1986. This promises to be the mother of all accrediting agencies since it has the task of analysing all vocational knowledge and training in the United Kingdom, manual and professional, paid and unpaid, into component 'competences' and arranging these 'competences' on a standard classification of five grades. In effect, it aims to construct a national grid of technical knowledge and to monitor, review and accredit all forms of accreditation. The Thatcher era was marked by the growth of central state control over a wide range of hitherto self-governing bodies. The NCVQ is surely one of its more remarkable creations, indeed of any state anywhere. This and other state bodies, however, have the distinctive aim of monitoring private bodies and their use of delegated public power and public funds. The comments that follow refer only to the accrediting that involves a relationship between professional practitioners and academics.

Formal steps in the process

The steps in this form of 'professional' accrediting may be outlined quite simply. They begin when an institution starts to design or amend a degree or course which it hopes will enable those who pass it to fulfil the academic requirements for membership of a professional association and thereby to obtain the qualification offered by this body. At the initial stage those designing the course usually probe their network of academic and professional contacts to discover the formal and informal rules and precedents of the accrediting committee of the professional body. Etiquette forbids direct contact with members concerned with accrediting but course designers may, and usually do, speak to the secretariat of the professional body. In all probability they will also discuss their plans with practising members of the profession among local employers, especially as many accrediting bodies now consider such discussions as essential to a successful proposal.

After submission, the proposal is reviewed by an accrediting committee within the professional body. It is a rare event for a proposal to be rejected outright at this stage. Most submissions, whatever the initial assessments of the accrediting committee, are followed by a panel visit in which all the matters raised by the committee about the course are put to the teachers, students and administrators, and the support services and facilities of the institution are briefly inspected. The panel then makes recommendations to the committee and the chair communicates their decision to the head of the institution submitting the proposal. Accreditation is for a fixed period, usually five years, and frequently, among engineering bodies, with detailed conditions attached. Some bodies insist on a brief annual written review from the institution. Some rejected applicants appeal or protest to the chair of the committee but decisions are never overturned.

Academics versus practitioners?

Accrediting bodies invariably consist of both academics and practitioners, though the proportions may vary and it seems to be a cardinal rule of all of them that visiting panels should always be drawn from both sides.

Accreditation is therefore a meeting point of the two branches of the professions and, in the light of all the discussion of the inadequacies and difficulties of vocational education in Britain, presumably also a potential flashpoint. If there were to be significant differences between the two branches of the professions one might expect them to surface first in the deliberations and decisions of the accreditation committees and panels.

There are some discernible differences among academic and practising accountants. 'We see different things when we look at proposals,' one board member observed, and he did not find it difficult to give examples of the different emphases of the two groups. Inflation accounting, for example, was 'all the rage in the seventies and eighties but academics now only want to teach its principles and concepts, not the technical details and specific standards, many of which are out of date anyway'. Practising accountants tend to be rather suspicious of examination innovations such as continuous assessment, fearing that they are lowering the high hurdles that they themselves had to jump when they entered the profession.

However, none of the bodies can recall deep or recurring divisions along these lines. Many of the academic members are themselves professionally qualified and often former practitioners or occasional consultants, so the identities of the two sides are usually blurred. Nevertheless, the failure, so far, to register any of the symptoms that government policy is designed to correct is somewhat curious. The informants consistently fail to identify permanent battle-lines between academics and practitioners. One accounting body carried out a systematic review of its curricula and examination standards, in which members evaluated 'blindly', and, although significant differences emerged, these did not collectively differentiate practitioners and academics.

Academics probably participate in the work of accrediting bodies with more commitment than their practitioner colleagues since they have a closer personal interest in the deliberations and decisions. Many of them see it as a way in which they can keep in touch with what is happening in other institutions. Their employers are, moreover, usually more willing than those of practitioners to tolerate the considerable time that these duties may entail. This raises the possibility that there has been a subtle, unnoticed academic take-over of the process, in which busy professional practitioners defer to the concerns and arguments of their more committed academic colleagues, so that what appears to be an external validation is in practice a comfortable form of academic self-regulation. In the grass-roots revolt of the membership of the Institute of Chartered Accountants of England and Wales (ICAE&W) in 1991 to prevent further extension of accrediting into the professional and more practical stage of their training, the suspicion was frequently aired.

In the case of engineers, this seems an improbable notion. To begin with, the evaluation of degree proposals includes a number of formal checks to ensure that the degree or course submitted for accreditation gives details of the employment pattern of students, of staff links with industry, of contact with practising engineers during the planning of the proposals and of student exposure to current industrial practice via visits, industrially related projects and workshops.

Moreover, at the instigation of the Engineering Council, engineering departments seeking accreditation for their degrees have been encouraged to establish permanent industrial advisory boards, preferably formally constituted with special responsibilities for the supervision and assessment of project work. Currently, for example, about one-third of engineering faculties seeking the approval of the Institution of Mechanical Engineers have formally established such bodies, which meet regularly and comment freely on the work of the departments; about one-third have informal and casual arrangements which the institution is urging be put on a formal and regular footing; and about one-third have neither formal nor informal institutional arrangements and rely on personal contacts between staff and practising engineers, through consultancy, visits or placements.

In these circumstances, it seems difficult to imagine how the academics could take over the accreditation process. Among accountants and solicitors, the practitioner involvement is neither as formal nor as extensive as among engineers and there is therefore more possibility of the academics getting their own way. Certainly, there is more suspicion among accountants: hence the ICAE&W grass-roots revolt against the accrediting of professional stage courses.

In general, academics and practitioners do not seem to constitute separate, let alone adversary, parties, but two branches of the same profession, with a very large measure of agreement about the proper content of the academic foundation of university education. They have little difficulty in establishing rules and conventions about the evaluation of degrees. In short, it seems to be an effective and legitimate form of partnership and, since the decisions of these bodies are never contested beyond the occasional protest of a dean or principal, one must assume that it enjoys a fair degree of legitimacy. There has been no inkling of the kind of protest sometimes made by American colleges (Velvel 1992).

Professional and public interest

This apparent legitimacy does not rest on state authority. In both theory and practice, it has sometimes proved difficult to disentangle public and private power in discussions of professional regulation. Since the power of the professions derives from their charters, they can, in a sense, all be said to be dependent on delegated state power. However, one can only observe that boards do not behave as though they are acting with any form of public authority. The only reference to statutory authority has been a reminder from a Law Society informant that the Society exercised accrediting powers with regard to training (i.e. the more practical training that follows the first degree) under the Solicitors Act. Otherwise, the institution is remarkable for absence of appeal to statutory or legal supports. There are no civil servants on accrediting committees and panels, there is no reporting to government departments, no statutory basis for their decisions and no appellate process for aggrieved applicants.

The entire process seems to be an exclusively professional one. There are no interested lay persons to represent the public interest. While such persons may be involved in umbrella organizations that have ultimate responsibility for the exercise of the powers of the professional bodies, they are not involved in the day-to-day accrediting work. If the public interest is involved, then it has still to be determined by discussion and negotiation between the teaching and practising branches of the profession.

In Britain there has never been much evidence of a definable public concern or public interest in the standard or content of degrees, except in the rather remote sense that it is in the public interest to have properly qualified professionals. In the United States, the public interest was evident to a greater extent from the very beginning of both medical and legal accreditation, for reasons already mentioned. The proliferation of professional schools meant that students might enrol for inferior or bogus professional qualifications and that patients, litigants and clients might employ their graduates. The public interest has now been extended to include affirmative action criteria and has erupted into bitter public controversies after the denial of accreditation on these grounds by one regional accrediting association to Baruch College, New York (Orlans 1993).

In Britain, however, degree proposals have never been assessed on such grounds, only on the more immediate and exclusively professional basis of having confidence in the knowledge, skills and competence of future colleagues. Minority representation on existing degree courses or elsewhere in the college has not been a criterion by which a degree has been accredited. However, as the NCVQ extends its powers to connect all professional qualifications to its proposed national grid of vocational qualifications, public interest criteria will become more explicit in accreditation procedures.

The NCVQ requires that there be a demonstrable connection between any required syllabus and the knowledge actually used by those who are qualified by it. The accountancy accrediting bodies are therefore engaged in a minute analysis and ranking of the distinct 'competences' actually utilized by their members and a consequent revision of the courses. Moreover, the NCVQ applies positive, equal opportunities criteria in the evaluation of the work of all subsidiary accrediting agencies and is hostile towards any traditional assessment arrangements that might disadvantage applicants on grounds of age, physical or sensory disabilities or learning difficulties, or of having to interrupt their vocational training.

Over the long run, the effect of the NCVQ procedures will be to deemphasize and limit professional judgement in the process of accreditation since the evaluation of the degree will come to depend more on survey research and the state agency that has instigated, commissioned and approved its findings than on senior, experienced members of the professions who have donated their time to accrediting bodies. Universities will pre-sumably frame their proposals with these 'competences' in mind. In that case it is difficult to see why accrediting panels need to be recruited at all, since anyone with the ability to interpret survey data could do it, recent graduates or even civil servants.

However that may be, accrediting bodies still behave at present as though their power exclusively derives from, and is exercised exclusively on behalf of, the members of their profession. The ultimate explanation of difficult decisions is usually 'our responsibility to our members', the ultimate barrier 'what the profession will live with'. Moreover, the whole accrediting pro-cedure is described and explained with an ideology that emphasizes its voluntary and advisory nature, the give and take and the dialogue that it involves with those submitting the application. Decisions are said to rest on convincing argument, on persuasion and consent, 'even if we do have teeth and sometimes use them'. In a sense, the relationship with the institution seems to borrow much from the relations between individual professional practitioners and their clients. There is often an element of control in the professional–client relationship and, for obvious reasons, accrediting simi-larly cannot be an entirely voluntary and cooperative procedure.

Failure to secure accreditation may mean that the degrees or courses in question are not viable and will have to be amended or abandoned. The number of non-accredited degrees appears to be declining. An engineering dean referred to accreditation as 'a bandwagon that's rolling' and pointed out that applicants are now more likely than they once were to ask whether a given degree is accredited. A member of an accrediting board claimed that more employing organizations now insist on their engineers having IMechE and CEng status: 'It's make or break for their careers . . . it's the qualification for upper echelons of managers.' Obviously, if these comments prove to be correct there will be a progressive increase in the power of the boards as universities lose the option of continuing with non-accredited degrees and courses.

Whether that is true or not, the professional, collegial ideology seems to be important to the continuation of accreditation in its present form, since it depends largely on the goodwill and voluntary participation of members of the profession. Most accrediting bodies have had some difficulty in at-tracting and keeping practitioners – especially the more senior, experienced and successful representatives of the profession that they prefer. One ac-counting body considered paying its volunteers but shelved its plans when it found that members, especially non-graduate members, felt it was their duty to help their profession in this way. One of their officers suggested that the difference between graduates and non-graduates in this respect was that 'the non-graduates feel they owe everything they have, everything they are, to their professional body and therefore have a stronger sense of obligation . . . they feel they should repay their debt to their profession so to speak. Graduates don't seem to feel this so strongly, if at all.'

The practitioners who donate their time usually serve as individual members of their profession rather than as representatives of their companies, although in accounting there is a more committed sub-group who are training managers or partners from the large firms. The primary interest of the practitioners seems to be the future individual members of the profession. Although they refer to providing the sorts of engineers or accountants that firms or industries need, the notion that they are ensuring that an individual has the basic academic skills to make a successful career seems to be deeply embedded. Employers are, in fact, rarely mentioned by name and seem to play only a secondary part and then in only rather exceptional circumstances, such as when the proposal to an engineering board comes from an institution adjacent to a large employer of its graduates. In these circumstances it helps an institution if the relationship can be seen to lend support to a proposal. One engineering panel, for instance, disliked the amount of continuous assessment in a proposal since in their view it gave insufficient guarantees as to standards. However, on hearing that the local employer was entirely happy with the quality of its graduates and the course was supported by employers, 'We still had doubts but we gave way.'

Employers may, of course, exercise influence in a number of other ways, for instance via endowed chairs or student sponsorship. And they have the opportunity to shape professional education during the training stage that follows the academic foundation provided by a university degree. The Law Society is currently reforming its training stage and intends to involve local practitioners extensively. A more thorough study of accrediting might also reveal a significant difference between professions that have a small number of very large firms, the most notable instance being the Institute of Chartered Accountants of England and Wales, and those that still have significant numbers of small partnerships or fee-for-service practitioners, such as the Law Society. Initially at least, there does not appear to be a defined employer interest in the academic stage of professional education that can be sharply distinguished from that of academics. There is therefore nothing comparable with the collective action of American employers to make engineering education more to their liking, which involved a virtual takeover of the professional associations (Layton 1969: 54–5).

Does it change anything?

The final and most important question is: what might the effects of accreditation be? This is not easy to answer. To begin with there is an impact on educational institutions prior to the submission of the proposal, a sort of anticipatory editing and evaluation, a self-censorship exercised as those proposing the course endeavour to present something that they think will be acceptable to the accrediting body. Obviously, it is difficult to pin down this process. Moreover, the entire accrediting procedure is confidential; there are no public records of rejected and amended proposals that would enable one to determine in exactly what way the accreditation process made universities amend their original proposals. The key evidence would be provided by asking representative sample institutions to disclose what they wished to do but could not do and what they were forced to do by the conditions attached to the accreditation.

Awaiting this kind of evidence, one may first note the case against the process, namely that it prevents or restrains curriculum innovation, that it imposes an undesirable standardization in professional degrees. And since accreditation panels exclude younger members who might be more *au fait* with current practice in favour of more experienced practitioners who have 'some authority, some clout', the charge can be made that they are out of date, defenders of traditional and conservative curricula rather than agents of change.

On the basis of a very limited number of interviews, it is only possible to observe that board members are sensitive to the charge that they might be imposing an undesirable uniformity or preventing innovation, and strongly affirm that they have no wish or reason to use their power in this manner. They are noticeably more prescriptive when talking about staff/student ratios, examination arrangements, the philosophy, structure and coherence of a proposal, or library and other support facilities than when talking about the content of degree curricula. Both the accountants and the solicitors reasonably defend themselves by pointing out that their core requirements refer only to part of a degree and any institution that wishes to innovate still has plenty of opportunity to do so elsewhere in the degree. Both engineers and accountants can point to the introduction of new management courses in recent years to rebut the charge that they resist curriculum innovation, though this is an ambiguous defence. In both cases these seem to have been the product of external prompting: by the Finniston Report in the case of engineers and by an inquiry prompted by the NCVQ into 'competences' in the case of accountants. All three, however, have accepted cooperation with other disciplines, such as business studies or languages, in their degrees and in corroboration point to the diversity of the curricula they have approved.

Innovations must, however, ultimately stop when they threaten the core of specialist knowledge that anyone aspiring to be an engineer, accountant or solicitor must master before he or she can be allowed to proceed to the practical part of the training. All see themselves as the custodians of this essential knowledge and are resolute in its defence. One ground for objecting to an engineering proposal is that it does not contain the core amount of mechanical engineering that is considered necessary for an accredited degree.

We'll say to them, 'If you don't include thermodynamics or thermo-fluids in your course, we regard them as vital and essential, sorry we will reject your application but you might try and accredit with another engineering body.' Or we might observe that the final year project doesn't have sufficient engineering. It is too open-ended, and must be integrated with the rest of the programme. We rarely have to say this twice. Now and then, a university will fire a shot across the bows to innovate and see if we will accept it. Sometimes yes, sometimes no. They take it back and revise it. They fly a kite and hope we might bend our rules. We can't. It's a responsibility to our membership.

An accounting board member admitted that there might be a certain 'lag' in responding to curriculum innovations: 'After all we accredit on behalf of six accounting professional bodies and have to carry them all with us, but don't get the idea we are stopping curriculum leaders. We're putting barriers against those who rush into the field with insufficient thought or resources.' This idea that the board is a defence against hasty administrative decisions rather than bold curriculum innovations of teachers also surfaced in the engineers' comments. There is a body of opinion among them favouring more innovation via a four-year master of engineering degree. They are therefore unanimously hostile to the idea of a two-year degree, aired recently by a minister.

Until the evidence for the prosecution is collected and presented these views seem to offer a plausible and persuasive defence. Accreditation provides a courteous collegial and continuous working relationship between academics and practitioners, enlists substantial voluntary support, relies to a considerable extent on discussion, consent and trust, interprets its mandate flexibly, accepts well-considered innovations that respect core or fundamental disciplinary knowledge and helps to communicate best practice through the system. Sometimes it defends academics against administrators and may even be prepared to do so against the state. It is also administered by self-effacing secretariats and has the tacit consent, at least, of the governed.

A historical and political issue

Clearly, we still have much to learn about the way accreditation has prevented or promoted change within universities, and about the relationships that it has created and is still creating between academic institutions and the world of work; especially, one might add, among engineers, since they seem to be the most innovative of the three professions considered here in making accreditation the basis of an extensive and permanent set of relationships between academics and practitioners. On both historical and policy grounds there is a strong case for trying to learn more about it.

Over the past decade state control has been extended not only over higher education in the manner described above, but also over the practitioners' own corporate bodies, especially for solicitors (Burrage 1992c). Accreditation has not escaped this extension of state power. The ever-extending reach of the NCVQ has been mentioned above but there are other examples in the accreditation of lawyers, teachers and social workers via the Lord Chancellor's Advisory Committee, the Council for the Accreditation of Teacher Education and the Central Council for Education and

Training in Social Workers. Collectively, these constitute a shift in the balance of public and private power of considerable historical significance and merit further research simply so that we may better understand what has happened in recent years.

They merit attention on political grounds because public policy in a democracy consists of an informed choice between alternatives and there clearly is a choice to be made between the forms of government and finance imposed on the universities and their accrediting arrangements with professions. These are not, to be sure, alternative ways of performing identical functions. However, their aims overlap, since both are endeavouring to relate academic curricula to the world of work, while the means by which they have sought to do this are strikingly different. The Government puts all its faith in change from above, in new imperative and contractual relationships, whereas accreditation rests on a shared interest in a particular body of knowledge, on professional collegiality and common interest. Whatever changes it may promote obviously rely more on participation and consent.

If there is to be any sensible discussion and review of present policy, we must identify the relative strengths and weaknesses of these two methods of change, their appropriate spheres of competence and their future promise.

References

Barnett, C. (1986) *The Audit of War: the Illusion and Reality of Britain as a Great Nation.* London, Macmillan.

Burrage, M. (1992a) 'States as users of knowledge: engineers and lawyers in France and England', in R. Torstendahl (ed.) *State Theory and State History.* London, Sage.

Burrage, M. (1992b) 'From practice to school-based professional education: patterns of conflict and accommodation in England, France, and the United States', in S. Rothblatt and B. Wittrock (eds) *Universities in Europe and North America.* Cambridge, Cambridge University Press.

Burrage, M. (1992c) 'Mrs Thatcher against deep structures: ideology, impact and ironies of her eleven-year confrontation with the professions', Institute of Governmental Studies Working Paper, University of California, Berkeley.

Burrage, M., Jarausch, K. and Siegrist, H. (1990) 'An actor-based framework for the study of the professions', in M. Burrage and R. Torstendahl (eds) *Professions in Theory and History: Rethinking the Study of the Professions.* London, Sage.

de Ville, H.G. (chairman) (1986) *Review of Vocational Qualifications in England and Wales.* Report by the Working Group. London, HMSO.

Duffy, C. (1979) *Siege Warfare: the Fortress in the Early Modern World 1494–1660.* London, Routledge and Kegan Paul.

Finniston Report (1980) *Engineering Our Future,* Cmnd 7794. London, HMSO.

Layton, E. (1969) 'Science, business and the American engineer', in R. Perrucci and J.E. Gerstl (eds) *The Engineers and the Social System.* New York, Wiley.

Lundgreen, P. (1990) 'Engineering education in Europe and the USA, 1750–1930: the rise to dominance of school culture and the engineering professions', *Annals of Science,* 47(1), 33–75.

Noble, D.F. (1977) *America By Design: Science, Technology and the Rise of Corporate Capitalism.* Oxford, Oxford University Press.

Orlans, H. (1992) 'Accreditation in higher education: the issue of diversity', *Minerva*, 30(4), 512–30.

Prais, S.J. and Steedman, H. (1985) 'Vocational training in France and Britain: the building trades', National Institute of Economic and Social Research Discussion Paper No. 105.

Simon, B. (1988) *Bending the Rules: the Baker Reform of Education.* London, Lawrence and Wishart.

Stewart, W.A.C. (1989) *Higher Education in Postwar Britain.* London, Macmillan.

Van den Berghe, W. (1986) *Engineering Manpower.* Paris, UNESCO.

Velvel, L.R. (1992) *The Deeply Unsatisfactory Nature of Legal Education Today: a Self-study Report on the Problems of Legal Education and on the Steps the Massachusetts School of Law Has Taken to Overcome Them.* Andover, Massachusetts School of Law.

Weiner, M.J. (1985) *English Culture and the Decline of the Industrial Spirit, 1850–1980.* Harmondsworth, Penguin.

Woodworth, R.J. (1973) 'Some influences on the reform of schools of law and medicine, 1890 to 1930', *Sociological Quarterly*, 14, 496–516.

Conclusion

10

Freedom and Accountability in Professional Curricula

Tony Becher

Introduction

In this concluding chapter, an attempt will be made to draw together a number of the salient points made by the previous contributions, and to relate them to the theme of professional accountability. This concept shares with that of professionality itself a wealth of different interpretations (Becher and Maclure 1979; Kogan 1988). It will here be taken to relate specifically to the obligation of professionals, individually and collectively, to justify their actions and decisions to legitimate audiences.

These audiences can conveniently be categorized, paraphrasing Becher *et al.* (1981), as fellow professionals, government agencies or employers, and clients (as we shall see later, they comprise a subset of the key interest groups noted by contributors, but omitting or eliding some of them). According to the same source, the corresponding forms of accountability can be designated as professional (or collegial), contractual (or political) and moral. The first of these – the acknowledgement by the individual of his or her obligations to members of the same occupational group – is relatively uncontested, and is given concrete expression in the existence of professional associations whose functions include the promotion of collective interests and the maintenance of a favourable public image. It calls among other things for a level of conduct that does not bring the profession itself into disrepute. The third, moral accountability, is concerned with answerability to the individuals or organizations to whom the professional concerned provides specialist services. In its traditional form, that answerability has tended to be guarded, limited and conducted mainly on the provider's terms. A steady diminution in public trust, and in the willingness of individuals to be treated in an apparently patronizing manner, has in recent years encouraged consumers to take a more militant and questioning stance.

It is, however, with contractual or political accountability – and in particular with the relationship between governmental agencies and the professions – that this volume is by definition primarily concerned. Even allowing for the evident differences between national traditions which influence the relationships between the state and professional activity, and the comparably significant contrasts between the nature and standing of individual professions, there is a general consensus among contributors that this form of accountability is growing in strength and significance, at least in Western European countries.

The means by which governments, whether national, regional or local, set out to control the activities of the professions are many and diverse, as are the motives for seeking such control. What many of them have in common is a focus on education and training and on certification – that is, the conditions under which specialized (and marketable) qualifications are awarded. The training institutions, even where they are not under the direct authority of a government agency, are relatively easy targets because of their significant dependence on public funds and, in many countries, on other forms of state patronage. So it is with the curricula of professional programmes (taking the term in its widest sense to include access, teaching resources and examinations as well as the nature of what is taught) that the following discussion is centrally concerned. The closely related process of accreditation – the ways in which course provision is monitored and approved – is a major theme running through a number of contributions, but given particular attention in those by Burrage and El-Khawas.

For the rest, the nature of professionalism itself, and some of the issues to which it gives rise, the tensions between theory and practice in professional education, and questions of relative status and its implications, are among the other themes singled out for brief discussion.

Characteristics and issues of professionalism

In a sharp caricature of traditional sentiments about the professions, Siegrist begins his chapter by portraying them as reflecting 'core values', and applying 'rational knowledge . . . "regardless of person" ', as comprising the elite of secularized culture, reflecting the processes of modernism and rationalism. He goes on to remind his readers that the ideal concept of a profession embodies both expertise and a sense of ethical values (including impartiality and altruism), and presupposes a specialized educational background. Professions, viewed within this frame of reference, monitor their own standards, and enjoy 'freedom from external supervision' as well as control over their admissions and licensing. Being the unique providers of certain specialized services, they are able to lay claim to special rewards and status.

This predominantly Parsonian view, as Siegrist goes on to argue, has been strongly contested in subsequent sociological literature, to which Johnson (1972) and Larson (1977) are among the most frequently cited contributors. It is possible, as this body of material suggests, to portray the professions in a much less favourable light, as power-seeking, self-interested guilds concerned with the colonization and mystification of areas of knowledge as well as with the vigorous pursuit of financial advantage, and ready to protect their own members, save in cases of extreme and evident misconduct, against the legitimate grievances of their clients.

Which interpretation is adopted – or whether some intermediate position would appear more credible – will be at least to some extent a function of the reader's own experience and set of values. What is not perhaps seriously in contest is that, as both Taylor's and Torstendahl's accounts underline, the exercise of any profession is dependent on both particular knowledge and specialized techniques or skills, and that its collective interests are affected by its forms of organization and the degree to which it can remain selective and exclusive. On the latter issues of organization and exclusion, Torstendahl gives an interesting historical account of the emergence of professional engineering bodies in Britain as primarily social gatherings of employers, whose membership of elite groups afforded them a value on the market: it was only later that practitioners were admitted to the various specialized institutes and that entry was controlled by public examinations.

In a number of countries, as Siegrist points out, professions were from their early stages of emergence controlled by governmentally established councils, which did not necessarily perform the same functions as autonomous professional bodies. In some cases, accordingly, voluntary associations sprang up to complement, or sometimes to compete with, the councils themselves. The picture is confused and untidy: in Britain alone, different patterns currently exist between medicine (with the General Medical Council as a statutory body and the British Medical Association as an up-market trade union), education (with unrequited aspirations for a General Teaching Council, an existing official accreditation body, as described by Taylor, and a number of competing teachers' unions) and social work (with a publicly appointed accrediting body and no strong countervailing professional association). Siegrist draws a contrast here between 'leading privately practising professions' and others, in their relative reluctance to introduce union-like organizations as against seemingly more prestigious professional bodies.

Regardless of forms of organization, it was the case in many countries that protectionist attitudes, closed entry and continuing political demands for autonomy and for the sanctioning of special privileges persisted well into the post-war period. They were, however, increasingly contested by changing political and public values, and perhaps even – as Henkel implies – by a newly emergent philosophical world-view. She goes on to argue that, on an international scale, 'the combined forces of managerialism, market philosophies, consumerism and concomitant social change' are having their effect on the boundaries, roles and power of the professions. More specifically, Taylor notes that free-market economists in the early 1970s were already suggesting that professions constitute 'a producer's monopoly which works against the interest of consumers'.

What all this seems to amount to is a significant shift in traditional attitudes towards, and conventional notions of, professionality (Burrage and
Torstendahl 1990). In general, the air of respect with which the pronounce-
ments of doctors, lawyers, teachers and the like may in the past have been
greeted seems to have been replaced by a more questioning stance on the
part of both clients and representatives of government. If professions are,
as a number of contributors suggest, being opened up by deregulation to
wider market competition and in many countries are subject at the same
time to closer official scrutiny, then certain evident consequences follow for
the process of initial education and training. It is accordingly to a review of
what previous chapters have had to say on the issue of professional knowledge that we shall now turn.

Pure and applied knowledge

Any profession embodies both theoretical and practical skills, but the balance
between them varies significantly from one to another; so, not surprisingly,
does the nature of the interplay between the two in the process of initial
education and training (Becher 1990). Perhaps particularly in the UK, now
long dominated by an uncompromisingly utilitarian administration, the
theory–practice division is – as Henkel argues – becoming blurred. The
emphasis on 'transferable skills' is, she points out, altering the perceived
relationship 'between the university and the world of work . . . so that
they are no longer distinct'. In tracing the philosophical underpinnings of
this move to promote the status of practical experience, she points to 'a
shared need to reconceptualize the relationship between pure and applied
knowledge'.

Taylor's chapter documents a series of changes in initial teacher education,
and shows certain similarities to Henkel's account of social work. As he
acknowledges, 'the education of all kinds of teachers is now fully integrated
into university level studies' in many countries. There is, however, a strong
countervailing tendency in England and Wales for the central authorities to
insist on a predominantly school-based pattern of training, in which the
academic component is relegated to a minor and subsidiary role. This owes
more to a political distrust of what is portrayed as bogus and irrelevant
theorizing than it does to the concept, derived from the research of Schön
(1987) and others, of the reflective practitioner drawing primarily upon
'knowledge-in-action'.

There are evident dangers in downplaying the knowledge element and
according practical experience too great a degree of primacy in professional
curricula. The main ones lie in the consequent limitations in developing a
coherent conceptual framework, as opposed to a mere collection of rules of
thumb, and in the associated difficulties of conducting systematic and critical
investigations into alternative professional strategies. An over-reliance
on craft skills and established tradition may also stand in the way of

much-needed changes to ingrained but outdated practice. There is of course the inverse problem of a tendency towards over-academicization in professional schools, to which consideration also needs to be given. At this point, however, it is useful to recall not only the great variety between one profession and another in the resolution of the theory–practice balance, but also the remarkable disparities to be found within a single professional field.

The point is perhaps most clearly underlined in Lonbay's account of legal education, which (unlike the initial stages of a number of other vocational subjects, including nursing as well as social work and teaching) currently tends to separate the academic component quite sharply from the practical. As his comparative analyses of the length of professional training in the law between different EC countries clearly demonstrate, the ratios between university-based and post-university provision vary considerably. Spain is placed at one extreme, showing a balance entirely in favour of academic study (with a five-year degree course and no practical requirement before qualification). The UK, not surprisingly, represents the other extreme, with an even weighting between the two (three years for the degree and another three to attain qualified status). The UK, along with Italy, enjoys the shortest total training period, and also the shortest degree programme, with four other countries requiring two years longer. On this evidence, harmonization of curricula seems still a long way off.

It is Vang's contribution that offers the fullest discussion of the dilemmas to which a strong emphasis on theoretical training for professionals gives rise. In medicine, he suggests, it is the imperatives of biomedical research which have created an unstable cycle of development in which academic issues have been overemphasized and professional values distorted. The lure and the rewards of research activity tend to take senior staff away from undergraduate teaching, leaving students in the hands of junior teachers with relatively little experience of either frontline enquiry or medical practice. His observations on the need for a shift from the current emphasis on curing disease to one on promoting health are of particular interest, linked as they are to proposed changes in the curriculum and in the way in which practitioners would have to carry out their work. He sees a shift towards problem-based learning as a promising way forward, particularly if developed in conjunction with the use of sophisticated data retrieval systems and open learning techniques. Among its direct benefits, this promises to encourage a move back to something like an earlier apprenticeship model and to promote a closer relationship between research and teaching. It should also leave more space to develop the kinds of teamwork and communication skills demanded by a growing, and to a large degree governmentally sponsored, emphasis on primary care.

An imbalance in professional curricula towards an overly academic approach may result in part from a concern, in the university setting, of the staff involved to comply with the norms and expectations of colleagues in non-vocational subjects (Harman 1989). On the basis of Vang's arguments, the result may be for research requirements to distract attention from teaching and to distort the curriculum by tilting it in the direction of esoteric knowledge with little or no practical relevance. But too drastic a shift in the opposite direction, as portrayed by Henkel, involving 'a substantial shift of power from the higher education sector', has its own attendant penalties. The more that professional and post-professional courses are deregulated to include programmes entirely based on the workplace, and the more higher education is relegated to a service role, the weaker the pretensions become of social work to aspire to the title of a profession. Indeed, as Henkel acknowledges, only a minuscule proportion of social workers embark on post-qualifying courses, and the Government's rejection in 1988 of a proposal to increase the two-year basic training period to three has effectively removed the hopes of classifying social work as a profession under the terms of the relevant EC directive. The effects of these considerations on the quality of recruitment remain to be systematically explored, though it seems easy enough to predict them.

It is perhaps significant that the question of an overemphasis on theoretical issues has arisen in this volume in relation to medicine, while the issue of an undue weighting on practical experience has been most clearly underlined in connection with teaching and social work. The inference seems to be that the distinction is connected with the relative status of various professions. It is that question which may next be usefully addressed.

Matters of status

The social standing accorded to a profession is of considerable significance. The higher its status, the greater the degree of public trust it is likely to enjoy; and since trust is closely related to accountability, the more it is likely to be allowed the freedom to pursue its own affairs. Conversely, where the level of trust is reduced – as seems to be happening in the USA in relation to law and medicine – there are increased demands for the imposition of external controls and a diminution in the esteem in which members of the professional community are held.

A number of contributions highlight the key factors that help to determine status. One of the most obvious is the degree to which the relevant knowledge base is seen as 'hard' rather than 'soft', technical, specialized and arcane rather than straightforward and commonsensical. Medicine scores highly on this count, while some of the more marginal professions, such as nursing, social work and teaching, suffer from the tendency of lay persons to consider that, without much difficulty, they could tackle the job as well as those who claim to be qualified. The use of technical jargon – a notable characteristic of both law and medicine – can be seen as a useful device for mystification in this context.

As far as engineering is concerned, Torstendahl's chapter brings home the emphasis in continental countries on formal technical education, reflecting a belief in 'not only know-how but also, or rather, know-what'. Graduation from a teaching institution, even in the early nineteenth century, was an asset on the labour market and 'a mark of status of great importance'. He contrasts the contemporary situation in Britain, where theoretical knowledge was not much valued, and where – as Burrage notes – 'compared with engineers abroad they were accorded an extremely low status in both industry and British society at large'. A similar contrast is drawn by Henkel in her references to the 'strong and prestigious' intellectual base for social work in Germany, developed within the pedagogic professional tradition in continental Europe, as against a knowledge structure lacking in rigour and 'susceptible to shifts in dominant ideologies', which condemns British social work to marginality.

Graduate qualifications undoubtedly play some part in the quest for raising professional prestige, as the recent pressure in the UK to establish new university departments in such fields as accountancy, pharmacy and nursing implies. The failure of social work in Britain to establish itself in the graduate sector undoubtedly set back its hopes of improved recognition; but on the other hand, the fact that teaching became an all-graduate profession in the 1970s does not seem greatly to have improved its image. And while architecture is a well-regarded profession in Sweden, it is noted by Svensson as having the lowest proportion of graduates among the six professions he discusses. Within the same country, Elzinga (1990) argues that the move towards 'the scientification of nursing knowledge' in an effort to enhance the image of nursing may have backfired by cutting off research from 'its necessary base in daily practice'. On this miscellaneous evidence it would seem that education to degree level is an inconclusive factor in achieving recognition as a well-established profession.

A public image of respectability – perhaps indeed of some degree of conservatism – is another consideration. The emphasis noted by Taylor on 'the teacher as an agent of progressive social and political change', and the accompanying 'wish to demystify professional power', will have done little to halt the decline in the credibility of teaching. Equally, the 'egalitarian and anti-intellectualist lobby' that Henkel identifies in British social work is a further element in casting doubt on its pretensions as a profession.

The term 'closure' is used in sociological writing to denote a form of exclusiveness which not only screens entry to a group but demarcates it effectively from its potential rivals and competitors. One of the main stages in the development of a profession, as Torstendahl's case study of engineering demonstrates, is to employ closure to achieve a specialized and protected title that clearly identifies membership and imposes significant demands on its achievement. Medicine offers a good example of both processes, whereas social work – in Britain at least – shows the opposite tendency. It lacks, in Henkel's words, 'an authoritative definition of professional boundaries' and its sphere of operation is numerically dominated by unskilled or semi-skilled care staff.

The extent of apparent unity and coherence within the professional group is another element in the complex determination of status levels. Here again British social work would appear to score badly, revealing its domestic quarrels to the public view in a politically inept manner. This tendency has for the most part been successfully avoided even by those established professions that are internally divided into hospital doctors and general practitioners, barristers and solicitors, several varieties of engineer, and so on. Teaching in the UK does not come out well on this score either, in that it is fragmented into a number of rival and often flagrantly competing unions. Public confidence, which is, as suggested earlier, a significant element in the determination of professional credibility, is readily destroyed when the veneer of collective unity is seen to have been split. This in turn can trigger off demands to install accountability procedures.

The existence of a sizeable private sector is touched on by a number of contributors as a factor relevant to professional status. As Henkel argues, 'Professional autonomy is far easier to sustain by the large numbers of social workers employed in voluntary organizations' in Germany, as against 'the overwhelming majority employed by the state' in Britain and Scandinavia. As earlier noted, those working in private practice have tended to favour professional associations, rather than unions, in what Siegrist describes as 'their fight against outside control on the part of the state'. Statutory general councils have served, he suggests, in the uncomfortable dual role of 'a useful instrument of indirect control' for governments and 'a means to safeguarding their autonomy' for professions. The existence of such a body is itself an indicator of status, denied to and sought after by those groups who have not yet achieved full professional recognition.

The granting of official licences to practise is another symbol of exclusivity. The absence of licensing for social workers in all but three EC countries (Germany, Greece and Luxembourg) is taken by Henkel as a sign of a lack of official endorsement, while Svensson records that only doctors and psychologists in Sweden are certificated: the other four professional groups discussed in his chapter (lawyers, architects, teachers and social workers) are not.

It would appear, then, that the acquisition of professional credibility, and the status that accompanies it, is a subtle exercise not easily reduced to a simple set of procedural rules. The type of specialized knowledge involved is undeniably an important factor, but not a determining one. Political issues also appear to loom large, in the sense that recognition can be seen as calling upon the careful management of a collective image as well as embodying a struggle for power and influence. The exploration of the various interests concerned is a relevant issue here.

Significant interest groups

Three contributors make a point of reviewing the main interest groups involved in the process of professionalization and the subsequent controls exercised on professional activity. In the case of social work in Britain,

which lacks an institutionalized profession within which standards and criteria could be established, Henkel identifies the other key agencies (with
whom the relevant training council had to achieve 'a negotiated order') as
public sector unions, higher education and local government (the main
employers). Burrage, writing on professions more generally, lists as 'interested
parties or major players': practitioners and professors (those who apply
specialist knowledge and those who purvey it); the state; and the users
(clients, employers and the like). Siegrist comes up with a very similar
grouping: members of the profession and their associations; educational
institutions; state/government and the legislature; clients and client organizations; and the media and public opinion.

The relative importance of these diverse groups varies over time, across
nations and between one profession and another. El-Khawas records the
limited role of the US federal government in issues of professional education,
but notes that state governments are substantially involved, as are a number
of private agencies. Burrage observes that British employers have traditionally
taken little interest in the content and certification of professional programmes in engineering. As against this, Henkel portrays the employers –
in the case of social work comprising almost exclusively local government
agencies – as playing a central role. Here, the uncertain status of the profession itself has been further undermined by its inability clearly to demarcate
its boundaries with other miscellaneous groups involved in social care. In
Germany, as Torstendahl points out, the professional association of engineers
– the *Verein Deutscher Ingenieure* – waged a notably successful political
campaign to raise the status of engineering education. Its British counterparts were less effective in promoting the interests of their members in this
respect.

While the groups concerned are for the most part engaged in a discreet
process of jockeying for political advantage, the relationships between them
occasionally become conflictual – as in the case of the divergent attitudes
of local authorities and higher education institutions during the 1970s
towards the increasing academic emphasis in social work training in the
UK. It would seem that something of a zero-sum game is played out in this
particular arena. Thus, as Lonbay suggests, as the influence of government
decreases that of the profession is enhanced, and the universities tend to
gain greater control over curricular policy. Svensson refers to another source
of tension, namely that between 'the power of the faculties' and 'the position
of the practitioners and . . . the associations'. Here again, academicization is
the issue at stake.

Client interests seem to be most effectively deployed where the profession
itself is weak. In teaching, Taylor draws attention to left-wing concerns to
'demystify professional power in the interests of greater democratic participation in schooling' and to open the schools to community control. On
the right, the system is assailed with demands for 'greater parental choice
and the importation of market disciplines'. In England and Wales, political
intervention has been deployed to support the latter demands, imposing

extensive changes on teacher education, including the introduction of competency-based courses and institutional accreditation. As El-Khawas also indicates in the very different context of the USA, the level of accountability in this field is high to the point of becoming counter-productive.

Where the professional group is more strongly entrenched, as in the case of medicine, Vang suggests that the state may decide to intervene on behalf of the clients, interpreting their needs and acting in what appear to be their interests. Hence there is a growing policy emphasis, in medical education, on a reorientation towards primary health care, based on a concern with 'the extent to which [the health care system] reflects social values, and perhaps also the political values of the government'. It is, however, noticeable, in a comparison of his account with Taylor's, how much more circumspectly the powers of the relevant authorities are deployed than they are in the case of teaching. These are, however, only two examples of a much wider issue concerning the power relationships between governments and the professions.

Patterns of state–professional relationship

History can be seen to play a major part in the interplay between professional agencies and the state. The form that this interplay takes is, predictably, variable between one nation and another, but both Siegrist and Burrage identify three main traditions, originating respectively in continental Europe, the UK and the USA. Without any direct collusion, the accounts they offer are broadly similar.

Siegrist writes of the continental European governments in the late eighteenth and early nineteenth centuries as establishing 'a rational and unified state apparatus of rule, government, law and culture'. As part of the process, central legislation drastically transformed the existing and subsequently established professions, imposing compulsory curricula, examinations and licensing regulations, and controlling the structure of the employment market. In the early stages, training was limited to that provided by the state-controlled professional schools, which was predominantly theoretical: it was only later that the requirement for practical experience before qualification was added. Burrage locates the origins of this process of governmental appropriation in Napoleonic France, singling out engineers, lawyers and the medical profession as prime examples.

Burrage contrasts the history of professionalism in Britain as one in which 'the state was content to let private individuals . . . organize their profession as they saw fit', adding that its 'responsibilities and interest extended little beyond granting the representative body of practitioners power of self-government'. Siegrist similarly identifies the key features as close collegiality, functioning in a context of 'decentralized elites and a weak state', with strongly autonomous professional associations which defined entry qualifications and supervised ethical standards and conduct.

The American approach was different again. Here, as Siegrist notes, 'the institutions which had been imported from England were swept away by the egalitarian movement of the 1830s', and liberal market principles were given freer reign, undermining 'the position of privilege enjoyed by the expert over his or her consumer'. Burrage offers a somewhat more drastic account, in which – at least for medicine and law – 'the practitioner-controlled and practice-based systems of training' were 'effectively destroyed', with the resulting collapse of most of the practitioner associations. As a result, much of the power and control over professional education passed to the universities, enabling them to 'act like entrepreneurs and sell specialist knowledge'.

In summarizing the three models, Burrage suggests that 'France has been state-led, while Britain has been practitioner-led, and the United States has been school-led.' Siegrist uses different terms, but to similar effect, writing of 'professionalization from above, by the state, in many countries on the European continent', 'the harmonious and gradual transformation of the old corporative professions in England' and 'the liberal professionalization achieved by the occupational groups in the USA'. It is perhaps worth observing the parallelism – even if not too much should be made of it – between each of these models and the three main forms of accountability outlined at the beginning of this chapter. The continental European model seems to lean heavily on contractual or political accountability to government agencies; the English model appears to emphasize professional or collegial accountability to members of the same occupational group; and the American model places greater stress on moral accountability to clients, if only through the agency of the market place.

These broad-brush presentations are further refined by Torstendahl, whose contribution draws attention to some significant historical differences not only between, for example, Germany and France in the process of professionalization of engineers, but also within France and Sweden in the types of technological education developed respectively by the state and by commercial interests. But he too underlines the relatively limited historical role of the state in Britain, confined mainly to the award of Royal Charters to favoured professional groups and the marginal involvement of the Ministry of Education in the monitoring of professional examinations in engineering. Henkel similarly confirms the directive role of continental European governments in social work – in the cases of France, Denmark and Spain amounting to legislative control of curricula and examinations – while in Britain the central training agency was allowed 'semi-independence from central government' and – at least initially – a relationship in which 'central government remained at arm's length' from the control of professional education.

Forms of and reasons for state control

It is against this historical background that the current patterns of governmental involvement in professional curricula can usefully be reviewed. The traditional relationships seem, on the evidence of previous chapters, to be changing in all three cases. In parts of continental Europe the trend is towards less direct modes of control, while in Britain intervention of various kinds has increased. The US federal government has always played a marginal role in education, but as El-Khawas indicates, state governments are now beginning to assume quite extensive powers of professional accreditation, including licensing, assessment, programme approval and external review.

Lonbay records 'considerable variation in the autonomy of institutions in curriculum matters as regards legal education', citing funding patterns and the existence of private sector institutions as important variables, but noting that in most EC member states, 'Parliament . . . establishes the basic minimum curriculum'. Control may be exerted variously through detailed specification of course content or broader approval of main topics, through state examinations or the official authorization of degree courses. However, in his judgement, 'the extent of state control has been weakening' in countries that have previously adopted a centralized approach to professional training for the law.

Examples of trends in the opposite direction in Britain are given by Burrage in relation to engineering, Taylor in respect of teaching and Henkel in connection with social work. In a rough and ready attempt to control the behaviour of universities in the direction of vocational relevance, and to contest 'the long-standing British prejudice against vocational education in general and engineering in particular', the Thatcher Government introduced strong industrial representation on the funding and governing bodies of higher education institutions (a move that Burrage notes as puzzling, since employers had previously taken little interest in technical education, despite ample opportunity to do so). Taylor's chapter documents, from a position of close, first-hand knowledge, the steady escalation since the early 1980s of political pressure on teacher education, involving not only the levels of funding for training provision and the control of qualifications but also the laying down of detailed specifications for course design and required competencies for achieving qualified status. Henkel in turn records, in the period from 1987 onwards, 'decisive moves by central government to assert its authority in social work education', including a restructuring of its central training agency and the setting out of 'agreed strategic objectives'. In both teaching and social work, educational institutions are no longer in control of the curriculum and 'performance in the workplace' is heavily emphasized.

Vang has a number of interesting comments to make on 'the government's attitude to, and policy on, knowledge formation and knowledge dissemination', seeing these as a 'fundamental factor governing the development' of the professions in general and the health services in particular. He points out that the state has a legitimate interest in medical research and development, and is able to control it through indirect measures – using mainly economic means for biomedical enquiry and statutory regulation for clinical investigations. However, he sees the tendency, which may be convenient to governments, to separate education from research as counter-productive. He also refers to the frustrations arising in many countries from over-regulation, the fragmentation of academic leadership and the concentration of power in government.

His observation that governments are properly more concerned with quantity than with quality in medical education – with avoiding 'any significant under- or over-production of physicians' and with 'the achievement of a regional balance of provision' – is echoed in relation to other professional groups. In the USA, according to El-Khawas, there has been pressure from policy-makers in some states for the introduction of 'enrolment limits in certain fields, including engineering and law'. In their concern for the recruitment of teachers from minority groups, a number of states have introduced special incentives: El-Khawas provides a detailed account of the stipulated requirements in Massachusetts. However, the tendency for government to maintain a close control of student numbers in professional fields is not universal. In Sweden, manpower planning – once a central feature of national policy in higher education – has been progressively relaxed. Moreover, as Taylor comments, 'in recent years demographic profiles and economic conditions in many developed countries have reduced the importance of teacher supply as a policy priority'. 'Government attention', he adds, 'tends now to be focused as much on quality as on quantity' – thus neatly reversing the relative priorities noted by Vang.

The control of overall numbers, however loose and approximate it may be, remains of legitimate interest both to the state authorities and to the professional associations. From the governmental point of view, an excess of students in training represents a needless expense and a potential source of articulate and troublesome unemployed people; from the profession's own point of view, it represents a potential reduction in market value. As against that, a shortage of trained professionals may give rise to strong protests from consumers (and voters), to which government would have to respond; and while the professionals themselves may be served by a modest level of under-recruitment, which tends to increase the saleability of their skills, they might beyond a certain point become heavily overburdened and find themselves having to contend with a demand for rival paraprofessional services.

In terms of attempted quality control, the National Council for Vocational Qualifications (NCVQ) is, in Burrage's estimation, a 'most ambitious state intervention' – and what is more, as a phenomenon of the Thatcher era in Britain, 'one of its more remarkable creations, indeed of any state anywhere'. Its remit is to produce appropriate competencies for all forms of vocational and professional training, classified into five levels of complexity. It promises, as Burrage graphically observes, 'to be the mother of all accrediting agencies'. Whether or not its critics are right to discern in it a threat to 'holistic and reflective conceptions of practice and a sharp downgrading of the role of higher education', it clearly exemplifies the more widespread tendency of governments to move from the control of professional education through a concern with 'input and process' to a concern with 'outcome and assessment' (as Henkel puts it); or towards deregulation of curricula accompanied by 'publicly accessible accreditation procedures, reviews and quality control problems' (according to Vang's account). Svensson offers his own variation on the same theme, when he writes of the shift, in Sweden, from a policy of structuring and regulating 'the activities of higher education in advance' to the introduction of audit and evaluation mechanisms; from 'governance *ante hoc* to governance *post hoc*'.

Accreditation processes

Accreditation, while it is a relatively novel phenomenon in continental Europe, is long established in both the United Kingdom and the USA. It takes a multiplicity of forms, encompassing both ends of the spectrum from *ante hoc* to *post hoc* control. But although there are similarities between the British and the American interpretations of the concept, there are also significant differences. In the latter, as Burrage argues, it has primarily been used to regulate a competitive market in professional credentials. In the former, it has served mainly as a means of monitoring the academic sub-contractors of professional bodies.

Historically, practitioners were able in Britain 'to assume exclusive responsibility for the training and certification of entrants to the professions'. Accreditation was 'part of the long process of adaptation and reconciliation between practitioners and professors', calling for minimal involvement of either government or the lay public. Burrage represents it in benign terms as 'a courteous, collegial and continuous working relationship between academics and practitioners', based on mutual trust and open to well-considered innovation. He finds accreditation board members to be sensitive to the charge of restraining curriculum innovation or imposing undesirable standardization. However, he acknowledges that there is a weakness in the extent to which the current system depends on good will, and especially on the involvement of 'the more senior, experienced and successful representatives of the profession'; and he notes the consequent possibility that in accountancy 'there has been a subtle, unnoticed academic takeover', reducing an apparent process of external validation to 'a comfortable form of academic self-regulation'.

Frequently expressed political concerns of 'cosiness', leading to demands for more rigorous forms of accountability, have been manifested in the less well-defended professions – notably teaching and social work – by the imposition of official accrediting agencies strongly dominated by governmental interests and politically correct lay representatives. More generally, Burrage foresees that, as NCVQ develops and extends its activities, 'public interest criteria will become more explicit in accreditation procedures', that the scope for professional judgement will be limited, and that accrediting panels will be effectively sidelined. The reductionism inherent in the insistence on measuring competencies, as against developing the conceptual understanding necessary to underpin capable professional work, suggests that the damage will not be limited only to the process of accreditation.

The chapter by El-Khawas offers a lucid guide through the complex jungle of accreditation procedures in the USA. Even though the federal government takes little part in the proceedings, the governments of individual states are active in asserting their authority over the recognition of professional courses and the monitoring of individual skills. State agencies overlap confusingly with voluntary general accrediting organizations and with bodies concerned with specific professional requirements; and practice varies widely from one state to another. State or state-approved accreditation is given enhanced importance by being tied to institutional funding procedures. Individual entrants to a profession may be subject to completion of a state-approved programme, a certifying examination, minimal course entry requirements and demands for continuing certification.

El-Khawas refers to 'the belief that state governments should not interfere in substantive academic matters', but her subsequent comments indicate the increasing specificity of state requirements. It is scarcely surprising that universities complain about an excessive degree of scrutiny, and that the critics of external review argue that it is 'both burdensome and harmful to good educational practice'. The burden has fallen heavily on the process of teacher education, for which she provides a detailed case study. Here, as elsewhere, state approval of courses is a potent mechanism, since its absence precludes subsequent entry of graduates to the profession. Many states also issue detailed guidelines for the acceptability of teacher education programmes, and some in addition stipulate minimum exit requirements. In addition, education faculties have to contend with the (non-statutory but more or less obligatory) National Council for Accreditation of Teacher Education, which enjoins them to meet eighteen standards and ninety-four criteria. Perhaps even their transatlantic counterparts, labouring under the similarly titled but statutory Council for the Accreditation of Teacher Education, whose work is described in Taylor's chapter, are not noticeably worse off.

The international dimension

One of the themes touched on by a number of contributors is the extent to which professions span national boundaries. It seems evident, from what has been written, that most if not all professions are in practice shaped by indigenous traditions and cultural expectations, even if they appear in principle to be dealing with universal issues. Lonbay, for example, observes that 'legal education transmits national cultures', while Vang points out that many medical tasks concern culture-related illnesses, and that diseases are 'to a large extent a function of local and cultural circumstances'. Both authors, however, go on to explore the contrary assertion that, in some important respects, professions and professional education are phenomena which transcend geographical boundaries. Lonbay notes that there are 'common features in the national legal orders in Europe resulting from historical connections between countries', and Vang acknowledges that 'medicine has in some of its aspects become an international discipline'.

The familiar contention that knowledge knows no frontiers is not strongly represented in this book. The emphasis, in discussing internationalization, seems to be more on convergent legislative and political structures than on common knowledge content. The European Commission is seen to have played a significant part in the process of 'harmonization' of professional qualifications, though its influence, as Lonbay observes, is often indirect. Henkel remarks that in social work Britain is characteristically out of line with the minimum training period and regulatory conditions laid down by the relevant EC general directive.

The pressure from students is seen as a potent force for convergence: Lonbay couples this with a concern to participate in 'cross-border links and courses' such as those promoted by Erasmus and Tempus. 'The advent of European Community law', he adds, 'has led to an increasing contact and mutual cooperation of legal practitioners across national borders.' Vang sees 'some degree of internationalization of initial medical education in Europe . . . as an important step towards the free movement of professionally qualified people between the European countries', and welcomes international networking as 'a strong incentive for the development of new ideas and for mutual learning'.

There seems to be no clear direction of accountability for the developments in professional education stimulated by international collaboration, except perhaps a shadowy obligation to fellow professionals and a responsiveness to students as a special category of client. So far, the European Commission has not sought to exert authoritative managerial powers, though Siegrist suggests that 'the transnational and trans-government bureaucracy of the European Community, and the lobbies circling round it, are generating new issues and forces, which present countries and professions with unfamiliar challenges'. But regardless of national relationships with Brussels, the development of closer linkages between those concerned with professional education in different countries is likely, as Vang acknowledges, to be as much dependent on language policies at the school level – or on intensive provision within university programmes – as it is on attempts to bring qualification requirements into line. And that is an issue over which it may be difficult for any government, whether national or international, to exercise any effective short-term control.

The limits of accountability

Those contributing to this volume have offered a broadly consistent picture of the relationship between governments and professional education as one involving a significant element of contractual accountability. The historic arrangements in the United Kingdom before the political and cultural watershed of the 1980s, in which successive governments chose to leave the professions to their own devices, intervening only to safeguard their monopolistic status, can be seen in retrospect as an anomaly. Even in the market-driven and decentralized culture of the USA, as El-Khawas makes plain, the governments of individual states may impose quite heavy demands on professional schools.

Eraut (1992) argues cogently that it is intrinsic to the nature of professions to be accountable, especially in terms of moral answerability to their clients. Insofar as the latter do not find it easy to defend their collective interests, action on their behalf seems reasonable enough. However, a number of contributors pose questions about how far either the market or government is an appropriate surrogate. The former is at best an uncertain mechanism, and the issue of how the latter's surveillance is best exercised remains an unresolved problem.

It is when the professions aspire to conduct their initial training in universities, as many of them now do, that further complications arise. If accountability is a defining feature of professions, it is an essential characteristic of universities – as Barnett (1992) contends – that both learners and teachers should be enabled to emancipate themselves from the passive acceptance of received knowledge through cultivating the propensity for independent critical thought. The consequent emphasis on academic freedom can prove uncomfortable to governments and professions alike, but it can also be an important source of innovative conceptions, fruitful discoveries and more thoughtful practice.

A weakening of the intellectual base of a profession's development, as embodied in its new recruits, is liable to prove doubly disadvantageous. As Henkel's chapter exemplifies, it can have the effect of downgrading research and of reducing the educational process to one of mechanistic technical training – a transformation likely to be encouraged in Britain by the ideological commitment of the National Council for Vocational Qualifications to the measurement of predetermined sets of competencies. A profession that follows this path, away from the mainstream and central values of higher education, renders itself less attractive to those able students who are the very ones it should be seeking to recruit.

There is a further problem related to top-down policies in general, of which requirements for contractual accountability are a subset: namely that unless they are based on careful consultation and negotiation they are likely to be covertly undermined. Writing of those subject to externally dictated requirements, Marris (1975) maintains that 'collectively, they have great power to subvert, constrain or ignore changes they do not accept, because, after all, they do the work. If innovation is imposed upon them, without the chance to assimilate it to their experience, to argue it out, adapt it to their own interpretation of their working lives, they will do their best to fend it off.' Elmore (1979) reinforces the point: 'Unless the initiators of a policy can galvanize the energy, attention and skills of those affected by it, thereby bringing these resources into a loosely structured bargaining area, the effects of a policy are unlikely to be anything but weak and diffuse . . . bargaining . . . is a key element of implementation.' Bringing the argument nearer home, Clark (1983), in an account specifically related to universities, emphasizes the nature of higher education as an inherently collegial enterprise, and identifies one aspect of academic freedom as collective resilience against coercive demands from central policy-makers: 'many centrally announced reforms leave no lasting deposit because internal constituencies are not effectively summoned to support them. When a system is bottom-heavy, groups at the grass-roots are key participants in implementing policies and reforms.'

There seem, in summary, to be three main dangers in excessive governmental demands for accountability in professional education: a reduction in the potentiality for self-critical development and for change that goes beyond incremental practice-led modifications of established routines; a scaling down of professional programmes to the level of training rather than higher education in the full sense, with a resultant failure to attract students of the calibre needed to ensure healthy survival of the profession itself; and the unintended promotion of a black economy in which seemingly unreasonable demands are met with conformity in appearance but subversion in reality. None of these outcomes could be seen as advantageous to either the professions or the governments concerned.

There is a necessary tension in all this between accountability and freedom. It can be healthy rather than destructive, but the balance is a delicate one. If, as the slogan runs, the price of freedom is eternal vigilance, it is also the case that, in education for the professions, the price of vigilance is some measure of enduring freedom.

References

Barnett, R.A. (1992) *The Idea of Higher Education.* Buckingham, Open University Press.
Becher, T. (1990) 'Professional education in a comparative context', in R. Torstendahl and M. Burrage (eds) *The Formation of the Professions.* London, Sage.
Becher, T., Eraut, M. and Knight, J. (1981) *Policies for Educational Accountability.* London, Heinemann.
Becher, T. and Maclure, S. (eds) (1979) *Accountability in Education.* Slough, NFER Publications.
Burrage, M. and Torstendahl, R. (1990) *Professions in Theory and History.* London, Sage.
Clark, B.R. (1983) *The Higher Education System.* Berkeley, University of California Press.
Elmore, R.F. (1979) 'Backward mapping: implementation research and policy decisions', *Political Science Quarterly,* 94, 4.
Elzinga, A. (1990) 'The knowledge aspects of professionalisation', in R. Torstendahl and M. Burrage (eds) *The Formation of the Professions.* London, Sage.
Eraut, M. (1992) 'Developing the professions: training, quality and accountability', mimeo, University of Sussex.

Harman, K.M. (1989) 'Professional versus academic values', *Higher Education*, 18, 491–509.

Johnson, T.J. (1972) *Professions and Power*. London, Macmillan.

Kogan, M. (1988) *Educational Accountability: an Analytic Overview*, 2nd edn. London, Hutchinson.

Larson, M.S. (1977) *The Rise of Professionalism*. Berkeley, University of California Press.

Marris, P. (1975) *Loss and Change*. London, Routledge.

Schön, D. (1987) *Educating the Reflective Practitioner*. San Francisco, Jossey Bass.

Index

The Society for Research into Higher Education

The Society for Research into Higher Education exists to stimulate and coordinate research into all aspects of higher education. It aims to improve the quality of higher education through the encouragement of debate and publication on issues of policy, on the organization and management of higher education institutions, and on the curriculum and teaching methods.

The Society's income is derived from subscriptions, sales of its books and journals, conference fees and grants. It receives no subsidies, and is wholly independent. Its individual members include teachers, researchers, managers and students. Its corporate members are institutions of higher education, research institutes, professional, industrial and governmental bodies. Members are not only from the UK, but from elsewhere in Europe, from America, Canada and Australasia, and it regards its international work as amongst its most important activities.

Under the imprint *SRHE & Open University Press*, the Society is a specialist publisher of research, having some 45 titles in print. The Editorial Board of the Society's Imprint seeks authoritative research or study in the above fields. It offers competitive royalties, a highly recognizable format in both hardback and paperback and the world-wide reputation of the Open University Press.

The Society also publishes *Studies in Higher Education* (three times a year), which is mainly concerned with academic issues, *Higher Education Quarterly* (formerly *Universities Quarterly*), mainly concerned with policy issues, *Research into Higher Education Abstracts* (three times a year), and *SRHE News* (four times a year).

The Society holds a major annual conference in December, jointly with an institution of higher education. In 1991, the topic was 'Research and Higher Education in Europe', with the University of Leicester. In 1992, it was 'Learning to Effect' with Nottingham Trent University, and in 1993, 'Governments and the Higher Education Curriculum: Evolving Partnerships' at the University of Sussex in Brighton. Future conferences include, in 1994, 'The Student Experience' at the University of York.

The Society's committees, study groups and branches are run by the members. The groups at present include:

Teacher Education Study Group
Continuing Education Group
Staff Development Group
Excellence in Teaching and Learning

Benefits to members

Individual

Individual members receive:

- *SRHE News*, the Society's publications list, conference details and other material included in mailings.
- Greatly reduced rates for *Studies in Higher Education* and *Higher Education Quarterly*.
- A 35% discount on all Open University Press & SRHE publications.
- Free copies of the Precedings – commissioned papers on the theme of the Annual Conference.
- Free copies of *Research into Higher Education Abstracts*.
- Reduced rates for conferences.
- Extensive contacts and scope for facilitating initiatives.
- Reduced reciprocal memberships.

Corporate

Corporate members receive:

- All benefits of individual members, plus
- Free copies of *Studies in Higher Education*.
- Unlimited copies of the Society's publications at reduced rates.
- Special rates for its members e.g. to the Annual Conference.

Membership details: SRHE, 344–354 Gray's Inn Road, London, WC1X 8BP, UK. Tel: 071–837 7880

Catalogue: SRHE & Open University Press, Celtic Court, 22 Ballmoor, Buckingham MK18 1XW. Tel: (0280) 823388

DEVELOPING PROFESSIONAL EDUCATION

Hazel Bines and David Watson

Institutions of higher education are currently having to react speedily and creatively to a range of demands connected with education for intending and already qualified professionals. In addition to traditional requirements for continuous professional development and updating, there is a growing awareness of skills needs, interprofessional cooperation, and innovative learning styles. This volume examines the context, development and management of a portfolio of professional courses. It draws on a number of practical case studies from one institution, Oxford Polytechnic, and emphasizes the necessity of a planned institutional framework including an overarching strategy for professional education. The overall design of the book identifies key issues and objectives and shows in practical ways how institutions can act to meet them. It should be of interest to those involved in the development and management of professional courses at both the course and departmental/ institutional levels, as well as to others with a broad interest in issues of professional practice.

'I am sure it will prove of value to all parties involved in the vital task of developing professional education.'

Sir Bryan Nicholson

Contents
The changing shape of professional education – Issues in course design – Course delivery and assessment – Management issues – Interprofessionalism – The future: problems and prospects – Appendix – Index.

192pp   0 335 09710 3 (Paperback)   0 335 09711 1 (Hardback)

THE FUTURE OF HIGHER EDUCATION

Tom Schuller (ed.)

Increasingly, the social and economic well-being of the country depends on the educational qualities of the population. Education has risen swiftly to near the top of the political agenda. Yet in education, as in so many other areas of policy, the debate in Britain has lacked a longer term perspective. This volume addresses itself to that lack in relation to higher education. Its contributors cover an enormous range of experience in teaching, research and management, in universities, polytechnics and colleges.

The Future of Higher Education focuses on three key themes:

- Access. There is widespread consensus on the need to expand the system, but how is this to be achieved and what are the implications for the structure and content of higher education?
- Governance. Change is essential at institutional and system level, but of what kind and how is it to be brought about?
- Quality. Remarkably, fundamental questions remain to be answered about what we mean by quality in higher education, and how it is to be maintained.

The volume challenges all those concerned with education to debate the priorities for the future of higher education.

Contents

Reassessing the future – Finished and unfinished business – Widening the access argument – Access and institutional change – Access: an overview – Governance and sectoral differentiation – Governance: the institutional viewpoint – Governance: an overview – The future and further education – Quality in higher education – Quality and qualities: an overview – Access, quality and governance: one institution's struggle for progress – Appendix – References – Index.

Contributors

Sir Christopher Ball, Tessa Blackstone, Colin Flint, Andrew McPherson, Pauline Perry, Elizabeth Reid, Michael Richardson, Tom Schuller, Peter Scott, Michael Shattock, William H. Stubbs, Gareth Williams.

144pp   0 335 09793 6 (Paperback)   0 335 09794 4 (Hardback)

VISIONS OF POST-COMPULSORY EDUCATION

Ian McNay (ed.)

Significant changes have occurred in the last ten years in post-compulsory education, and a new framework has been set for the next ten. This book reviews these changes and poses questions about the future balance between change and continuity. One major section is devoted to views from different sectors of activity and provision – universities, polytechnics, other colleges, further education, adult education, vocational education, staff development, and local education authorities. Two are written specifically from a European viewpoint and international comparisons are drawn upon by several other authors. The other main section examines key cross-sectoral issues: access, quality, technology, structure, management, and internationalism. A central argument of the book is that it is essential that the recent emphasis on competition be balanced by cooperation (or partnership) not just to preserve collective autonomy out of defensive self-interest, nor to allow economies through rationalization, but to preserve the availability of diverse provision and contribute positively to enhanced quality and service.

Contents

A: Retrospective – The 1980s: change, contradiction, confusion and their legacy – B: Perspective: Views from interested parties – Universities: Responsibility and motivation – The exploding community: The university idea and the smashing of the academic atom – The polytechnics – Other colleges – Further education: navigating the 1990s – Policy for vocational education and training: 'have tail to wag – where's the dog?' – Adult education and European communities – Enabling learning: raising the profile of staff development. A trainer's view – Competition, collaboration, communities: the involvement of LEAs in post-compulsory education – C: Prospective: Views on key issues – Access: growth, outreach and openness – Quality: the search for quality – Technology: technological utopias in post-compulsory education – Structure: restructuring and resourcing – Management: under new management? – The world: post-compulsory education and the international community – Bibliography – Index.

Contributors

Judith Bell, Jennifer Bone, David Bradshaw, Robert Cuthbert, John Gray, David Hawkridge, Ian McNay, David Morrell, Leni Oglesby, John Othick, Alan Parker, David Parkes, Tom Schuller, Gisela Shaw, Lorna Unwin.

192pp   0 335 09778 2 (Paperback)   0 335 09779 0 (Hardback)